Intermediate & Higher RMPS

MORALITY IN THE MODERN WORLD

Joe Walker

Cartoons by Moira Munro

Hodder Gibson

A MEMBER OF THE HODDER HEADLINE GROUP

The Publishers would like to thank the following for permission to reproduce copyright material:

Photo credits

Page 11 © Maggie Hardie/Rex Features; page 14 © Circa Religion PhotoLibrary/John Smith; page 20 © Michael Freeman/Corbis; page 32 © Roman Soumar/Corbis; page 47 left © Getty Images; page 47 right © TopFoto/Image Works; page 49 © Toby Melville/PA/Empics; page 53 top © Equal Opportunities Commission; page 53 bottom © Time&Life Pictures/Getty Images; page 57 © BBC; page 61 © epa/Corbis; page 66 © Hulton-Deutsch Collection/Corbis; page 75 © SIPA/Rex Features; page 77 © Stephanie Sinclair/Corbis; page 88 © Hodder Education; page 92 © AFP/Getty Images: page 95 © PA/TopFoto; page 101 © John Powell/Rex Features; page 110 © Express Syndication/Associated Newspapers; page 112 © Mirrorpix.com; page 115 © Bettmann/Corbis; page 121 © Getty Images; page 132 © Steve Raymer/Corbis; page 136 © Lee Snider/The Image Works/TopFoto; page 138 © Ben Edwards/Getty Images; page 140 © National Geographic/Getty Images; page 147 © TopFoto/Image Works; page 148 © Christian Aid; page 157 © Sipa Press/Rex Features; page 158 © Rex Features; page 162 © Marcel Mettelsiefen/epa/Corbis; page 164 © AFP/Getty Images; page 165 © Dung Vo Trung/Sygma/Corbis; page 166 © Kael Alford/Panos Pictures; page 171 © Shelter; page 180 © James Fraser/Rex; page 184 © Rex Features; page 203 © AJPhoto/Science Photo Library; page 205 © Rex Features; page 206 © John Cole/Science Photo Library; page 211 © Tony Gentile/Reuters/Corbis; page 218 © AFP/Getty Images; page 228 © Jack Kurtz/Zuma/Corbis; page 229 top © David Turnley/Corbis; page 229 bottom © Empics; page 232 © Reuters/Corbis; page 233 © Rex Features; page 235 © Getty Images; page 237 © Rex Features; page 238 © Luc Gnago/Reuters/Corbis; page 250 © Getty Images; page 252 © Rex Features; page 254 © CDC/Phil/Corbis; page 256 © AFP/Getty Images; page 259 © TopFoto; page 261 © Getty Images; page 267 © Rex Features

Acknowledgements

I'd like to thank Lorna and David again for all their support during the often all-consuming writing of this book. Thanks also to Dharmacarini Anagarika Kalyanavaca, Director of the Edinburgh Buddhist Centre, Dr June Maxwell of the Humanist Society of Scotland for running knowledgeable eyes over the materials, especially in relation to their own world-views. Any errors or muddled bits remain, as ever, my fault – but as always I'll happily put them right in the second printing – though you'll need to buy enough copies of this one first. Thanks also to Jane Arnold, Tonto to my Lone Ranger at Liberton High School and the pupils of Liberton who are often unwitting guinea pigs for ideas and draft materials. Thanks are also due in great measure to John Mitchell, Katherine Bennett and all the staff at Hodder Gibson. Without these folks, committed as they are to Scottish education, Scottish pupils would too often have to make do with textbooks from 'down south' with the sometimes – perhaps rather dubious – claim of being 'also suitable for Scottish Certificate Work'. Thanks to Moira Munro for the funky artwork again – she seems to be able to get the image just right and get what's going on in my head – no mean feat. Thanks to all you RMPS staff across the country – beleaguered as we often are from all sides – for your support for my many textual incarnations. Remember that what we're doing is indeed, 'noble, good and true', and we remain the front line crack troops in society's duty to get our young people clued up about these important moral issues. Battle on!

Joe Walker
joe.walker@liberton.edin.sch.uk

Hodder Headline's policy is to use papers that are natural, renewable and recyclable roducts and made from wood grown in sustainable forests. The logging and manufacturing processes are expected to conform to the environmental regulations of the country of origin.

Orders: please contact Bookpoint Ltd, 130 Milton Park, Abingdon, Oxon OX14 4SB. Telephone: (44) 01235 827720. Fax: (44) 01235 400454. Lines are open 9.00 – 5.00, Monday to Saturday, with a 24-hour message answering service. Visit our website at www.hoddereducation.co.uk. Hodder Gibson can be contacted direct on: Tel: 0141 848 1609; Fax: 0141 889 6315; email: hoddergibson@hodder.co.uk

First published in 2007 by
Hodder Gibson, an imprint of Hodder Education
and a member of the Hodder Headline Group,
An hachette Livre UK Company,
2a Christie Street
Paisley PA1 1NB

Impression number 5 4 3 2 1
Year 2011 2010 2009 2008 2007

Cover illustration by Oliver Burston/Debut Art
Cartoons © Moira Munro 2007
Illustration by Tony Wilkins
Typeset in Garamond 12pt by Fakenham Photosetting Limited, Fakenham, Norfolk
Printed in Great Britain by CPI Bath.

A catalogue record for this title is available from the British Library

ISBN-13: 978 0340 939 222

Contents

TEACHER'S INTRODUCTION

Phew! What a marathon effort this was... Obviously these are complex topics involving a wide range of information and diverse, often conflicting, viewpoints on the issues. Each topic area could run to a whole book on its own, but the economics of Scottish RMPS and publishing just couldn't sustain that. I think however, that the book covers all you need for the SQA Course of the same name. Those of you doing the full course will want to go beyond the book to the many other sources and resources that are available nowadays – including the Internet. There's no shortage of material on each topic, but it's not always very pupil-friendly, whereas I hope this book is. For pupils following the full course, I hope that it sets them off on the right tracks and keeps them from getting sidelined into areas which aren't related to the course they're following. For them, you might also want to use the free LTS Support materials to develop their understanding. I have kept an eye on these materials as I have been writing this book because I wanted this book not to duplicate what's there (even the *Morality in the Modern World Support Materials* I wrote for LTS – or those I reviewed for others!). Partly this has been so that we maximise the opportunities for pupils through avoiding pointless duplication, but also so that no one thinks of nobbling me over copyright!

Bear in mind that the arrangements documents do not specify which religious viewpoints should be covered – so I've decided to refer to Christianity and Buddhism throughout. This is mainly because these two religions remain the most popular options studied in schools at this level. The exam cannot ask about specific religions, so these are as good as any in helping pupils to understand a religious viewpoint. For anyone focusing on Islam, *Making Moral Decisions* has Muslim responses to the moral issues there – some of which are also topics in Morality in the Modern World. If you want to use Judaism, Hinduism or Sikhism as the religious viewpoints then you're on your own I'm afraid – but there are many sources on the Internet which should provide help. I would have liked to cover all six faiths, but your poor pupils would have been struggling with the weight of the book as a consequence!

Of course, I hope that this book will be taken up like its predecessor *Making Moral Decisions* was – as a textbook for use with core RE pupils where a number of topics are covered throughout the years, and – just like *Making Moral Decisions* – bought in the same vast numbers! Because I expect this to happen, I have decided to accompany this book with a Teacher Book which is designed to offer additional work for pupils in the form of photocopiable worksheets based on the main textbook. This should help teachers differentiate the material in the book more widely. The Teacher Book is focused mainly on making the book more accessible for Intermediate 1 and core RE pupils, but should also be an extra source of less 'schooly' things to do for Intermediate 2 and Higher candidates. So feel free to buy that too – you need only one copy per school after all.

CHAPTER 1 The Relationship between Religion and Moral Values

The Euthyphro Dilemma

Rab and Donnie bought some tickets for Grease in London at the Apollo theatre through a very dubious Internet site. Unfortunately, what they actually bought was tickets to the Acropolis in Greece via London (then Lithuania and Iceland – an odd route they thought. . .) So, instead of singing along to 'Summer lovin' had me ablaze' they're experiencing the ablaze bit – cos it's 35 degrees in the shade – but there's not much chance of any kind of summer lovin' for them. Probably has something to do with the fact that they are dressed for Grease, in slicked hair, black leather jackets and spangled trousers, which looks somewhat out of place on the steps of the Acropolis in Athens where they are proving to be something of a tourist attraction. . .

Rab: Well Donnie, we've surpassed wurselves whis time eh?

Donnie: No hauf. Could huv been worse though – this is no bad this Necropolis.

Rab: Acropolis ya numpty.

Donnie: Whatever. Ah thought when that taxi driver said acropolis we were goin tae a nightclub?

Rab: Don't even think aboot anything tae dae wi cream eggs Donnie – they'd melt here anyway.

Donnie: Aye. Mind you, your comment at that guy in the skirt nearly got us a right doin'.

➜

Rab: How wis ah tae know that he's a crack Greek soldier – wearin a skirt and slippers wi pom-poms?

Donnie: Might have helped if ye'd contacted yer brain before ye opened your gub.

Rab: It wis just a bit of a harmless wind-up...

Donnie: This, comin' fae somebody who could pass for Elvis wi sunstroke.

Rab: Anyway, how come you're always tellin' me what's right and wrong. First it was eatin' burgers. Then it wis meditatin, then it wis the right course of action wi a cream egg...

Donnie: Ah tell ye so that you can understand the difference between right and wrong and this will make yer life immeasurably easier Rab.

Rab: And which God gave you the divine command oh great one?

Donnie: The gods of the Ocropolis maybe – they ancient Geeks knew a thing or two about the nature of morality and aw that...

Rab: Once again, Donnie, it's Acropolis and its Greeks.. whit are ye oan aboot anyway?

Donnie: The ancient Greek gods Rab – they never liked what's wrong.

Rab: But these gods – did they no do aw sorts of dodgy stuff? Were they no a bit nippy sometimes? As far as ah remember they were always playing with humans like they were their wee toys – they hud some right funny ideas aboot right and wrong did they no?

Donnie: True, but they had great moral virtue.

Rab: Ah don't think so – they were always fightin' each other and fallin oot and killin' people off and doin' nasty practical jokes.

Donnie: Bit like your cousin Maigret then eh?

Rab: Aye, and ah wouldny take her advice aboot whit's right either.

Donnie: Right enough – but these Gods couldny organise a three legged race – they couldny huv agreed aboot what's right and what's wrong could they?

Rab: But they all agreed aboot certain things like it's wrong tae kill people.

Donnie: Huv you hud too much sun? They hud some right nasty wars aboot here though – did ye no see that film 'Troy Story'? And these gods – they were always on one side or another were they no?

Rab: I ah suppose so, but I don't think they really approved of aw the killin' – pretty wrong aw that stuff.

Donnie: But the big problem Rab is this: Wis sumthin' wrong because the gods said it was, or did they only say it wis wrong because it already wis?

➜

Rab: Ah see your point there Donnie – like the chicken and the cream egg problem eh?

Donnie: aw no cream eggs again Rab...

Rab: Never mind that – here's that guy wi the pom-poms comin'. Run Donnie...

Euthyphro Has a Dilemma

No, not something he needs medication for. As ever, Rab and Donnie have hit upon the essential bits of a very famous argument in moral thinking, this is known as the Euthyphro dilemma. It was identified by the philosopher Plato, in *The Last Days of Socrates.* As they did in those days, Socrates stops and asks a young man Euthyphro what he thought was 'right' (or 'holy' which was one way of describing right in the olden days). Euthyphro talked about what the gods would think was right. Funnily enough, Euthyphro must have been quite a moral guy because he was taking his dad to court because his dad had mistreated one of his slaves. On the other hand, Socrates was about to be tried for the 'crime' of stirring up trouble in the city's youths – he could face the death penalty for this. But if Socrates was going to be executed for doing 'wrong' then he wanted to find out if the people of Athens knew what 'wrong' actually meant. This was one of the reasons he asked Euthyphro such a complicated set of questions and got into a right old argument.

Basically Euthyphro suggests that what is right is what the gods would be pleased with. Socrates ends the argument by asking Euthyphro **if the gods command what is right because it is right or if it is right only because the gods command it**. Euthyphro left with a dilemma – and probably the start of a headache too. Now, the Greek gods don't figure very highly these days (except maybe when the Olympic flame is being kindled by the rays of the sun on Mount Olympus), but the issue remains. Is something right because it is approved of (or commanded) by a divine being (or group of beings) or does God (or gods) command only things which are right? Should religious people do things which their god commands them to do even if they otherwise think that what they're being asked to do is wrong? Or should they doubt that the command has come from their god if they believe that the command is wrong? Not easy.

Euthyphro's Problem

Not only did the poor guy have a dilemma, he also had a very practical problem as well. Suppose Euthyphro was hanging about the Acropolis and he hears a godlike voice telling him to whip out his dagger and kill the next person who passes him. He is convinced that he has heard the voice of the gods and he has been brought up always to obey the commands of the gods, because they only command what's right. Should he do the killing? Even if he thinks it is wrong (which he does) the gods wouldn't command it if it was wrong, would they?

Talk Point 1

Forget about whether you believe in gods or not – if there was such a thing as a God do you think he/she/it/they would command you to do something which was wrong?

Morality and Killing

The philosopher Peter Singer states: 'People often say that life is sacred. They very rarely mean what they say'. It is true that there's probably a rule prohibiting killing in almost all religions. But… almost every religion also allows for exclusions to this rule in certain circumstances, for example, to protect the innocent in war or end the life of someone in intolerable pain. So what's going on? Is killing right or wrong? Would a god command it? Again, this depends who you ask. Some religious people understand their faith's no killing rule to be **absolute** – that means it never wavers and always applies. If you're going to war should you kill the enemy? Not according to these people. If someone is dying and in unspeakable pain should you bring their life to an early end? Not according to these people. Killing is absolutely wrong in all circumstances. Other religious people wouldn't agree. Their view would be that killing depends on lots of things and so is **relative** to the situation. What if someone is about to kill an innocent child? Should you stop them even if it means killing the person? Yes, according to these people. Also, if somebody is dying and in serious pain then their life can be ended too. They believe that killing depends upon the situation you find yourself in. Buddhists talk about skilful means. This means that what is right for one person in one situation might not be right for another person in another situation. So killing might be relative.

So might a god command a religious person to kill? Yes possibly. Might killing be the right thing to do in some situations? Yes possibly.

Time Out 1

Is there anything which you think is always wrong no matter what? Or is what's right and wrong related to the situation?

What is probably true for religious people is that the act of killing would be closely linked to the possible reason for the killing. Some reasons might be more likely to be supported by your faith than others. It's all a very grey area indeed. This means that the theory and the practice of killing can be linked in peculiar ways. Here are some examples:

- It is wrong in theory to kill, but sometimes the situation demands it.
- It is wrong in theory to kill and so it is wrong to do it no matter what the situation.

- It is theoretically right to kill in certain situations and so right to actually do so.
- It is theoretically right to kill in certain situations but it is actually wrong to do so (!)

All of this also applies completely to non-religious people (in other words, those people with viewpoints independent of religious belief) too. They might be just as likely as religious people to think that life is a very precious thing which should be protected at all times and at all costs. They don't think that this is because life is a gift from any kind of god, but it is just special in itself. In fact, many non-religious people will argue that their view of life is even more focused than religious people because they believe that we have only one life. There's no heaven or hell afterwards, no rebirth, no reincarnation, no more chances to get out of life what it can offer, which makes it even more special.

Time Out 2

Is it more important to do the right thing if you believe in an afterlife?

Divine Command Theory

Euthyphro's dilemma raised the issue of how divine beings are linked to right and wrong. Most religions around today fall into the 'my god would never do that' category. Most of these religions think of their God/gods as perfectly good. This means that their God always does what is good and always expects the same from his followers. In fact, it would be pretty hard to be any kind of god nowadays if you were not perfectly good – that's part of the job description. Now, if such a God commanded you to do wrong then the alarm bells should be ringing, shouldn't they? Unfortunately it's not that simple. First of all, let's think about how religious people are likely to hear from their God:

- directly as a voice or vision or a sense of God being present
- indirectly through something happening which is interpreted as 'God talking to you'
- as an answer to prayer
- through the study of sacred texts
- through the teachings of a member of your faith or the guidance of a guru/priest/minister and so on
- through the historical teachings of your faith.

Now in every single one of these cases it is possible that you might feel you're being directed to do something which is a bit morally suspicious. Should you do whatever it is because you think it came from God? There are plenty of examples of all sorts of dodgy things being done by people throughout the ages because they thought God told them to, but does that mean that they were all wrong or liars?

Take the issue of stealing. Would a perfectly good God command you to steal?

Answer 1: Yes, because there might be situations where you have no choice in order for you to survive.

Answer 2: Yes, because there might be situations where you rob from the rich to give to the poor and this is the right thing to do.

Answer 3: No, because instead of commanding you to steal, God should just provide you with what you need some other way.

Answer 4: No, because if God says it's okay to steal you could just give up working and take up nicking as a profession (and you couldn't complain when someone pinched something from you).

Talk Point 2

What do you think of these four answers?

So what's a religious person to do? Follow blindly, accepting everything? Doubt and question everything? Disobey God if they disagree with something?

For most religious people, this is a complex question with no easy answer. The only sensible solution is to put more than one feature of their faith together and see if they can get at the truth. So, if you heard a voice claiming to be God telling you to do something wrong you would cross-check that with other aspects of your faith, like your holy books and the teachers of your religion. All religions would think that this would make sense, after all, the religions with a God believe that their God gave you a brain which you are allowed to use. So the probable answer to the Euthyphro dilemma for a religious person goes something like this:

- God is good.
- God commands you only to do good.
- It is possible for God to command you to do something which does not seem to be good.
- God has his reasons for this (because he's got a far better understanding than you of what *good* is).
- Don't try to out-think God*.

(* By the way, this also works in Buddhism. The idea of skilful actions means that you could end up doing something which is normally wrong because you are doing it for the right reason.)

Time Out 3

What makes something good? Outcome? Intention? Something else?

What you do with what you think God is telling you (no matter how you think this is being done) is related to two further key ideas in moral decision-making: Autonomy and Heteronomy.

Check Your Learning

1. In your own words, explain Euthyphro's dilemma.
2. In your opinion, what makes something right or wrong?
3. Do you think there are any things which are always wrong?
4. Do you think morality is fixed or flexible?
5. From what you've read so far, would a religious person be more against killing than a non-religious person?
6. Do you think some ways a religious person 'hears' from God are more likely than others?
7. How should a religious person respond if they believe their God is telling them to do something 'wrong'?
8. Why should a religious person 'use their brain' when thinking about right and wrong?
9. In your opinion, do you think Divine Command Theory makes sense? Explain.

Autonomy and Heteronomy

Jackie is in fifth year and has issues. She describes her approach to life on a phone call...

I'll do exactly what I want. I make my own rules. I'm fed up with my ma telling me what to do, what to think, where to go, who to go with and 'by the way there's no danger you're going out looking like that young lady...' Blah Blah Blah. And school. Be here, be there, do this homework, read this crappy book, learn this stuff that you'll never ever need to know about for the rest of eternity. And teachers. Study hard so you can be like me – what an aspiration, what a dream to live. And my pals. Try this makeup, fancy him do you? What is it with you anyway?

Just get out of my face world.

I'll do it all my way – exactly as I please.

What was that?

What do you mean 'What if everyone did it like that?'

Who cares about everyone?

I care about me

Laws and rules, yeah yeah, making the world a nicer place, yeah yeah, all sugar and spice, yeah yeah

Oh wait a minute – here's my ma – what'll it be now – clean your room. Make your bed.

'Yeah, sure ma, I'll go shopping with you. Can we go to the new topshop?'

Gotta go. See ya later!

The process of changing from a child to an adult means you have to go through a troublesome stage called the teens! Here, one of the tricky things to come to terms with is that what you want has usually got to fit in with what everyone else wants, not to mention what is actually possible. You have to decide what you think is the difference between right and wrong and act on that decision in loads of ways. *Moral autonomy is all about using reason to work out what is right and wrong and not simply following a set of rules.* Autonomy means doing things your own way. The word is actually two words which mean being a law unto yourself. In practice, this means that your moral values are not linked to any kind of religious belief or founded on any religious principles. So how might the autonomous being make a moral decision?

By using *reason* – this simply means thinking it through. It might use very formal rules of logic like 'If X then Y unless Z', or might be a little more loosely applied. Using reason could well involve the following:

- What is the most appropriate course of action to take in this situation at this time for this person?
- Which course of action might have the best outcome?
- Which course of action might have the best motivation?
- Might one course of action produce a better outcome for the majority even at the expense of a minority?
- Are there any general rules about what makes an action right or wrong which could be applied in this situation?
- How flexible should our ideas about right and wrong be?
- Are there some things which are always right or wrong? (moral absolutes) Or is everything related to the situation we're in and so our moral choices can change about a lot? (moral relativism)
- Should a moral decision be based on self-interest alone or take into account the interests of others?

And so it goes on. Using reason to make your moral decisions is seen by many as the best way – because you take as many things as possible into account and make your decision based on all the facts and being flexible about the choice you make. Others think that it's a little too flexible and opens up right and wrong to personal whims, likes and dislikes.

Talk Point 3

Does reason seem to you like a good way to make moral decisions?

To work it through, here's a wee moral problem to think through. Let's see if we can use reason as outlined in the bullet points above to come up with a moral choice which everyone agrees with.

The government of Baboonia has decided that people are living too long. It can no longer afford to look after its ageing population. So, it comes up with a solution. Everyone will have their every need provided for by the government up until the age of 30. Life will be sweet in every respect. No one will be cold, hungry or have to do without anything in life. The price which will have to be paid for this is that when you get to 30 you have to be killed.

Have the Baboonians got the right idea?

What Do Christians Think About Moral Autonomy?

It really depends on what kind of Christian you are... and just how far your autonomy goes.

One the one hand, some Christians would say that being a law unto ourselves is the problem. God's teachings through the Bible should be the source of our decisions about what is right and wrong. We can't just make up right and wrong as we go along, even if we have reasoned it all out very carefully. This is called Moral Relativism and is the idea that some things can be right in one situation and wrong in another – there are no absolutes (things which are always right or always wrong). It's this kind of moral pleasing ourselves which separates humans from their creator. To get back on God's side we need to follow his moral teachings, not our own. It's faith in what God wants us to do that's needed not some kind of mental gymnastics which try to work out what we should do in any situation.

But, other Christians would call this simplistic: God gave us brains so that we could work things out for ourselves. We have to be sensible about right and wrong, they are not always straightforward ideas. So, for many Christians standing on our own two (moral) feet is exactly what *God wants us to do* – not hang on his every word frightened to make our own decisions. Many Christians believe that it is possible to have faith and use your reason to work out your moral choices. In fact, you need to because even making a decision as a Christian means taking loads of different and complex ideas into account. Bishop Richard Holloway says that we should 'leave religion out of ethics', which might seem like a funny idea coming from a holy man, but there you go.

Bishop Richard Holloway

Source 1

'...it is better to leave God out of the moral debate and find good human reasons for supporting the system or approach we advocate, without having recourse to divinely clinching arguments...'

Godless Morality*, *R Holloway, Canongate 1999 p20

He says that we should do something called 'ethical jazz', which means listening to others and fitting in to the overall moral tune – finding things we agree on and blending our disagreements into something creative. Our morality should be based on what makes sense, not on some slavish sticking to the rule book without using our brains.

Jesus also probably argued that people should decide for themselves what is right – he often asked people what they thought about things and how they understood scriptures in his day. So for many Christians, autonomy is part of moral decision-making. You have to make your own decisions about right and wrong, you have to work things out. But this doesn't just mean grabbing what's right and wrong out of the air. Your morality must be based on firm principles and these exist for Christians in the Bible, the teachings of important teachers throughout Christian history, the tradition of the church, prayer, study, reflection and so on. Christians should decide for themselves what is right and wrong – but this must always be based on a good understanding of what Christianity is all about.

An example of this is that during World War II many Christians in Europe hid people from the Nazis. When soldiers searched their houses they lied on purpose so that the people they were hiding weren't found, taken and killed. Now most Christians think lying is wrong, but in this case it made sense. Although the Bible clearly says in the commandments – you shall not bear false witness (lie) – it would be wise to break this if doing so would help people. So, you have to make the decision about lying according to the situation – moral autonomy. In Christianity, moral autonomy means that you ignore one moral rule (such as lying) if it comes into conflict with some other and maybe greater moral rule (saving lives). That doesn't mean doing your own thing willy-nilly, but it does mean thinking for yourself and trying to make sense of the moral teachings of Christianity so reasoning it out. But, don't forget, many other Christians think that basing morality on the situation is dodgy and could lead to problems – if the Bible says that lying is wrong, then you should never ever lie.

What Do Buddhists Think About Moral Autonomy?

For Buddhists it's a lot easier. The Buddha himself said that you should try his teachings out for yourself and if you find they don't work for you then you should try something else. Buddhism is all about your own efforts to strive towards enlightenment and so you have to be a law unto yourself. Buddhists also live by the idea of skilful means, which sounds very like the example of hiding people from the Nazis you read about above... For Buddhists, what is right depends on the situation, the people involved, what you think the outcomes might be and so on. For example, it would be right to give a starving person some money, but it might not be right if that person was an alcoholic and you had a good idea that he'd be off to buy booze with the money. If doing something is likely to result in good kamma (for you or the recipient) then its right – if the same action results in bad kamma for anyone then its wrong.

But here too there are some things you should check first: skilful means doesn't just mean a moral free-for-all where anything goes. Buddhists say that you're more likely to do the right thing if your actions are based on love, kindness and wisdom. There is also the teaching of the Buddha to take into account and the teachings of other Buddhist leaders and saints even. There are scriptures and traditions to use to help you too – so you do make your own decisions, but not entirely alone so to speak.

Source 2

[The principle of skilful means is]... knowing what the best thing to do is in any particular situation. In Buddhism, morality, insight and intention are the keywords rather than obedience.

101 Key ideas in Buddhism, Mel Thompson, Hodder & Stoughton 2000 p77

So, although moral autonomy is the idea that you should make decisions based on reason, many religious people think that you need reason to work out what their faith teaches!

Viewpoints Independent Of Religious Belief On Moral Autonomy

Those who have no religious belief do, however, have a belief system. It doesn't involve God, gods, rituals or anything 'spiritual', but it'll definitely involve morality. For people such as Humanists, moral autonomy is what it's all about. There is no God or gods guiding you, just you. You make your own decisions based on what you think is right. It might not always be easy but it is what makes us human and it's something we should celebrate. However, again this doesn't mean picking what's right and wrong out of your bathtub, but drawing together all sorts of different things to arrive at a workable decision.

Humanists do have moral sets of considerations and guidelines about their moral choices. They believe in equality fairness, justice, that human life is precious and is worthy of protection, among lots of other things. So Humanists decide what is right and wrong based on what is best for human society and the survival of the human species and what helps us thrive as humans. Every moral choice therefore would have to be put through some kind of checklist which looks at the possible outcomes of the action, and if they are mostly positive or negative and for whom. Of course, Humanists stress the importance of applying reason and logic to moral decision-making and absolutely reject any appeal to a 'higher power' up there.

Source 3

The modern Utilitarian philosopher Peter Singer explains that ethics **IS NOT:**

- *A set of prohibitions*
- *A system which is good in theory but not in practice*
- *Something which has to be linked to religion*

Instead he says that ethics **IS:**

- Living according to a set of standards about right and wrong which we can defend and justify
- Living in a way which brings benefit beyond just to yourself
- Living in a way which 'requires us to go beyond 'I' and 'You' to the universal law, the universalisable judgement, the standpoint of the impartial spectator or ideal observer, or whatever we choose to call it.'

Practical Ethics 2nd Edition, Peter Singer: CUP 1998 p14

Singer means that ethics is about making justifiable decisions based on positive outcomes for those involved in the consequences of the decision. So for viewpoints independent of religious belief, the whole point is independence in deciding what's right for yourself and not basing it on any teachings which are unquestionable in all situations.

Time Out 4

What are the major similarities and differences in these three ways of making moral decisions?

Moral Heteronomy

All this means is basing your moral decisions on a range of different things and not just acting as a law unto yourself. This kind of decision-making might involve working with others to arrive at choices or basing your decisions on many sources of guidance and information. Of course, you still make the decisions for yourself – but you just do so in the context of some other sources of guidance and support. Heteronomy means making decisions based on rules and guidance from outside yourself. This means you are more likely to appeal to an outside set of beliefs and morals, such as those found within religions.

What Do Christians Think About Moral Heteronomy?

Christians will be comfortable about this. They would argue that God directs them towards doing the right thing. This might be through the scriptures or more directly through the answer to prayer. As a Christian, you are also supported by the Christian community in helping you to make your decisions – both the community around the world and the community of Christians through the ages. Your decisions can be based on help and advice from these sources. This helps you not to feel isolated in your decision and might give you the moral support necessary to make difficult moral choices.

Source 4

The Archbishop of Canterbury, Prof. Rowan Williams – leader of the Anglican Church argues that making a moral decision is about learning to live 'in Christ'. In practice, this means doing what you think Jesus might have done in the same situation as well as working out what would build up the Christian Community overall.

Can we then begin thinking about our ethical conflicts in terms of our understanding of the Body of Christ? The first implication, as I have suggested, is to do with how we actually decide what we are to do, what standard we appeal to. An ethic of the Body of Christ asks that we first examine how any proposed action or any proposed style or policy of action measures up to two concerns: how does it manifest the selfless holiness of God in Christ? And how can it serve as a gift that builds up the community called to show that holiness in its corporate life?

www.anglicancommunion.org/acns/lambeth/lc035.html

Talk Point 4

How might thinking 'What would Jesus do?' be helpful/unhelpful for a Christian when making a moral decision?

What Do Buddhists Think About Moral Heteronomy?

For Buddhists, the faith is built around taking 'refuge' in the Buddha, the dhamma and the sangha. All three involve looking to other sources to help you make decisions about right and wrong. Buddhists do not expect you to make decisions on your own – even though each decision is yours – they believe that the teachings of the Buddha help and guide and set an example and that the community of Buddhists – the sangha can support you and encourage you in making good moral decisions.

Viewpoints Independent Of Religious Belief On Moral Heteronomy

Humanists too, believe that we don't make decisions about right and wrong in isolation – and you could argue that there are Humanist 'sets of considerations' which people can draw upon to help them make moral choices. We consult others, we learn the lessons of human history and we match up what we think with what is written in guiding documents from organisations like the United Nations. The Humanist community worldwide also has shared moral values – just as religions do (but not with any divine involvement of course) and these values can act as guidance for the Humanist in making a moral decision, just as scriptures and religious leaders can guide those from religious traditions.

Time Out 5

Find out about the UN Declaration of Human Rights. Choose one of the articles in this and explain how it would guide your moral decision-making.

Check Your Learning

1. What is moral autonomy?
2. Do you think of yourself as morally autonomous?
3. Why might someone think that reason is a good way to decide what's right and wrong?
4. Why might someone think that reason is not a good way to decide what's right and wrong?
5. What should the government of Baboonia do in the example you've read?
6. What would a Christian think of someone who was 'a law unto themselves'?
7. What do you think of Richard Hollway's argument about leaving God out of morality? What should a Christian think of it?
8. How does the Buddhist belief in kamma link to the idea of moral autonomy?
9. Explain Peter Singer's views about what acting morally means.
10. Explain the difference between moral autonomy and moral heteronomy.
11. What things might Buddhists and Christians take into account when making moral decisions?

CHAPTER 1 Guiding Principles for Morality

Doing unto others? What am I to do?
I don't know if you'll like it
Cos sadly I'm not you
I could do what makes me happy
What fills me full of cheer
But maybe you'd just groo and puke
With your allergy to beer

I could read my holy parchments – books and papers short and tall
I could use each one to guide me
In how to help me have it all
...But they're very confusing
I've got Bibles Dhammapadas, Torahs all around the house
Does this make me heteronomous?

Or maybe virtue ethics is the meaning of this game
Being good or doing good
I thought they were the same?
Old Aristotle had the right idea
His wise old mind had seen
Long ago
That even in this scary world you must seek the Golden Mean

And what of Jerry Bentham, for still today he's stuffed
On his chair in a glass case

→

And yet he's mighty chuffed
He stood up for the greater good
For the majority
But he's been gone for many years
And couldn't come for tea

Then there's Kant (why can't he?) and this is what he taught
That right and wrong exist for themselves
Of right because they ought
To be done by all no matter when, or where or what
Kant said that good should make us live
and be reliable
Because the categorical imperative
Is absolutely universalisable

So when you're choosing right from wrong
Make sure your guide is clear
Avoid bad choices, negatives and choosing out of fear
Choose to win not fail
Make good decisions, not bad
That's the moral in this tale.

When we try to make a moral decision what are we thinking about? All sorts of different and sometimes conflicting reasons why we should do X instead of Y are likely to pop up in our muddled brains. Moral issues aren't easy to cope with and don't have simple answers. Why is morality so complicated? Here are just a few reasons...

For many people, having some kind of guidance about making moral decisions is helpful, it stops us blundering about in the dark trying to work out what's right to do... Here are some Guiding Principles – think of them as signposts along the way to doing the right thing.

Talk Point

5

How do people in your class make moral decisions?

Recipe For A Moral Decision...

You need all the facts, sometimes they aren't there and sometimes they are but you don't understand them. It takes a clever scientist with years of specialised training to work out how to do genetic engineering – so how can ordinary Joe Public decide whether what the scientist is doing is right or wrong – especially as some clever scientists give us one bit of advice about it and others give us the opposite advice!

You need to have some idea about the possible consequences of any moral decision. Who will it affect? How? When? Where? For how long? Again – who can tell? It's sometimes just too difficult to predict 'what will happen if...?'

But when we make any moral decision we have to decide – based on what? Whose advice? What laws?

You might need to sacrifice one thing for another and so the consequences of your decision might have to be bad for some and good for others. Is that fair? Can you make a decision which is right which you know will cause harm (of the maybe very serious type) for some (or millions?). Should you have rules you never break? Rules you sometimes break, or no rules at all? Are your ideas of 'right' and 'wrong' never-changing or just hooked to the situation in which you've got to make a decision?

Sacred Texts

In religions, there are usually sacred scriptures which teach the followers how to tell right from wrong. The problem is that views about these scriptures differ between religions and even within a religion there are differences of opinion about how important they are.

Christianity

Some Christians believe that the scriptures (Old and New Testaments) were sent directly from God to those who wrote them down. So what's in them has great moral importance and should be followed as closely as possible. But there's letters and history and poetry and songs. Other Christians think that they are just a general guide to how to live and some are more useful than others when it comes to making moral decisions (compare Leviticus with Song of Songs for example). Some Christians also worry about how the scriptures are used. They say there's a difference between taking the scriptures as a 'whole package' – trying to find general themes and picking out bits of the Bible to suit what you thought in the first place. Some might say that there's a Bible verse for every occasion and scripture teachings are not meant to be understood apart from the time, place and situation in which they were written. Also, Christian scriptures were written long ago and some of today's moral issues wouldn't even have been imagined then. You might try to match up the message with the modern problem but that means you'll have to work out carefully what the message was and so what it might mean today – and that's not going to be easy.

So, you can use scripture as a guide or as an unchangeable set of laws – two different ideas – but which one's best? Jesus himself stuck to the laws of the Hebrew Bible (what Christians call the Old Testament), but was also prepared to bend those laws when he thought it made sense to do so. Also, what's in Christian scriptures and what isn't is not agreed on by all Christians – so what is a Christian to make of it all? Christians do 'follow the scriptures' when making a moral decision, but there are very different ways in which they do so. A Christian would use their scriptures but compare what is written with what seems right in the modern world – or check with their religious teachers or other Christians, for example.

Time Out 6

Find out about the Song of Songs and Paul's Letter to the Galatians. Explain how each one gives moral guidance to Christians.

Buddhism

One of the problems with Buddhism, like Christianity, is what's in and what isn't. There are many Buddhist scriptures: some are the sayings of the Buddha; some the memories of his followers; some stories about what he did when alive (or in previous rebirths); some are writings of great Buddhist teachers or leaders. In trying to work out what the scriptures teach, Buddhists can be in the same muddy water as Christians – what did it originally mean? How can I link it to a modern situation? Is it part of an overall theme about how to live or is it just an isolated lonely verse which doesn't mean much in itself? Buddhists also disagree about what counts as sacred scripture and what doesn't. For Buddhists, there's an added problem. In Buddhism, the scriptures are only guides. The whole point of Buddhism is that you try things out for yourself by putting them into practice. There are Buddhists who don't read any of the scriptures: for them, being a Buddhist is all about learning what's right and wrong for yourself, maybe with the help of a spiritual teacher or through meditation and reflection. Choosing right from wrong might be helped by being able to point to a particular scripture – but then again, maybe not…

Viewpoints Independent of Religious Belief

Of course there are no sacred scriptures here, no books which are on high (or even from on high). But that's not to say that such viewpoints do not have written texts which act as a starting-point to help people make decisions about right and wrong. No point in re-inventing the wheel every time you make a moral decision, someone else may have thought it all through before and suggested a way forward – why ignore it – it's a good start. For example, Utilitarians will refer to the work of writers like J. Bentham and J.S. Mill – Humanists will take into account views of other secular philosophers. Also, documents like the United Nations Declaration of Human Rights will give people a point at which to start in their moral decision-making. There's no need to follow anything that's written, however, and no writing can ever take the place of a personal choice about morality. But non-religious people might use written sources to help them make moral decisions, it's just that they think these sources are in no way sacred (at least not in the religious sense anyway).

Source 5

Whereas the peoples of the United Nations have in the Charter reaffirmed their faith in fundamental human rights, in the dignity and worth of the human person and in the equal rights of men and women and have determined to promote social progress and better standards of life in larger freedom

United Nations Declaration of Human Rights

Check Your Learning

1 Describe how a Christian might use sacred scriptures to arrive at a moral decision.

2 What problems are there for Christians in using their scriptures?

3 How might a Christian work out if the moral teachings of their scriptures would still apply today?

4 Did Jesus always stick to his holy books? What does this mean for Christians?

5 Do scriptures mean the same thing to Buddhists and Christians?

6 How might a Buddhist use his scriptures to help him make a moral decision?

7 Do people who are not religious have no written sources of guidance about moral decision-making at all?

Golden Rule

Katie sees someone collapse in the street. She goes and helps them. Later she's asked why she did this and she replies in a matter of fact way: 'I hope someone else would do the same for me in the same situation'.

The Golden Rule exists in both religions and in non-religious belief systems. It comes in two forms and one is more positive than the other:

- Positive – do to others what you would like them to do to you.
- Negative – do not do to others what you would not like them to do to you.

The Golden Rule is based on a simple idea – psychologists call it mutual reciprocity (so be glad the Golden Rule is less of a mouthful!). All this means is that your behaviour towards others should be guided by what you would and would not like. If you don't fancy it being done to you, why would anyone else like it? If it's pleasing to you, it's probably pleasing to others too. The Golden Rule is simple but effective – imagine a world where everyone, before they made any kind of moral decision, thought to themselves 'Would I like the consequences of this decision?' If their decision passed this test, then it might be something which everyone would be OK with – if not, then maybe they'd need to think again. The Golden Rule in action would mean thinking about what others would and wouldn't like before you make any moral decisions. So, you'd probably not be very selfish or thoughtless and put the needs of others high on your list when deciding on a course of action – not a bad way to make moral decisions. The only problem with the Golden Rule is that it suffers from the same difficulties as any moral decision …

Problems With The Golden Rule

What you like done to you might be the opposite of what someone else likes done to them – people have different likes and dislikes. This might be linked to their culture or their upbringing or who knows what else.

You'd have to be sure of (all) the possible consequences of your moral choices to make sure that they were likely to result in the best for others. Maybe your choice will actually be bad for people, even if you meant it to be good!

Although there are problems, some say that the Golden Rule is a good way to make moral decisions because at least your intention is right, and that's half the battle. If you make choices for the right reasons then it is (possibly) more likely that those choices will be the right ones. At least it's a way of deciding right from wrong based on the needs of others rather than your own – and has the added benefit that your own needs will be met too if everyone else is applying the Golden Rule as well!

Christianity

Do as you would be done by is a central Christian theme. Jesus specifically taught the Golden Rule. One of the most important ideas in Christianity is putting the needs of others before your own. The death of Jesus for all mankind is thought of as the best example of this – a life sacrificed so that others could have life – so Christians too should be expected to 'die to their old life' so that they can have a new life in Christ. Christians should live their lives in a selfless way, thinking about the consequences of their actions for others and taking that into account before making a decision. That's the model Jesus lived – so they should follow it. Christians should live their lives the way they would expect others to live theirs.

Buddhism

Buddhists too should put the Golden Rule high up on their list of reasons for making a moral decision. This is because your moral choices affect not only others but yourself too. Kammic consequences follow all choices and you want each choice to produce the best possible kamma for you and all beings. Making decisions based on the interests of others is therefore crucial. Also, in Buddhism the intention of an action is an important part in making it right or wrong. It's very hard to predict all the possible consequences of your choices, but if you mean well then you've started off on the right foot. The Golden Rule means well even if it doesn't always work out that way.

Talk Point 6

Can you think of an example where you might do something because that's what you'd like, but someone else might not?

Source 6

Buddhism: A state which is not pleasant or enjoyable for me will not be so for another; and how can I impose on another a state which is not enjoyable to me? (Samyutta Nikaya, V).

Christianity: All things whatsoever ye would that others should do to you, do ye even so to them (Matthew 7:12)

Quoted at: www.interfaith-centre.org

Viewpoints Independent of Religious Belief

Some might say that the Golden Rule existed long before religion did. Humans have always thought about how their choices might affect others, it makes sense to. If you depend on others in the human family for your survival, then you should make choices which benefit everyone. If we have a common humanity, then probably people will have more or less the same likes and dislikes, no matter where or when they live. Humans do share many values: the importance of freedom, fairness, protection from harm and so on. If we share these values then making a decision based on the Golden Rule is a fairly safe way to make sure that you do the right thing for everyone. People who base their moral decisions on viewpoints independent of religious belief use reason to work out what's right and wrong. It seems a fairly obvious bit of reasoning that if you didn't like something being done to you, it's probably true that no one else would either.

Source 7

The Golden Rule requires kindness and care for the less fortunate, because this is what we would want in their situation, and it discourages actions like lying and theft because no one wants to be lied to or to have their property stolen. It is simple and clear, and works well in practice. Humanists seek to live good lives without religious or superstitious beliefs. They use reason, experience and respect for others when thinking about moral issues, not obedience to dogmatic rules. They are impressed by the fact that we find this very useful basic principle everywhere. It appears to be based on our common humanity, using our need to be treated well by others and our aspiration to live harmoniously with others as its foundation. It can be worked out by anyone, anywhere, by thinking about our understanding of ourselves and other people. It does not need to be given to us by sacred texts or a god.

British Humanist Association www.humanism.org.uk/site/cms/contentViewArticle.asp?article=1222

Check Your Learning

1. What is the Golden Rule?
2. Explain how the Golden Rule can be expressed positively or negatively.
3. Have you ever put the Golden Rule into practice?
4. Why would a Christian follow the Golden Rule?
5. What might this mean for a Christian in practice?
6. How might kammic consequences link to the Golden Rule?
7. In what way could the Golden Rule be considered 'reasonable'?
8. Why might a Humanist follow the Golden Rule?

Virtue Ethics

Human Excellence

Virtue ethics starts with a simple enough distinction: that it's easier to work out what makes a person good than what makes an action good. Moral actions involve so many things: intention, consequences, the rights of the few against the rights of the many. Being a *moral person* is much simpler, you work out what that is and then you make your moral choices so they reflect what a good person would do. Aristotle, the Greek philosopher, was very keen on virtue ethics: what is good is what is good for you and what is bad is what is bad for you. So to act morally you need to be a moral person. You can't of course just decide to be one of these – you need to learn how to. Aristotle said that every good thing exists between two bad things, he believed that what was right was sitting in the middle of the two wrongs.

So, when making a moral decision what you're aiming for is an average between two bad options, which will be the good. This average he called the Golden Mean. Quite simply it's like this. Suppose you could choose either to live a simple life of poverty or one of fabulous wealth. Which would be right according to virtue ethics? Well neither actually. If you're too poor then that's bad – you'll be a burden to others and maybe do some bad things to escape your poverty. But if you're fabulously wealthy then maybe you'll become very selfish as you try to protect your wealth, maybe you'll eat too much and become a health burden to others. So, the solution is that what is right is something in between the two: the mean of the two. Neither too wealthy nor too poor – and so causing none of the problems that the extremes of either can cause – for you and everyone else.

Alasdair MacIntyre (1929–) has picked up Aristotle's idea. He believes that what is right is what a moral person would do and so a moral choice should be based on the idea of a moral person instead of the idea of a moral action.

Time Out 7

What characteristics and qualities would a 'good person' have?

The Problem With Virtue Ethics

The problem of course is: can everybody really agree on what the Golden Mean is? Bad and good aren't mathematical ideas, they are much more complicated than that (feel free to tell your maths teacher). How can you decide what is the mean between two bads if you can't give a value to bad (or good for that matter)? Also, would it ever be possible for everyone to agree what a good person is? Your good might be my bad. Isn't it just silly to think that we can agree about what a good person might be, if we can't even agree what a good and bad action is? On the other hand, maybe this is just nice and simple and we shouldn't be thinking too hard about it and running it through some kind of philosophy machine. Maybe we can all agree what a good person is and, if so, then knowing what one is will help us to know what one does. And then we can copy it...

Christianity

Christians have often treaded a difficult path between two extremes. Christians may be peace-loving, but realise that there may be times when to maintain peace, war is necessary. Christians forgive others, but also realise that punishment is sometimes called for too. Jesus' actions towards the woman caught in adultery suggest a golden mean approach. He could have joined in the stoning, upholding the Jewish Law, or he could have let the woman off without a word. He did neither. He did save the woman's life, but instructed her to go and sin no more. In fact, perhaps he was also suggesting that she help herself avoid doing bad things by becoming a good person – and so following the principles of virtue ethics. Christians also follow the teachings of Jesus because he was, in their opinion, the ideal moral being. He was an example of how to be good and so they try to copy his actions in their own lives.

Source 8

The Orthodox Christian Church suggests that being a Christian is about finding a way between extremes – the extremes of fanaticism and letting the world walk all over you.

If we look at the history of the New Testament Church, we see that She treads the royal path, finds the golden mean, which is in humility. And humility is neither in fanaticism nor in humiliation. The Church in Her Saints neither feels hatred for those who hate Her, nor does She give way weakly to humiliating pressures from outside

www.orthodoxengland.btinternet.co.uk/ocet20.htm

Buddhism

You might be forgiven for thinking that the Buddha had heard of Aristotle. In Buddhism, one of the most important ideas is that of the Middle Path (or Middle Way). This is the idea that the best course of action usually lies between two extremes – each as bad as the other. Before Siddattha Guatama became the Buddha, he tried starving himself and then overindulgence as ways to try to get enlightened. He eventually gave both of these up as equally pointless extremes. He found a middle way between both as his way. Throughout Buddhism this Middle Way idea is strong. Your moral choices should lie between extremes – which sounds very like the Golden Mean of course.

Talk Point

In your own life, are there any examples of you following a 'Golden Mean'?

Source 9

[The Buddha] came to see that the most productive course was a middle way between extremes... The most appropriate lifestyle, accordingly, would be one of moderation in which the appetites were neither denied nor indulged to excess.

Buddhism: A Very Short Introduction, D Keown, OUP 1996 p24

Viewpoints Independent of Religious Belief

Humanists argue that human nature can lead to good or bad results, but Humanists believe that where humans are happy, contented, free, safe and so on, their behaviour will improve. The Humanist ideal is a world where people use their reason to work out the best course of action. This doesn't mean just going with the flow – it is based on solid humanist principles of fairness, equality, justice and so on... If you follow these reasonable principles, then you will become a good person, and aiming to become such a person will lead to you making good moral choices.

Source 10

[Elizabeth] Anscombe called for a return to a different way of doing philosophy. Taking her inspiration from Aristotle, she called for a return to concepts such as character, virtue and flourishing. She also emphasized the importance of the emotions and understanding moral psychology. With the exception of this emphasis on moral psychology, Anscombe's recommendations that we place virtue more centrally in our understanding of morality were taken up by a number of philosophers. The resulting body of theories and ideas has come to be known as virtue ethics.

www.utm.edu/research/iep/v/virtue.htm#SH1a

Check Your Learning

1. Which philosopher came up with the idea of the Golden Mean?
2. What does the Golden Mean mean?
3. How does Alasdair MacIntyre think you should make a moral decision?
4. Explain ONE problem with the idea of the Golden Mean.
5. Why would a Christian copy Jesus?
6. What do Buddhists mean by the Middle Way?
7. How would a Humanist argue that you can become a good person?
8. How would you define a virtuous person?

Utilitarian Ethics

Consequences

John Burbleblott, a well- known genius, is tinkering about in his garden shed one day making a machine. Putting the last bolt in place, he straps himself in and presses the start button. Kazam! He travels back in time – back, in fact, to the very day that one little Adolf Hitler was lying in his cot, having been born just a few hours ago. Now, being a genius, John knows that fiddling about with time is tricky, because you never know what the consequences of your actions might be – but surely, in this case, he should really do something about this small child, who he alone knows is going to turn out to be one of history's nastiest ever pieces of work...

Source 11

An action may be said to be conformable to the principle of utility, or for shortness sake, to utility, (meaning with respect to the community at large) when the tendency it has to augment the happiness of the community is greater than any it has to diminish it

An Introduction to the Principles and Morals of Legislation, J Bentham, quoted in 'John Stuart Mill, Utilitarianism' Mary Warnock (Ed): Fount 1979 p35

Talk Point 8

What should John do?

Now some of you probably leapt to the conclusion that John should rid the world of this known threat to the future, but others of you might have been more cautious. Who's to know what all the possible consequences of your actions might be – you might make things better – or worse. Maybe if you get rid of young Hitler, you make a space for an even more dangerous person to claw his way to power, maybe someone who will be responsible for even more terrible things than Hitler was. So the problem with consequences is that they are very hard to predict. What looks like the right thing to do in any one situation might be the worst thing you could do. Also, the consequences of an action are not in your control, but the reason you choose to act in one way rather than another is. This too can cause problems, because the consequences you want from an action might not be the consequences anyone else wants.

Utilitarians say that our moral choices should be based on getting the greatest good (or pleasure or happiness) for the greatest number of people. This is called the Principle of Utility.

Talk Point 9

Have you ever tried to do something good which backfired on you?

There are three main types of Utilitarianism:

- **Act Utilitarianism**. This is where the probable consequences of your actions decide whether your actions were right or wrong. If your actions are likely to lead to the greatest good for the greatest number then they're probably right. So, for example imagine you're in charge of transport for the government. Traffic in the village of Merrypickle is pretty bad and there have been many accidents in the village where thundering trucks have caused mayhem and destruction. Someone has suggested that you build a bypass around Merrypickle, and you think this is a good idea. However, this has to go through Old Farmer McSporran's fields – land which has been in his family for generations. You decide to go ahead with the bypass. You know it's a shame for Farmer McSporran, but the needs of the many (everyone else in Merrypickle) outweigh the needs of the few (Farmer McSporran and his family). Your action is right, at least in terms of act utilitarianism.
- **Rule Utilitarianism**. Rules are designed to promote good outcomes (the greatest good for the greatest number). Some rules obviously do this, like the one about not stealing from other people. Obviously following this rule is good because if we all followed it, then no one would ever have anything stolen from them and everyone would be happy. But what if you and your family were starving and too poor to buy food – would this rule be so helpful then? Again, the problem is that we all have to agree on what a good outcome is so that our rules are made up to make sure that good outcomes are the consequences.

Time Out 8

In many schools, wearing school uniform is a rule. What are the beneficial consequences of wearing school uniform? Who for? Does wearing school uniform lead to the greatest good for the greatest number? Would a Utilitarian support the wearing of school uniform?

- **Preference Utilitarianism**. Sometimes it's difficult to judge how any moral decision might affect the majority or the minority. Some people's tastes might be very different. Preference Utilitarianism gets round this by applying the idea of the greatest good for the greatest number only to those involved in the situation - so the right thing to do is what maximises the happiness of those involved – according to what their preferences are.

The Problem With Utilitarianism

Who decides what pleasure or happiness is? One person's pleasure might be another person's torture.

Is it ever possible to fully predict all the possible outcomes of a moral decision? We can't see into the future and something which is good for the majority in the short-term might be terrible for the majority in the long-term and so cancel out the good in the first place! Who decides what to take into account when trying to work out if a decision will produce a balance of happiness over misery?

What about the minority? Utilitarianism suggests that the good of the many outweighs the good of the few – is that fair? This might mean that minority groups or individuals get 'sacrificed' for the greater good – what kind of society does that? Maybe such a society is bad because it allows the minority to be squashed for everyone else's benefit – who would be safe then?

Christianity

Christian morality often seems very Utilitarian in nature. The idea of sacrifice is important in Christianity and this could be seen as Act Utilitarianism. In fact, you could argue that the suffering and death of Jesus was a Utilitarian act. God allowed his son to suffer and die for the good of all, he was prepared to sacrifice a minority (Jesus) for the good of all his other children (mankind). As well as this, there are many examples in Christianity where the greater good is important. In war, for example, many Christians will accept (if with sadness) the death of some for the good of others, and will risk the lives of soldiers and enemy civilians in order to bring about a good outcome. Christians positively encourage the idea of self-sacrifice if it is going to lead to the greater good – those who act for the happiness of others – even at the expense of their own happiness are considered heroes in Christianity. For Christians, the big problem with Utilitarianism is what happens to the minority.

Christians traditionally champion the rights of the weak and vulnerable, who are often in the minority, so they'd be very wary of any harmful effects on the minority caused by following Utilitarian principles. Even if a Christian based his morality on the idea, 'what would Jesus do?' then that's going to mean trying to work out consequences of actions and whether they'll lead to the greatest good or not.

Source 12

Justice is Christian love using its head, calculating its duties obligations, opportunities, resources...on this basis it becomes plain that as the love ethic searches seriously for a social policy it must form a coalition with utilitarianism. It takes over from Bentham and Mill the strategic principle of 'the greatest good of the greatest number'.

Joseph Fletcher Situational Ethics: The New Morality; Louisville: Westminster John Knox Press 1966 p95

Buddhism

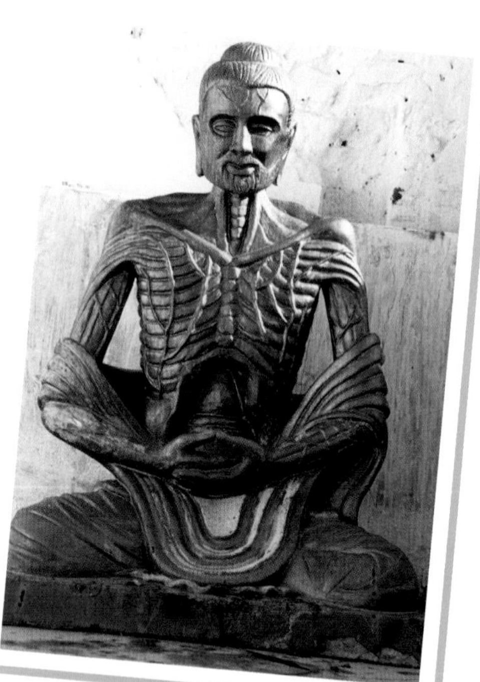

Buddhism is very interested in outcomes. If actions have kammic consequences, then doing the right thing is all about maximising good kamma (a kind of pleasure?) for as many as possible. However, Buddhists would be wary of the idea of sacrifice – the Buddha tried starving and punishing himself to find enlightenment but didn't think it was the right way at all.

That's not to say that Buddhists won't work tirelessly for the good of others, or put the needs of the majority above the needs of the minority. The Buddha also left his wife and young son to go out into the world and seek enlightenment. You could say that he sacrificed his own son and wife's happiness so that he could go off and find a way for everyone to be happy. The principle of skilful actions could be thought of as a form of Preference Utilitarianism because here you try to work out what is right for those involved in the possible outcome of any moral decision. Skilful actions don't rely on unchanging rules, they depend upon what you think is most likely to produce the best outcome in any situation according to those involved in the situation. Buddhists too would be concerned about what Utilitarianism means for the minority. Buddhism seeks the happiness of all beings, not some at the expense of others.

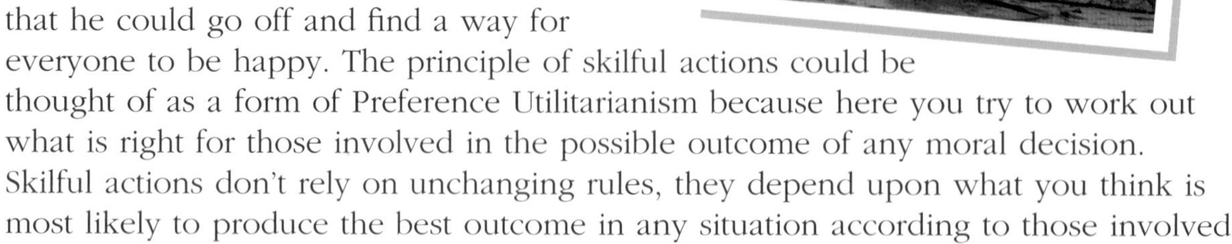

Talk Point 10

Have you ever used the principle of skilful actions when making a moral decision?

Viewpoints Independent of Religious Belief

Utilitarianism is in itself a moral theory independent of religious belief. Modern Utilitarians like Peter Singer argue for a form of Preference Utilitarianism.

Source 13

The way of thinking I have outlined is a form of utilitarianism. It differs from classical utilitarianism in that 'best consequences' is understood as meaning what, on balance, furthers the interests of those affected, rather than merely what increases pleasure and reduces pain... The utilitarian position is a minimal one, a first base that we reach by universalising self-interested decision-making

***Practical Ethics*, P Singer, Cambridge University Press, page 14, 1993**

Singer's view is that you try to take into account not only the possible consequences of any moral decision, but what the consequences are likely to be for those involved in the situation. This doesn't mean ignoring the implications for everyone else in the long-term, because what is decided in a particular situation could have implications for other similar situations in the future, or for the devising of laws and rules which might end up applying to all. But generally, for Singer, what matters is that our decisions in the first place are based on what's best for those who might be immediately affected by the outcome of the decision.

Humanist ethics also have a strong Preference Utilitarian element. Humanists believe that what is right is what is in your interests, provided that this doesn't mean just pushing other people's interests aside. Humanists argue for making decisions which benefit you, but not at the expense of others and taking into account likely consequences and the greater good.

Check Your Learning

1. What is the Principle of Utility?
2. Explain the difference between Act and Rule Utilitarianism
3. Why might someone argue that Preference Utilitarianism is the best kind?
4. Would they be right?
5. Explain ONE problem with Utilitarianism.
6. In what way(s) might a Christian act in a Utilitarian way?
7. Why might a Buddhist be wary of Utilitarianism?
8. Why does Peter Singer prefer Preference Utilitarianism?

Kantian Ethics

Duty and Reason

Your mum asks you to do the dishes. You could agree because you think it will make you a good person. You could agree because you want to avoid the consequences of not doing so (grounded, moaned at, allowance withdrawn and so on). You could agree because you'd like to think she'd help you out in some way if you asked. . .or you could agree because you felt that as her only child it was your duty to do so, and besides it would be a lovely world if everyone did what their mummies told them, wouldn't it? Of course, you could also let the dishes fly out of your hand crashing to the floor so you'd never be asked again, but let's not go there. . .

Talk Point

In this situation, is there any difference between what you would do and what you should do?

Immanuel Kant (1724–1804) was right into duty. He said that duty was a form of practical reason – in other words, you think about what's right to do in any situation based on how you think you *should* act. This isn't linked to consequences because consequences are far too difficult to predict and don't also take into account the motivation for your behaviour (maybe you're making selfish choices). So Kant believed that what was right was what you feel you *ought* to do in any given situation. He said that we could work out what we ought to do using pure practical reason.

Source 14

Kant sees self-development of virtues as its own reward, and ethics – action springing from the pure practical reason – is the sole means of bringing this about. The intention of his morality is to set aside all ego-centredness, and move towards an unconditional and universal sympathy.

Ethical Theory, M Thompson, Hodder & Stoughton 1999 p92

Kant didn't give us much idea of what he thought was right and wrong, only that we should develop an internal 'voice' which told us what we should do in any given situation. Our moral decisions would then be based on applying reason to the problem and coming up with what we *ought* to do in that situation. This would lead to a form of moral decision-making in which everyone could take part – which he called the *categorical imperative*. This categorical imperative can be summed up in Source 15:

Source 15

Act as if the maxim from which you were to act were to become through your will a general law

Critique of Pure Reason, Kant, 1788

Time Out 9

Can you think of any examples of things you do which everyone should do?

This is just the positive version of saying; 'What would it be like if everyone did that?' Kant argued that the imperative (something you *must* do) was categorical (applicable in *all* situations). What this means is that the moral decision you make in any situation is something you think it would be okay for everyone to do too. If so it's right. If you didn't think it would be okay for everyone everywhere then it would be wrong. This means that every moral decision has to be universally applicable or universalisable.

The Problem with Duty and Reason

Kant's way of working out right and wrong sounds a bit like a maths puzzle doesn't it? Can there be such a thing as pure reason and if there is, can we all apply it? Wouldn't you need to be some kind of philosophy professor or something? It's all very well to say that what is right is what we ought to do, but people could still have some mighty serious disagreements about what ought to be done in any situation. Is it really possible for us all to sit down and use 'ze little grey matter', like Hercule Poirot, to work out the right thing to do? In some situations where a moral choice is necessary a lightning flash of pure reason is the last thing you're likely to have. And what about duty? Ideas about duty vary across the world and between individuals. Is it really possible for everyone to agree on what ought to be done in a situation – seems unlikely. Kant's theory sounds like a clever piece of clear crisp logical thinking, but not so easy to apply to the slightly messier real world. Also, surely consequences do matter? Can we really apply a moral rule like not killing others to *every* situation?

Christianity

Christians place a lot of emphasis on duty too – doing what you think is right. They also have some very clear guiding principles in their moral decision-making. These come in the form of commandments and the teachings of Jesus. Christians do also follow ideas which sound like universalisable categorical imperatives, like you should love one another. But, these moral principles need some interpretation and may involve contradiction, which would give Kant a right old philosophical headache. For example, Christians think you *ought* to protect the weak and that you *ought* to preserve life. Unfortunately, doing one of these might mean you have to ignore the other – by killing someone who was threatening the weak for example – so both can't be categorical imperatives. On the other hand, Christians do believe that if everyone followed the maxim 'love one another' then that would in itself be the right thing to do. It's probably true to say that Christians would like a wee bit more moral flexibility than Kant's ideas allow.

Buddhism

The Buddha taught that you should try his teachings out and abandon them if they did not work for you. This sounds like the opposite of the categorical imperative. Buddhists don't have a duty to follow what the Buddha taught if they find that in practice it doesn't 'work' in any given moral situation. Buddhist ethics dislike absolutes like you *ought* always to do something or other. However, Buddhists talk about duty quite a lot, in fact, on becoming a Buddhist you're expected to accept the five duties of not killing, stealing and so on, and once you become a monk or nun, the number of duties go up considerably! Even so, Buddhists will modify these duties where it seems sensible to do so, (skilful actions) this means that although they ought to be done, they can't be considered as 'oughts' in the same way that Kant would.

Viewpoints Independent of Religious Belief

Humanists argue that we do have duties to others and that our common humanity should trigger how we relate to others and how we treat them. There probably are certain things which we all ought to do, like treat every human being as an equal. This isn't just so that we can benefit from the positive consequences of doing that but because certain fundamental human actions like it are right in themselves, they don't need any further justification. Humanists emphasise 'responsibilities' going hand in hand with 'rights'.

Source 16

Onora O'Neil, a modern Kantian Philosopher interprets Kant for today's world:

Duties (or obligations) are prior to rights

Starting premise:

We are all moral equals.

Rather than deriving:

Therefore, we all have equal rights.

Kant derives the deeper implication:

Therefore, we all have equal duties.

The basic principles of justice – like all ethical principles – are principles for all. We should not act on principles that are unfit to be principles for all.

www.sfu.ca/~etiffany/teaching/phil120/overheads_2_16_06.html

Check Your Learning

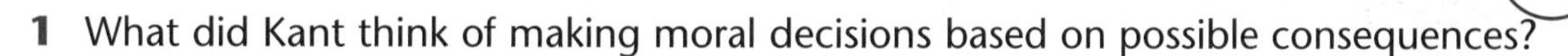

1. What did Kant think of making moral decisions based on possible consequences?
2. What did Kant mean by the categorical imperative?
3. What does it mean to say that a moral decision should be universalisable?
4. How likely is this?
5. Explain ONE problem with 'duty and reason' as ways of making moral decisions.
6. Is 'love one another' a categorical imperative?
7. What kinds of duties are Buddhists expected to follow?
8. Would a Humanist argue that there are certain things we just ought to do? Why?

Extension Activities

Knowledge, Understanding and Evaluation through Practical Activities

1 Draw your own illustrated cartoon which explains, in simple terms, The Euthyphro Dilemma.

2 Imagine a religious person feels that his God is asking him to do something very morally dubious. What should the religious person do? What things might they do to check if what they're being 'asked/ told' to do is right? Choose any religion you have studied.

3 Use the following moral problem and decide what you would do based on TWO of the Guiding Principles for Morality you have studied:

Bob is walking along the road one day minding his own business when a man who is very drunk approaches him. Bob is initially wary, but the drunk seems friendly enough. The man hands Bob a huge wad of money and walks off singing to himself. Bob looks at the money and quickly counts it: £10,000! Should Bob go and give the money back? Keep it? Hand it in somewhere?

4 Design an information leaflet (with a bit of humour!) entitled 'How to be a good person'.

5 Play a game of consequences using the following moral problems. For each one the problem should be read out and then someone starts off by saying the next thing that happened was... And the next person follows that and so on – keep it going as long as you like and be as ridiculous as you want the consequences can go on for the rest of the characters' lives if you like.

- *Kayleigh is a dancer. She's up for the lead part in the school show – but so is her rival Leanne. The auditions are about to begin. Someone hands Kayleigh a tub of itching powder and points knowingly at Leanne...*

Extension Activities continued

- *Someone in the class has thrown a pen at the teacher. The teacher asks everyone in the class to write anonymously on a piece of paper who did the dirty deed. There's one person you don't like in the class, but you know it wasn't him. Even so, you scrawl his name on the paper and hand it in. . .*

6 Design a poster split into two sections: Parents' Duties/Childrens' Duties.

7 Choose one religion you have studied or a viewpoint independent of religious belief and carry out some research leading to an extended report explaining how a follower of this faith/viewpoint would reach moral decisions. Explain:

- the central moral codes/principles of this faith/viewpoint
- the sources a follower might use when making a moral decision
- some practical examples of how a follower of this faith/viewpoint might put their morality into practice.

8 Choose one of the sources in this section. Respond to this source with your own justified viewpoint.

9 Have a class debate where five representatives – one supporting a guiding moral principle you have studied in this section – argue that their way of making a moral decision is the best way. Vote them off one by one.

10 Wibble, Wobble and Weeble arrive from the planet Onkxrt 3 (turn right at Jupiter) and ask you the following question: How do humans decide what's right and wrong? What would your answer be?

Unit Assessment Question

Higher

'The Golden Rule applies equally to religion as well as to those who make their moral decisions based on viewpoints independent of religious belief.'

How accurate is this statement?

4KU 6AE

Sample Exam Question

Higher

a) What is the central question in the Euthyphro Dilemma? **4KU**

b) Explain how TWO sources of moral guidance might respond to the question:

'Is it ever right to kill?' **6KU 4AE**

Homework

Discuss with at least four people how they decide what's right and wrong. Identify which of the principles you have studied in this section match their method of moral decision-making. You could, if you like, use one of the moral problems in this section as the basis for your discussion.

Personal Reflection

How do you make moral decisions? Do you think of yourself as a good person?

CHAPTER 2 Gender: Stereotyping of Male and Female Roles

Hi, how's it hangin? I'm Janet – just efter a hard day's work weldin steel reinforcements on the buildin site. Never mind, the pay's no bad and ye get a good skive in the lavvies huvin some banter wi the mates. Mibbe go oot for a wee bevvy efter work. Better no be too long though, or John'll be givin it like, 'And where have you been to this time of night eh? Your dinner's ruined. You could have phoned...' yak yak yak. True, I like my dinner on the table when I get hame. Meat and two veg – washed doon wi a can or two of special brew and a good big burp to clear ma tubes. Then settle tae the TV – some fitba on Sky Sports while John puts the weans tae bed. Sometimes I'm that knackered I just conk oot sleepin on the settee – man, dae I get an earful when I wake up! Canny wait tae the weekend though – Agnes is huvin a hen night – her last night of freedom before the old ball and chain – we've got a hunk-o-gram comin along – as long as her man doesny find oot eh? Gonny be a hard weekend – I'll mibbe huv tae throw a sickie on Monday. Mind you, if I dae that I might huv tae take the weans oot furra wee walk... boring...

Hello there, I'm John. Here at hame looking efter the weans while Janet's oot working hard, or so she says. Usual routine: Breakfast, get the weans dressed, mibbe story time or off to the community centre for the toddlers' group. Hame and grub. Then mibbe a nice cup of tea while the weans huv a snooze and a quick look at my mags. Run roon the place wi a duster and pick Janet's claithes aff the floor and get them inty the wash. Might just be time before the weans wake up tae get the dinner started. She's usually late – but you canny tell. Dinner's either cold or it's like, 'Wherrs ma dinner? Do ye no know I've been workin all day?' Then doin up the dishes – no in a dishwasher mind 'We canny afford wan of them' – well, no on the miserable house keeping money Janet gies me anyway. Ironing, get the weans tae bed – mibbe noo and again Janet'll dae the bathtimes – efter no very subtle promptin usually. Finally, tuck up wi a nice book and doze off tae sleep... I must change these sheets the morra though...

Talk Point 1

Can you identify with the Janet and John presented here?

The Historic and Contemporary Role of Men and Women in the Family

Confused? Some of you might recognise Janet and John, some of you won't. Some of you might think they are well over the top and that surely such people don't really exist... Some of you might wonder whether the printer has got the pictures the wrong way round and the names should be swapped around. Some of you might think that such roles existed in the past but (thankfully) don't now. It's all very hard to say because it depends on your own experience of the male and female role in the family. Historically, in the UK, it's probably true that the male and female role in the family was quite separate. There were probably always families who went against the trend but generally speaking, in public, families tended to have particular roles and functions which were considered to be the 'woman's' role or the 'man's' role. This wasn't a law or anything like that, just a set of social customs and norms which most people stuck to because that was considered 'normal' at the time. Any other kind of behaviours from men and women would have been considered weird and maybe even dangerous and subversive!

Traditional (historic) male role	Traditional (historic) female role
Man is head of the house and the breadwinner, so man goes out to work to support family. He is the financial provider. Probably made major decisions in the family and had the final say.	Woman is 'subordinate' to man and is the homemaker, so woman stays at home and looks after the home. She is dependent upon the man's income. Often had to defer to the man's decisions.
Man may 'support' woman in the upbringing of children by 'helping out' or 'babysitting' on occasion. Man more likely to spend time with male children and set 'male' examples to son(s) through rough/tough play involving a lack of emotion and so on. Will encourage son(s) to show 'manly' behaviour and engage in 'manly' things.	Woman's main responsibility is bringing up children and everything that goes with that. Possibly more likely to interact more with female children and set 'female' examples to daughter(s) such as kind, helping behaviours. Will encourage daughter(s) to be feminine and model behaviour and role on mother.
Man will probably have a life outside the home, apart from his family (perhaps including sons). This will fall into the category of 'masculine' activity, e.g. going to the football.	Woman will probably have a limited life outside the home. Will probably involve interaction with other women only and may be traditional 'female' activities.

All of these are **stereotypes**. A stereotype is a 'typical' example of something where you have gathered lots of different ideas or beliefs about a person or a group of people and applied them willy-nilly to everyone. And there's the problem... as soon as you have a stereotype you've stopped looking at people as individuals but as 'types'. You might then judge them according to how close to or far from their 'type' they are. Then people may feel that they have to conform to their type and this might lead to them being unfulfilled and unhappy. For example, all through history there have probably always been women who wanted to go out to work and men who wanted to stay at home and look after children. However, because these would be the opposite of the male/female stereotype people would have found it hard to do so in the past. Men would have suffered the contempt of other men who would have said that 'the wife wears the trousers in that relationship' – and women would have had a hard time in the man's world with people wondering why she was not 'at home looking after the children'.

Linked to the stereotype of what men and women *do* is the stereotype of what men and women *are*. Psychologists will tell you that gender is quite a complex issue. It is a complicated mixture of genetics (nature) and upbringing (nurture). No one is quite sure how important each of these is in making you 'male' or 'female' but what's fairly certain is that no two males or females are ever identical in terms of their gender. Add to this the individual differences of personality, social class, culture and so on, and the idea of male and female being totally separate in all respects starts to break down. However, in ordinary thinking, many people still refer to male and female qualities and characteristics. Males are generally described as active, tough, physical, aggressive, while females are said to be passive, soft, emotional and so on. There is some psychological evidence to support the idea that males and females have some different qualities and characteristics – but these qualities and characteristics can't be automatically applied to all males and all females. So, it doesn't make sense to base our treatment of men and women in the family on what we think male and female means.

Where Do Gender Stereotypes Come From?

What is male and female behaviour can be learned in a number of ways. Psychologists refer to the Social Learning Theory (SLT) which states that we learn behaviours by observing others. When we see their behaviours rewarded in some way, then we are likely to copy that behaviour so we get a similar reward. We can also learn our gender roles in other ways, for example, when our parents encourage us to act according to our gender by rewarding us for doing so (conditioning). With young children this is usually the way we learn gender roles. For example, girls might be encouraged to play with dolls and 'housey' things whereas boys might be encouraged to play more physically.

Our parents will reward boys for behaving like boys and so on. As we get older, we're more likely to learn what is appropriate behaviour for our gender from our peer group. In the teenage years, our friends are very likely to point out if we're a boy 'behaving like a girl' or a girl 'being a tomboy'. Whether these behaviours are encouraged or not will depend on the peer group we judge ourselves against.

Throughout life we will also learn gender appropriate behaviours through our exposure to the media. Newspapers, TV, movies, magazines will all clearly – or more subtly – show us what 'men' do and what 'women' do. The power of the media is significant in today's world and there's more of it. More TV channels, more magazines, the Internet – all of these can subtly (or not so subtly) influence what we think it means to be male or female. They can all influence us in our understanding of gender and can even *shape* our own gender without us even knowing it.

Some argue that nowadays, **media stereotypes** are far more varied than in the past. There are many examples of male role models who behave in 'female' ways and many examples of strong, powerful women for girls to copy. It is probably true that in the past women were portrayed by the media as meek, subservient and probably at home, whereas men would be portrayed as strong, independent and active in the world. However, again, some will say that the media is now more likely to present a more balanced picture of gender. Male and female role models these days are far more likely than in the past to display behaviours which do not traditionally 'fit' their gender.

Another important gender issue for many is the argument that women have traditionally been portrayed in the media as little more than sex objects. Some say this is still the case – though others reply that men are now just as likely to be treated in this way as women. Your average pop video, for example, is now just as likely to have a cavorting guy in it as a sexy woman. How the media portrays men and women will almost certainly affect how we 'see' men and women. If either gender is portrayed as an 'object' then the person or their gender is in danger of being dehumanised and so devalued. Some argue that men and women are equally stereotyped in the media as a whole, but others disagree, usually arguing that women are portrayed more negatively than men. This is still an area of hot debate however, for example, many claim that women are more likely to be judged by their looks, whereas men are more likely to be judged by their abilities.

Time Out

What do you think are 'male' and 'female' qualities?

Media Stereotyping

In the 21st century we are constantly bombarded with media images which influence our behaviour. The stereotyping of males and females is a significant part of that. From childhood, children's programmes reinforce 'girl stuff' and the same for boys. Adverts involving girls are far more likely to be for dolls and fashion items, whereas boys are more likely to advertise football-related toys and action games. In the teenage years, girls' programming tends to centre around make-up, fashion and chasing boys – whereas boys' shows are still tied to the active sporting image. The 'hero' in a movie is still far more likely to be a man than a woman (in some action movies, the men do dangerous deeds and the women seem to do nothing more than scream). Men tend to act tough in the movies – there are still not many movies where the main man is a caring, soft and gentle person. In 'horror' movies women are far more likely to be the victim, and in sports movies, women are rarely to be seen – unless the movie's about surfing and there are bikini-clad women galore. The traditional male and female roles in society are still central to media presentation of gender, and variations on this are usually presented as a little odd or the subject of humour. Women in the media still seem to have to pay attention to their looks whatever their age, whereas men can look as haggard as they like.

Recently there seems to have been a greater trend towards presenting women as the strong capable ones and men as, well, pretty useless – leading some men's groups to argue that men are now suffering the same sort of degrading stereotyping that women used to receive. Add to all this the 'objectification' (turning women into objects for male pleasure) of women in lads' magazines, and pornography and the fact that the portrayal of feminists in the media is still very negative, and you have a media which is still very unfriendly towards women.

The problem with all of this is that boys and girls constantly measure themselves against such portrayal of gender. It leads them to think that these are the ways in which they 'should' behave. So a strong determined girl might think she's not normal, as might a soft caring boy – if they're comparing themselves to their counterparts as portrayed in the media. Control over the portrayal of men and women in the media is difficult – especially with the lack of regulation over the internet. However, as far as TV and radio is concerned in the UK this used to be done – until 2003 - by the Independent Television Commission. This role is now carried out by Ofcom. In its Code of Standards (2005) it states:

Source 1

Care should be taken to foster tolerance and respect for difference and avoid the lazy adoption of stereotypes covering race, gender, age, religion or sexual orientation.

www.ofcom.org.uk

Also in the UK, the advertising standards authority regulates the presentation of gender issues in advertising in many different kinds of media (see www.asa.org.uk/asa/codes.htm).

Check Your Learning

1. Describe the traditional role of women in the home.
2. Do you think traditional male and female roles in the home still exist?
3. What is a stereotype?
4. Describe the traditional male stereotype.
5. How might children learn to be boys or girls?
6. In what ways does the media stereotype males and females?
7. How much of an influence do you think the media is in shaping people's gender?
8. Do you think enough attention is paid to men in gender equality discussion?

Talk Point

Who are your role models? Are they all the same gender as you?

The Changing Role of Men and Women in the Family

During WWI, while the men were off fighting, women took over many 'male' jobs. When the men came back, many women found they wanted to stay working. The argument that they 'couldn't do a man's job' had now been disproved. So many women went out to work and some men began to stay at home. This situation was repeated after WWII. In the economic depressions which occurred after the war and during the fifties, many women found they had to go out to work because they found they could not afford to live on one income. Also, many traditional 'male-dominated' heavy industries like shipbuilding went into decline. Many men found themselves out of work. New, lighter industries like electronics assembly attracted women far more than the men who'd been used to 'man's work'.

So, in the family, the roles were changing and more men had to stay at home while their wives became the breadwinners. In the swinging sixties, attitudes to male and female roles in the family were more relaxed. This was a time of changing opinions and practices. The old certainties of male and female roles in the family were being challenged on purpose. Many men were choosing to be househusbands and being more open about their 'feminine' sides. Male and female dancing became indistinguishable as did fashions and even hairstyles!

These changes to work practices and views about the role of men and women in the family and wider society have remained right up to the present day. It's now just as likely to be the man of the house who cooks, cleans and looks after the children and the woman who is the breadwinner. There's now more likely to be a sharing of the old traditional roles of men and women in the family, and people outside a family will think little of it.

However, some argue that the role of men and women in the family is still very traditional in many places and should be challenged. Some will say that Janet and John do exist, only Janet's speech would be swapped with John's in the real world. Many argue that the continued existence of violence against women in the home is an example of how power is still wielded (badly) by some men. They would say that society's failure to tackle violence against women properly is an example of how society still regards men as being the 'head of the house' and women as subservient to them. Also, many men who choose the 'female' role of home-maker are still discriminated against in society. They can be made fun of in the media and still treated as oddities. There are very few role models in society for men who are 'househusbands'.

Time Out  2

How 'traditional' are the roles of men and women in your family?

The Historic and Contemporary Role of Men and Women in the Workplace

Read this to your class and watch the puzzled looks you get when you ask the question at the end

Two people are in a car, a father and his only son. There is no one else in the car. Unfortunately the car crashes and the father is killed. The son is rushed to hospital in a critical state. As he is wheeled into surgery, the surgeon arrives in mask and surgical gloves, takes one look at the boy and exclaims: 'I can't do this operation... that's my son!'

How is this possible?

No matter how enlightened we are about the modern roles of men and women, some of us still have stereotypes about the male and female role in the workplace. How many people in your class (and how quickly) suggested that in the problem above, the surgeon was the boy's mother? For some people, the idea of the surgeon being female isn't the first thing that comes to mind because traditionally such roles would have been more likely to be done by a man. So, did women only start going out to work after the world wars? Not at all. Women have always gone out to work in the UK. Mostly this was due to economic need. Before the industrial revolution, when most work was agricultural, there was little difference between what a man did and what a woman did. In fact, many women worked in the fields and looked after the home too!

During the industrial revolution, the jobs which men and women did started to separate out more, with men doing more of the heavy physical work, though even here, women did dirty and dangerous jobs in the mills and factories of the time. A single woman without a husband would need to support herself and so she would go out to work to do so – unless she stayed at home and was provided for by her father. However, here is where the difference really began. Generally speaking, when a woman got married and left the parental home she was pretty much expected to give up work – unless there was some dire financial need which meant she had to carry on working. The provider role which had been her father's would now be her husband's. Certainly, as soon as she got pregnant it would be expected that she leave work and raise her children. She could expect social disapproval if she continued to work after giving birth – especially if she didn't have to work for financial reasons.

As people started to separate out a 'man's job' from 'women's work', the separation of the genders in the workplace became more obvious. This had practical implications too because it meant that women would be far less likely to reach the top in their chosen field of work if they were married and had children. This is because they would have long 'career breaks' where they looked after their children until they left the family home and so they missed out on the experience necessary for promotion. Also, many women were probably passed over for promotion (and sometimes even employment) because it would be 'feared' that they would get married, have children and leave. This meant that where women worked, they were generally in the lower paid, more menial jobs. Those women who did achieve position and wealth through work were often single women, or married women who could afford a nanny to bring up the children. Some argue that things are not really much different for women nowadays.

Economic Changes

Firstly, many men had to change their jobs because of changes in industry. The UK has seen a change in recent history from heavy to light industry. The demise of coal-mining, heavy construction and shipbuilding are to name but a few. These traditionally male worlds have been replaced with financial services, call centres and precision electronics. Many of these jobs have been taken up more by women than men. This has led to more women in certain industries than men. This has also led to more women reaching high positions in these new industries – though some argue that this is still more difficult for a woman to achieve.

Added to this is the general trend towards smaller families – meaning that women are taking shorter career breaks and so not losing out in the promotion stakes to the same extent. Also, after WWII, rationing and the opening up of world markets, people began to be able to buy all sorts of consumer goods which made their home lives easier – washing machines, dishwashers and other 'labour-saving' devices. This meant that housework took up less time and so people could spend more time at work if they wanted to. But... this new era of consumerism led to people wanting to buy more and to do that they had to earn more. For example, it soon became difficult for some people in some areas to afford to buy a home on one income and so many men and women had to go out to work – just to make ends meet – or rather to have the standard of living they were now getting used to.

These are all economic reasons why the role of women in the workplace changed. However, even economically, some say that the situation is still biased usually against women. Men are still far more likely to wield power in the workplace and they are still more likely to pay men more, promote them more and treat them better. The argument goes that people don't like to give up their economic advantages easily and if they can avoid doing so based on the fact of gender then they will.

Social Changes

So the work done by women during the World Wars proved that there was no such thing as a job that only a man could do. People began to think differently about what men and women could and should do in the workplace. Combine this with changes to how people began to understand and express being male and female and you have a recipe for change in the workplace. Not only were women finding that they could do and enjoyed 'traditionally male jobs', men were finding that they were sometimes just as good at 'traditionally female jobs'. Men actively took up jobs as nurses, secretaries and working with children. It all became much easier for men and women to do jobs which previously would have been (unofficially) closed to them. The old stereotypes of male and female were breaking down in general throughout British society and this led to changes in who did what where and how.

Some do argue however, that there are still jobs where men dominate and where women dominate. At the moment for example, the head teacher of a secondary school in Scotland is more likely to be male, whereas primary teachers are more likely to be female. Nursing is still a predominantly female occupation while engineering is more male-dominated. Managers are still more likely to be male and their secretary female. So, it seems that there are still jobs which are more likely to be done by men than women – though the reason why this is varies. Some argue that society is not doing enough to challenge gender roles in the workplace. They say, for example, that there should be greater efforts to encourage boys and girls at school to take subjects which are traditionally associated with the opposite gender.

3

What is the balance of male/female pupils in your school in:

- *Home Economics*
- *CDT?*

Legal Changes

The UK now has a whole range of laws which are designed to avoid gender discrimination in the workplace. This can either be when you apply for a job – where almost all jobs cannot be advertised as for males or females only. Many job applications now ask you for only the initials of your name, so that your gender can't be identified and contribute to whether you are interviewed or not. There is also a wide range of laws covering things like equal pay and equality of opportunity which are designed to get rid of any possibility of being treated differently because of your gender. These laws were not always there and so in the past, employers could discriminate against you based on your gender and get away with it. Not so now – although some equality campaigners still believe that gender equality doesn't yet exist in the workplace because employers are bending or ignoring equal opportunities laws. However, it is probably fair to say that widespread discrimination based on gender is far less likely in the UK now than it was in the past – and that at least we're heading in the right, fairer direction now.

Again, it is possible to argue that the role models presented in the media stereotype women in the workplace. Either women are shown as meek and submissive types in menial jobs, or when they are successful and powerful they are usually portrayed as strident and 'butch'. Powerful women are sometimes portrayed as women who have given up their 'feminine' qualities and taken on 'masculine' ones so that they can succeed in a 'man's world'. At the same time, men who do not fit the traditional working man image are just as likely to be presented as a bit wet if they stay at home and look after children. Although there are examples in the media of men doing 'women's' jobs and vice-versa, these role models are still in the minority.

Check Your Learning

1. Explain how male and female roles in the family changed in the 20th Century.
2. Why did the surgeon story confuse some people?
3. What evidence is there in what you have just read that women were treated unfairly in the workplace in the past?
4. What economic factors led to changing gender roles in the workplace?
5. Explain ONE social change which affected the balance of men and women in the workplace.
6. How might an employer avoid employing you (or not) based on your gender?
7. What messages does the media give about men and women at work?

UK Law on Equal Opportunities

Sex Discrimination Act (1975)

This Act makes it unlawful to discriminate against people because of their gender, it specifically covers:

- Education: schools can be single sex but they have to offer the same curriculum and mixed gender schools should ensure equality between the genders in all they do.
- Advertising: this must avoid all forms of gender discrimination.
- Employment: this relates to what job you can do and your pay and promotion chances (though there are some jobs which can be gender specific).
- Provision of housing, services, goods and facilities: in all of these cases there should be no form of discrimination based on your gender.
- Marriage: including the provision of maternity leave for women and paternity leave for men.
- Sexual harassment: any unwanted conduct or behaviour based on your gender or related to sex which is likely to cause you harm in some way.

Anyone who wants to bring a claim under the terms of this act in Scotland, would do so either through employment tribunals (if it is work-related) or through the

Sheriff Court system. You can get compensation if you are affected and the guilty party will have to put things right generally so that it does not fall foul of the law again. (Information based on www.eoc.org.uk.)

Equal Pay Act 1970

This Act aims to ensure that whether you are male or female you get the same pay and benefits as a member of the opposite gender doing the same job. It applies to people of any age and equally to full-time and part-time workers. It also covers maternity leave and treatment at work during pregnancy. It covers every imaginable possible difference between how men and women are paid and treated at work to ensure that there is complete quality between the genders (see www.eoc.org.uk).

EU Legislation

The UK is also a part of the European Union, which has specific laws on gender equality issues. Much of its documentation can be found at: www.ec.europa.eu. The EU, generally speaking, mirrors the already existing legislation in the UK. However, there are many cases cited which have gone to the European Court of Justice because the complainants have obviously been unsatisfied with their own nation-state's applications of gender equality law!

Equal Opportunities Commission (EOC)

This organisation was set up by the UK government in 1975 to put the Sex Discrimination Act (1975) into practice and ensure that it was being adhered to throughout the UK. Beside its logo is the slogan: Women. Men. Different. Equal.

It states:

'...we deal with sex discrimination and inequality related to gender, including good practice in the fair and equal treatment of men and women'. It states that its current priorities are to:

- close the pay gap between men and women
- open up job choices equally for men and women
- improve support for parents and carers
- secure a decent pension for everyone
- promote equality in public services
- investigate unlawful practices at work
- help people secure their rights
- campaign to modernise the law.

The EOC has run a poster campaign since it began challenging all forms of gender stereotyping (see www.eoc.org.uk). It challenges the whole concept of gender stereotyping saying:

'Sex stereotyping is making assumptions that women and men should play different roles in society. Such assumptions restrict individual choice, which leads to wasted and unfulfilled potential, to skills gaps and to lower pay for those jobs which are seen as 'women's work'. In short, stereotyping results in discrimination against both men and women.'

The report where you can find this quote can be found on the EOC website (use the search facility and use the keywords 'young people stereotyping'). This gives some fascinating information about how gender stereotyping is changing, but also about how it seems to be alive and kicking too. It quotes one 12 year old girl as saying, 'You don't get male nurses' and another 12 year old girl saying: 'There are some things that women are better at, like making beds, things like that, men are better at fixing the car'. On the other hand, it also quotes a grandfather who wished he could have his time over to change the kinds of things which led to gender stereotyping.

An International Perspective

So, some people argue there is much more gender equality in the UK – in the workplace and in the family – than ever before, even if there are still many abuses. However, if we look at the international scene we see a different picture, or do we? Firstly, in the world there have been a number of world leaders who have been female: Margaret Thatcher, Indira Gandhi, Mary Robertson and Germany's first ever female leader, Angela Merkel. But there are far more countries of the world which have never had a female leader, and some argue that the world's female leaders so far have not brought much benefit to the cause of women. Many say, for example, that Margaret Thatcher, the former British Prime Minister, was just as warlike (and ready to go to war) as a man. So the idea that if the world was run by women that wars would be far less likely seems not to be so true after all.

Most societies in the world remain strongly patriarchal (male dominated and led). There are some matriarchal societies in the world, mostly in Africa – though some argue that these are of little benefit to women as it simply means that the women have to be wives, mothers, homemakers and run things – while the men do very little. In fact, in some countries of the world, the stereotyping of men and women is even more obvious than it is in the UK. Many laws around the world seem to favour the rights of men over the rights of women. Some give almost unlimited power to husbands over their wives, which can lead to all kinds of domestic abuse. Many places in the world still openly discriminate against women in the workplace. In fact, when you look into it more carefully, the UK looks pretty enlightened about such issues!

The United Nations Convention on Ending All Forms of Discrimination Against Women (CEDAW)

The United Nations Charter has, as its first article, the claim that it exists to secure human rights for all, regardless of gender. It describes discrimination against women as:

'. . .any distinction, exclusion or restriction made on the basis of sex which has the effect or purpose of impairing or nullifying the recognition, enjoyment or exercise by women, irrespective of their marital status, on a basis of equality of men and women, of human rights and fundamental freedoms in the political, economic, social, cultural, civil or any other field.'

Once a nation has signed up to the convention, it commits itself to:

- Incorporating the principle of equality of men and women in law – abolishing discriminatory laws and making laws which are against discrimination.
- Establishing public institutions which protect women against discrimination.
- Ensuring elimination of all acts of discrimination against women anywhere in the country by anyone.

The full text of the Convention is at www.un.org/womenwatch/daw/cedaw/text/econvention.htm.

All these laws and regulations have sometimes led to positive discrimination where laws are put in place to give preference to one gender over another. Some argue that this is equally unfair, while others say that this is just putting history's wrongs right.

Check Your Learning

1 Explain TWO features of the *Sex Discrimination Act 1975*.

2 What does the *Equal Pay Act 1970* cover?

3 What might someone do if they felt that UK law failed them in a sex discrimination case?

4 What does the Equal Opportunities Commission do?

5 Does the fact that there have been female world leaders help or harm the case for equality for women?

6 Is positive discrimination any fairer than any other kind of discrimination?

The Historic and Contemporary Role of Men and Women in the Religious Community

Christianity

Christianity has a mixed history with respect to women. When Jesus chose his closest followers (the disciples) they were all male. This was not surprising as Jesus was a Jew living in a male-dominated Jewish world. However, he had female followers, even very close ones. In fact, Christians believe that after he rose from the dead he appeared first to the women who had come to anoint his dead body – an important message perhaps about the ability of women to spread the Christian message, or just a coincidence? Some modern feminist Christians argue that women had a far greater role in the life of Jesus but that they were 'written out' of the story by a Christian Church which had become male-dominated. We may never know.

The first Christians seemed to give important roles to women, and all through the history of Christianity women have played important roles as religious leaders, teachers, political figures and even saints. However, there have generally been different roles allocated to men and women in the Christian Church. It's not clear if this can be supported by Christian teaching or if it is just the result of custom and tradition. In the 11th Century the Roman Catholic Church in the 'West' split off from the Orthodox Church in the 'East'. Both however held on to the belief that women could not take up the important role of being a priest (though they could marry priests in the Orthodox tradition). In these two versions of Christianity, women cannot be priests even today. So, as they cannot be priests they cannot be Bishops, Cardinals, Patriarchs or Popes or any other such office in the church. The reasons why women are not permitted to be priests are based on:

- The fact that Jesus did not choose women as disciples suggests that he wanted a different role for women.
- The belief that the priest represents Jesus therefore must be male.
- The view that it goes against the Church's tradition to have female priests. Traditions are important and shouldn't be ditched just to follow current trends.
- Bible texts which might oppose women priests, for example, 1 Timothy 2:8-14; 1 Corinthians 14:34-35.

As you might expect, there are women and men who disagree with this within both denominations. They argue that:

- As women feel 'called' by God to the priesthood, the men who control God's church on earth should not stand in their (or God's) way.
- (Some argue) God is neither male nor female but has all the qualities of both. Therefore a woman can be God's representative just as well as a man.
- Women make up a significant proportion of the Church. It is therefore wrong to exclude them from any role in the Church.
- The Bible's teachings about the role of women represents the time in which those teachings were written. The Church needs to move with the times or it will

become irrelevant. A good way to move with the times would be to ordain women to the priesthood.
- Bible texts which might support women priests, for example, John 20:10-18; Galatians 3: 26-28; Acts 2:17-18.

Some groups within the Roman Catholic Church have ordained women into the priesthood, but they are generally excommunicated (excluded) from the Church for doing so. The female priests are not recognised as priests by the church. (You should know that in UK law, jobs like priests in religions are excluded from laws about sex discrimination and equal opportunities.)

Talk Point 4

Should Christian churches, as employers, have to stick to UK laws on sex discrimination?

This is not to say that women are not valued in Christianity. In these denominations the role of the woman in the home is stressed. She can however, play an important role in the Church in many other ways – running groups within the church, reading the bible and praying and carrying out important pastoral roles like visiting the sick and so on. Also, these traditions have religious orders of nuns, and some nuns can become 'head nuns' (they might be called 'Mother Superior' or 'Abbess'). These nuns play many important roles in the Church – from being out in the world helping the needy like Mother Teresa's Order, or cloistered in prayer and reflection like many Carmelite orders. However, all nuns have to take vows of poverty, chastity and so on, and consider themselves 'married' to the Church (though it is also possible to become a nun having been married and having had children).

In the West, the Christian church split in around 1520 into the Roman Catholic Church and the Protestant Churches. Some Protestant Churches (like the Church of England) held on to the ban on women becoming priests... However, some years ago, the Church of England voted to allow women to become priests. Some members of the church (male and female) were so disgusted about this that they left the Church. Others refused to attend churches where women were priests. Some even carried a card with them which stated that in an emergency – if a priest were needed – it had to be a male one. To some this seems like a bunch of people hopelessly out of touch with the modern world – but it could be argued that you can't muck about with your basic beliefs just to be 'modern'. Other Protestant denominations (since the split from Roman Catholicism) had very different attitudes to women. Some, like Methodists and the Church of Scotland, today have female clergy and some, like the Quakers, don't have clergy at all but a fully equal role for men and women in their church. Most Christian churches stress the importance of the role of being a mother for women – and this is why some churches have 'lesser' roles than being priests for women – like deacons and lay preachers, for example. However, in many churches, like the Church of Scotland it is possible to be a wife, a mother and a fully ordained minister in charge of a Church – it is even possible to become the head of the Church of Scotland, the Moderator (though you are only in this position for a year).

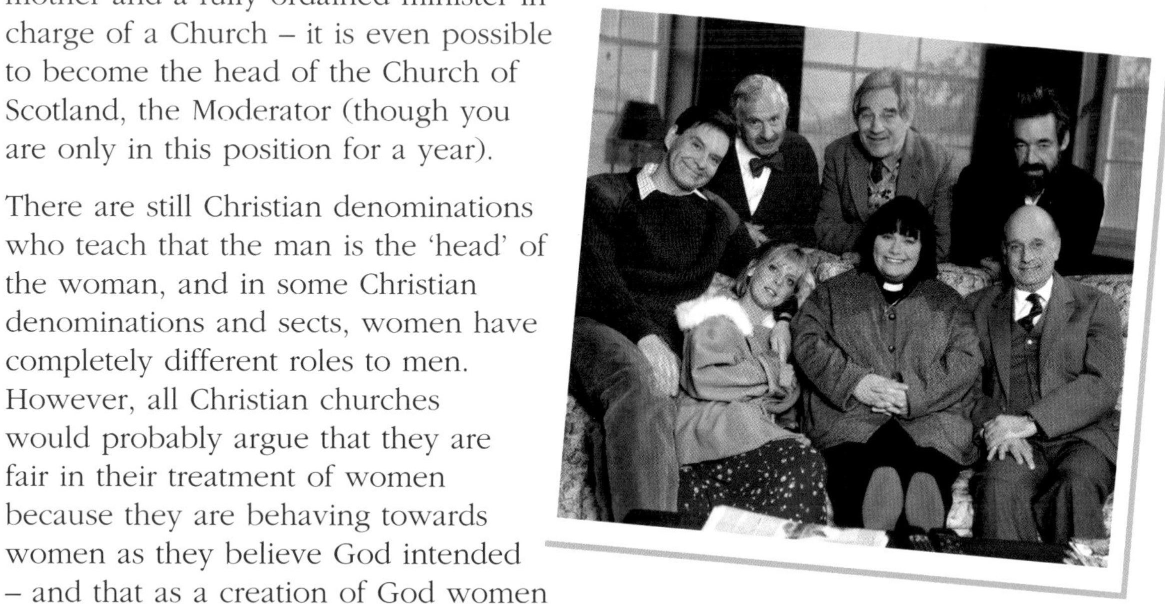

There are still Christian denominations who teach that the man is the 'head' of the woman, and in some Christian denominations and sects, women have completely different roles to men. However, all Christian churches would probably argue that they are fair in their treatment of women because they are behaving towards women as they believe God intended – and that as a creation of God women are to be valued as much as men. However, this doesn't mean, they argue, that men and women are equal or have the same responsibilities in life. Interestingly, the media has had a fun time with the portrayal of men and women in Christianity. The men who chose to be ministers or priests would either be shown as slightly dim or wet and drippy, hopelessly inept or dodgy drunks. In *Father Ted*, for example, almost all these stereotypes appeared. Rarely has there been a strong male role model in any TV programme or movie who has also been a member of the clergy. Women too have appeared as side-issues in such programmes – sometimes as women 'looking after' the priest or bossy housekeepers. So far, only with *the Vicar of Dibley* has there been any attempt to show a strong woman in a clerical role.

Buddhism

The Buddha had a similarly mixed attitude to women. He taught that anyone can be enlightened – male or female, but he warned his closest followers about the dangers women could pose in distracting them from following the eightfold path. Women did become followers of the Buddha and important ones at that. However, as Buddhism grew, spread and developed, it tended to adopt some of the social customs of the places it ended up – and this could mean a changed role within the faith for women. This means that in modern Buddhism, there are many female nuns. How 'high' they can become in their order is different according to the order they are in. Some can reach the highest offices while others seem to be treated as much lower in status than monks. Again, as in Christianity, there can be many lay roles for women in Buddhism (just as for men). Women can assist monks and nuns in many ways, and can teach the faith at the highest levels and do everyday practical work too.

Gender Roles Old and New – Advantages and Disadvantages

Of course, there are people in the UK and the world who believe that men and women are not equal. Some believe this for religious reasons and others for traditional or cultural ones. Some argue that the modern approach to gender equality doesn't really benefit people at all. Some argue that the old days – where the roles and identities of men and women were more clearly separated – was far better than today's 'gender-confused' world. How do they try to justify this argument?

Men and women are 'naturally' different. We have different skill and abilities. The modern trend of ignoring these differences and treating us as the same means that neither gender can fulfil its potential fully. For example, such people might argue that women are selected by nature to nurture children whilst men are not as good at this. So, children who are brought up by men are not getting the full deal. So, the 'old' gender roles were good because people knew where they stood – nowadays boys have no idea what kinds of qualities they're supposed to develop. Alternatively the 'new' gender roles are better because no one has to feel pressurised into one role or another – you can just be yourself instead of having to be 'a man' (or a woman).

Equality leads to a more stressful society and not a better one. Women are having to act 'unnaturally' in taking on roles more suited to men. This leads to negative impacts on relationships, the family and society as a whole. Equality comes at a price. Such people might argue that women should be protected from the stresses of life and gender equality doesn't do this. (Others would argue the opposite of course!)

Gender equality leads to men not acting like men and women losing their 'feminine qualities'. This is wrong, and will lead to a confused society. Some religious people argue that God did not create men and women as equals.

Each of these points contains a lot of scope for disagreement and debate. Most people in today's world are agreed that equality and fairness are just about opportunity. Women or men are not being forced into roles they don't want, but the world is being made a fairer place by ensuring that discrimination based on gender is fading away. Men and women are being given equal opportunities, whether they choose to take them or not is up to them. Boys and girls are free to imitate aspects of the role models which they feel most comfortable with. They're not being forced to imitate only their own gender.

The Moral Implications of Separate Gender Roles

The moral issues here are fairly straightforward – though putting them into practice is not!

Is it right to treat people differently because of their gender? Obviously if this leads to unfairness then no, but what is and isn't fair is sometimes difficult. Perhaps more gender equality leads to men and women still feeling forced to do what they don't want to. Maybe women who want to stay at home and raise children feel a pressure to go out and work. Maybe men who want to work feel a pressure to behave like a 'new man' and stay at home. Do we help or confuse children with mixed messages about gender? The messages which go out to children about how they should behave as boys or girls are sometimes contradictory – perhaps it might be easier if we stop talking about boys and girls altogether.

Should society's morals change with the times? Some people worry about 'moral relativism' – the idea that what is right and wrong can change according to time, place and situation. Perhaps there are some 'moral absolutes' which should never be challenged – like the different roles of men and women in society. If we meddle with what's right and wrong then we open up all sorts of worrying possibilities for the future. On the other hand, perhaps gender equality is a moral absolute (something which is non-negotiable) and perhaps gender equality has been the victim of moral relativism for too long. Perhaps the 'old, traditional ways' were wrong and should be swept away in the 21st Century and beyond.

Should gender become history? Perhaps in the future we will drop the terms man and woman and all that goes with them and just refer to people. Would this make the world a better place?

When you stereotype anything you ignore individual differences and treat everyone in the same group the same – that can't be right.

Christians and Gender

In the UK and many other western world countries it is often argued that the negative treatment of women has been based on a Christian morality which had gender inequality at the centre. Is that fair? You've already looked at the place of women in Christianity. What beliefs underlie this?

- *Eve* – the poor girl's got a lot to answer for if you listen to some Christians! Christians believe that God made man first. He then realised that he needed a mate and made Eve. Some Christians to this day therefore argue that this means that man is in charge of woman. Others say that this was an equal but different partnership and should be the model for male/female relationships today. However, according to the Genesis story, Eve persuaded Adam to disobey God and so they brought sin into the world. No matter what the Christian thinks of this story it has led throughout the history of Christianity to a secondary role for women. Many modern Christians argue that Adam and Eve were both equally responsible for bringing sin into the world and so Eve's actions are no justification for treating women differently.
- *The Old Testament* – mixed messages again. Women here are just as likely to be heroines like Esther or mighty rulers like Sheba or wives and mothers. The Old Testament was a strongly patriarchal society with clear divisions in the roles of men and women and it was this tradition into which Jesus was born.

- *Jesus* – he seemed to have an important place for his female followers, by his time, the segregation of men and women in society was pretty complete with the home/mother role of women being central. Society in the time of Jesus was very male-dominated and so many Christians believe that his treatment of women was very liberated and modern.
- *The letters of Paul* – another confusing area! In 1 Corinthians 14:34-36 Paul doesn't mince his words. He instructs that women should keep silent in Church and be taught by their husbands at home. Elsewhere he argues that women should cover their heads in Church and not hold certain positions. However, maybe most famously, in his letter to the Galatians he argues that '…in Christ there is neither male nor female… for all are one in Christ Jesus'. Some Christians have used Paul's teachings to keep men in charge in the faith and others to show that gender equality is the ideal. What's going on? Perhaps Paul had mixed views about women in the Church – perhaps he did see them as equal but different. He could have argued at the same time that men and women were equals in the eyes of God, but that this does not mean they have the same duties and responsibilities. On the other hand he was writing his letters to deal with specific situations in churches in different places. Maybe he never intended the whole Christian church everywhere to try to put all his teachings together.
- *Modern Feminist Christians* argue that beliefs about and the treatment of women have been twisted throughout Christian history by a Church dominated by men. They argue that women are a vital part of the church and can bring a level of understanding to the faith which men can't. Some Feminist Christians don't mince their words about their views on male domination in the Christian faith:

'God's Plan' is often a front for men's plans and a cover for inadequacy, ignorance and evil.'

Mary Daly, Feminist Christian (and all-round controversial figure – see www.marydaly.net)

Buddhists and Gender

Views of women differ according to the tradition of Buddhism. The world in which the Buddha lived was again very male-dominated and women had fairly lowly roles in society. The Buddha therefore was probably quite 'modern' in his treatment of women. He did warn his male disciples about the distracting possibilities of women in making a man stray off the right path – but this wasn't a criticism of women, more an attack on the feebleness of men. The eightfold path can be followed by women just as by men and both can achieve enlightenment. The early Buddhist nuns were freed from the tyranny of their male-dominated lives by the dhamma:

> 'Free I am free from the three crooked things: mortar, pestle and my crooked husband. I am free from birth and death and all that dragged me back.'
>
> Therigatha: The enlightenment songs of early bhikkunis (nuns)

Buddhism would not tolerate discrimination based on gender. This would be an example of wrong action, as well as something closer to the three root poisons than to loving kindness, generosity and selflessness. Also, Buddhism would not support the idea of separate working practices for men and women – it would only be concerned that whatever work was being done was 'right livelihood'. The Friends of the Western Buddhist Order FWBO states about Buddhism and Feminists:

> 'Feminism… could be described as a movement that demands… that women should have full access to all the facilities that they require for their development as human beings; it asserts that they should not be confined or limited to any particular range of facilities or activities; and it encourages them to take more initiative, be more independent, and to function as individuals in their own right, rather than being mere extensions or supports to the men in their lives. Feminism of this sort is quite compatible with Buddhism and the spiritual life.'

It argues that in the FWBO: 'no one should be excluded from the process of higher human development, whether on grounds of sex, race, colour, level of education or social position.'

www.fwbo.org/articles/feminism_and_buddhism.html

The organisation Sakyadhita, is the International Association of Buddhist Women. It exists to promote Buddhism generally, but also:

> 'To encourage and help educate women as teachers of the Buddhadharma. To

provide improved facilities for women to study and practice the teachings.' (www.sakyadhita.org)

Buddhism does, however, go one step beyond Christianity in the value it gives to women – there are female deities who embody female divine energy and are common in Tibetan Buddhism. For example, the deity Tara is a Boddhisattva (one who has attained Nibbana but not taken it up in order to help others attain it). In one version of her story, she was a princess named Jnanachandra who attained Nibbana, but was concerned at the lack of female Boddhisattvas and decided to put off Nibbana in order to become a female Boddhisattva. Others say that she is any of 21 female deities in the Buddhist tradition. In general, for Buddhists in everyday life there should be no discrimination based on gender.

A Viewpoint Independent of Religious Belief

Germaine Greer is a well-known feminist. In 1970, her book *The Female Eunuch* set out her vision of feminism some thirty years ago. She argued among other things, that women have not yet come to terms with the extent to which men hate them and just how much they are brought up to hate themselves. She suggested that women had been 'neutered' (just like eunuchs) by a male-dominated society that had kept them subservient for its own purposes – and that women had allowed this and should do so no longer, but rise up in revolt. In 1999 she wrote *The Whole Woman*, as a sequel to the female eunuch and states that this is the book she said she would never write. She mentions that although women have come a long way in the past 30 years, there are still issues that need to be resolved, because she is a little doubtful that modern equality is what it's claimed to be:

> 'From the beginning, feminists have been aware that the causes of female suffering can be grouped under the heading 'contradictory expectations'. The contradictions women face have never been more bruising than they are now. The career woman does not know if she has to do her job like a man or like herself. Is she supposed to change the organisation or knuckle down under it? Is she supposed to endure harassment or kick ass and take names? Is motherhood a privilege or a punishment? . . . The rhetoric of equality is being used in the name of political correctness to mask the hammering that women are taking. . . On every side speechless women endure endless hardship, grief and pain, in a world system that creates billions of losers for every handful of winners. It's time to get angry again.'
>
> *The Whole Woman*, Greer G, Doubleday 1999 p3

Greer wants nothing less than completely equal footing for women with men – in everything, everywhere.

The British Humanist Association states:

> Humanists support personal freedom. This must involve allowing everyone opportunities and choices in the worlds of education, employment and home. Girls and women should not have restricted roles imposed on them, but neither

should they feel that they have to do everything. Men, too, should have the choice of staying at home and looking after children if that is what they want. Within humanist organisations, men and women are treated equally (www.humanism.org.uk).

Check Your Learning

1 Why do some Christians object to women priests?
2 Are male Christians portrayed positively in the media?
3 Do you think that Buddhism is fairer to women than Christianity?
4 Choose one of the bullet points which tries to argue that the 'old ways' were better. Write a response to this from your own point of view.
5 Do you think our ideas of right and wrong should 'change with the times'?
6 Why might Eve be responsible for the treatment of women in Christianity today?
7 Explain what view(s) a Christian could have of women after reading Paul's letters in the Bible.
8 Explain the views of the FWBO on gender equality.
9 Why is Germaine Greer going to get angry again?

Extension Activities

Knowledge, Understanding and Evaluation through Practical Activities

1 Look at the Janet and John stimulus. Write a similar couple of speech bubbles which show gender stereotyping. However, this time, Janet and John are both posh and live life in very traditional male/female roles.
2 Make up a list of forty descriptive words (like tough/gentle etc.). Now give this list to people in your school (who are not studying gender issues!) and ask them to put each word into a 'mostly male' and 'mostly female' category. Do people still stereotype men and women today?
3 Go through some mail-order catalogues and find examples of how they identify whether toys are for boys or girls. Make up a display board showing your findings.
4 Make up a short illustrated talk about gender stereotyping in the media. You could use images or video/DVD clips to illustrate your talk.
5 Make up your own posters like the ones on the EOC website showing women doing traditionally 'male' jobs.
6 Make up an illustrated booklet about the changing role of men and women at work in the 20th (and 21st) Century.

Extension Activities continued

7 Make up your own simplified 'Guide to UK gender discrimination law for employers'.

8 You find you are paid less than a member of the opposite gender though doing the same job. Describe the course of action you would take and why.

9 Design a poster of famous women. Find examples particularly where women have succeeded in traditionally male roles e.g. world leaders, scientists etc.

10 Have a class debate: 'All Christian Churches should allow women to become priests'.

11 Boys, write a speech entitled 'Why women deserve equality'. Girls, write a speech entitled; 'Why men deserve equality'.

12 Do some further research into the viewpoints you have studied in this section and write a fact sheet on the three viewpoints and gender issues.

Unit Assessment Question

Intermediate 1: Name ONE religion you have studied. What does this religion say about the role of women in the religion? **2KU**

Intermediate 2: Explain ONE way in which the media might stereotype men *or* women. **2KU**

Higher: Should a religious person support the idea of women going out to work? **6AE**

Sample Exam Question

Intermediate 1: John stays at home while his wife goes out to work. Explain why someone might disagree with this. **4AE**

Intermediate 2: What does UK law say about equal pay? **4KU**

Higher: 'You cannot be a religious person and a feminist.' How accurate is this statement? **4KU 4AE**

Homework

Carry out a survey into people's views about some of the issues you have explored in this section.

Prepare a report of your findings.

Personal Reflection

In what ways do you conform to the stereotype of male or female?

CHAPTER 3 Gender: Economic Issues

Will Economic Equality Between the Sexes Lead to a More Just Society?

A page from the diary of Lady Cynthia Harris-FForde, partner of Lord Tarquin Harris-Fforde, Lord of Balsquishy Manor:

Oh dear heavens above another insufferable day as lady of the manor. Tarquin's been out shooting all day with his old school friends – though why they need to do so with a perfectly good range of game in the house already I simply do not know. And what of little old me? Yes, another day spent in frippery. I awoke at eight in the customary manner and was served breakfast by Agnes the housekeeper with my usual range of our own hens' eggs. Dressed and read this morning's Times. Tarquin had already risen and was out with his friends – I could hear the crack of the guns far off in the distance. I wandered around the house for a time, straightening up the odd piece of china which Agnes had dislodged from its customary location while doing her daily dusting. Margaret the cook asked me if I had any preference for lunch today. I'd be lunching alone as the men had their picnic with them and would set up table out in the wilds. Harrington was with them and he'd see to all that while the men had their hunting fun. Good old Harrington, he's been with the family since Tarquin was a child – what a dear. Had lunch and read a little while eating. Then wrote a letter to the children; another three months before they come home from boarding school for the summer. I think they rather enjoy being away from home.

In the afternoon I had some ladies visit from the local art appreciation society. I showed them around the manor – they seemed quite pleased at the chance to look at some of our paintings. I know very little about them of course, but they seemed to be quite knowledgeable at any rate. I had a brief snooze in the afternoon, just before tea. Margaret had made another delicious cake – Tarquin really should have some on his return I thought, although he may be late returning. These shooting days often end up with him and his friends staying over in the hunting lodge and making rather merry with the brandy. Well, as it turned out, they did stay on at the hunting lodge. I dare say I'll hear all about it tomorrow. I spent this evening reading a little more and writing up my diary – which is just like a best friend really. I'm very lucky you know. I don't want for anything really – all my material needs are met by Tarquin and the family's very old wealth. Isn't it rather amazing how wealth made so long ago can still sustain us in this day and age... I sometimes worry that I rather depend too much on Tarquin and the privilege which is my lot, but then, what else would I do... it's been like this for a very long time indeed...

The Historic Economic Relationship Between Men and Women in the UK

The traditional relationship between men and women in the UK has been that the man of the house is the breadwinner and the women the home maker. Men traditionally went out to work and left their wives at home. It was a common practice in Scotland for the man to give the woman housekeeping money. This was a proportion of his income which she would use to buy food and keep the house running smoothly. Women would often save something from this for treats for themselves – or wait until their partners thought to buy them something.

In some places – particularly in the west of Scotland – there was the tradition of the 'keepie back'. In this situation, the man would give most of his pay packet to the woman and keep back what he thought he needed for his own purposes – usually traditional male things like drinking and the football. In working class families at any rate, it was clear that men saw the money they earned as theirs and their women were dependent upon them for their economic survival. It is probably true that many men wielded this like a weapon, and that many women were stuck in poor relationships because they wouldn't be able to afford to live apart from their partners.

This level of economic dependence probably often led to women feeling powerless and depressed – caught in a world not of their making. Such situations were complicated things where men physically or mentally abused their wives. Many women 'put up with it' because they didn't see that they had any choice. Of course, most relationships probably didn't involve abuse, but still the fact that women were – consciously or not – 'kept in their place' by the economic power of men would be regarded as abuse by some. Girls grew up observing this relationship and usually ended up in the same kind of relationship themselves. These girls often simply moved at marriage from being supported by their father to being supported by their partner. This is one of the reasons why we say that a father 'gives away' his daughter to her partner during the wedding. Similarly, boys grew up expecting to be the breadwinner and taking on the responsibility for supporting a partner and family. Some of the 'side effects' of this kind of relationship were:

For Women

Women were often 'trapped' in a vicious circle of dependency. The longer they were out of work the less likely it became that they would ever work again as their skills would be out of date or out of practice. Many women worked before marriage but stopped on getting married.

Many women did not feel fulfilled (as society expected them to be) by the role of partner and mother. Many probably wanted more out of their lives, but were unable to achieve it because of their economic dependence on men.

Those women who did work were often working in dull menial jobs and paid a pittance. Partly this was because it was thought that a woman didn't need to earn as much as a man because she would have a man to support her. Employers might see her job as just for 'pin money' – extra income just to be frittered away. This wasn't always true of course. Many women had to work out of economic necessity – but their pay and conditions reflected the idea that their work was secondary to men's.

Many argue that this relationship of dependency was a significant contributor to women's health issues. Where a person feels trapped and without real purpose in life, there does seem to be an effect on their health. It's not completely clear why. Linked to this is the issue of violence against women. Men treated women as their 'property' and some thought this meant they could treat them however they wanted. In the past, laws probably didn't do much to stop men thinking this or following it through with action. The police would often dismiss such 'crimes' as 'a domestic'.

The creative power of many women was definitely stifled. No one is in any doubt today that the skills and abilities women can bring to the workplace are just as good as those men bring. Women are just as capable and intelligent as men. You have to wonder just what a loss it was to society to have some women 'chained to the kitchen sink' when they could have been (and would rather have been) out in the world doing something of earth-shattering importance.

For Men

It's probably true that many men felt equally trapped in this kind of relationship. There was pressure on men to bring in a wage. This might mean a man working long hard hours in a job he didn't like. He might compare his own breadwinning efforts with other men and feel that he wasn't doing enough. This probably led many men to be unhappy and unfulfilled. Also, men might be likely to put their own health issues to one side as they struggled to support their family. This could have serious effects on their health – especially as it often went with an unhealthy lifestyle where nutrition and relaxation took second place to working.

Many men therefore missed out on their children growing up – and only once it was too late did they realise what they'd missed. For children, a dad who wasn't around much because of work probably wasn't good – meaning they missed out on the things a dad can bring to a child's upbringing.

Just like women, the creative power of some men may have been wasted. Men missed out on their further education because this was really something only the rich could afford. If all your earnings went into supporting your family, then your own personal or educational development might be hindered. There might have been men with great things to offer the world if they hadn't been 'chained to their work'.

Check Your Learning

1. In what ways is Lady Cynthia dependent upon her husband?
2. How have women in Scotland traditionally got money when they don't work?
3. Why might economic dependency possibly lead to abuse?
4. Explain why some working women might not have been so well-treated at work as men.
5. In what ways could it be stressful on a man being the family's breadwinner?

The Class Issue

Some argue that the economic relationship between men and women was different according to which social class you were in. They might say that everything you've read on this topic so far is most likely linked to working class families. How true is this? Although working class women depended upon their men for their economic survival because of financial need – women in other classes were just as dependent but for different reasons. For example, the middle classes would have seen it as a statement that they had 'moved up in the world' where they could afford for the woman to stay at home. She wouldn't have to do some menial job to make ends meet (sometimes by doing work in the home) and so she was tied to the house by the need to appear wealthy enough to do so! Naturally this wasn't always the reality. Many middle class couples probably struggled economically but carried on 'to keep up appearances'. So these women remained just as dependent on their men as working class women.

In the upper classes, many women were also shackled to the manor house. Although neither partner needed to work – the social role of the lady of the house was quite well-defined and strict and many upper class women probably had to conform to a role which they didn't like because that's what was expected of them. Some might even argue that for these women it was even worse because they had no role at all. They didn't work, they depended on their partner's wealth for economic survival and they didn't even have to run a home or bring up children – they had employees to do this for them! Some would argue that Lady Cynthia in the stimulus is just as tied to the manor as any working class woman is to the kitchen sink.

Time Out

Do you think that working class men or women have a harder time of it than other classes? (Is social class important in the gender inequality issue?)

How Did Women Become Economically Dependent on Men?

In the past, childbirth and childhood were much more dangerous than they are now. Healthcare and prevention and cure of illness were far less advanced than today. People tended to have large families because it was expected that some children might not live much beyond their childhood. Children were a form of security. In the absence of pensions and welfare, it would be the job of your children to look after you in your old age. You therefore needed children for this. Also children would be able to help support the family economically. It is only within the last hundred years or so that working class children have not been sent out to work as soon as they were able. Because of this, many women spent a long period of their life bearing and rearing children. This kept them out of the workforce and men took that role as provider.

Even once families didn't have to be so big and children were not put to work, men retained the provider role because it had always been that way. Some men probably also enjoyed the 'power' it gave them over their wives and their families. For many people it also seemed more 'natural' for a man to be the provider and women to be responsible for child-rearing and home-making. If nature equipped only women to give birth and feed infants, then nature must intend women to do so. Also, as men were 'naturally' physically stronger, it seemed that nature had chosen them to work and women not to. Add to this religious beliefs and social customs about the role of men and women in the family and society and you have men as breadwinners and women at home (see previous section).

Contemporary Economic Relationships Between Men and Women in the UK

Some argue that things are no different now to what they were in the past. Women still depend on men for their economic survival, with all the problems and issues that such dependence brings. Some men and women seem caught in a 'time warp' where the advances in thinking about the roles of men and women in society seem to have passed them by. Some don't think about it, and their economic relationship is just what has grown and developed through habit – perhaps because that's the model they have from their parents. Others may choose to live in this way – with some men happy to be 'in charge' and who knows, some women happy to be 'kept' by their partner. Some make a positive choice to be this way and others don't. The level of choice you've made as a couple about your economic relationship can affect what that relationship means to you and how it affects you both. So in today's world, we still have very traditional families where women are economically dependent upon their men – just as they were in the past – but there are also differences too:

Female Breadwinners

In many families it is the woman who goes out to work these days. This might be because she has greater earning potential than the man because she has a better level of education or just works in a job or profession which involves higher earnings. This has been made possible partly because of changes in the education of girls throughout the years and partly through social changes which have made it more acceptable for women to go out to work. In such families, the decision that the woman goes out to work is a matter of choice – and it's probable that both the man and the woman are happy with this. However, in other families it is probably through economic necessity. Perhaps the man has lost his job or it doesn't make enough to support the whole family. In this kind of situation the effects of this changed relationship might be different. The man might feel useless and weak because he can't provide, and the woman might feel pressured to go out and work when she would rather raise the children. In these kinds of situations, all the problems associated with women being dependent upon men might be reversed so that the man suffers from all the consequences of lack of economic independence.

Both Working

In many families today this is far more common. Again, it can be a choice or through economic necessity. In some families this means that both the man and the woman will share household tasks equally – or pay people to do them. Childcare may be shared too, along with the use of nurseries and child-minders. However, it is still the case in some families that the woman will work as well as fulfil the home-maker role. This is particularly likely where she earns less than the man – but that's not always the case! For many modern women this takes away the economic dependency, but doesn't really make their lives that much easier.

Talk Point 1

Should the choice of which partner goes out to work be based only on financial issues?

Check Your Learning

1. Explain why a woman being dependent upon a man isn't just linked to one social class.
2. Why might middle class women have decided not to go out to work in the past?
3. Explain ONE major change in recent history between men and women in the workplace.
4. What could the practice of 'working mothers' mean for society generally? (positive and negative outcomes).
5. Why do some women have to work and still maintain the home?

What Would Economic Equality Mean for Society?

Some argue that where a woman depends on a man for her survival she is not empowered. This keeps control of society firmly in the hands of men – with all the negative stuff which that involves. Some argue that men are naturally more aggressive, warlike and uncaring. While they control society we will always be in danger of exploiting others and going to war. A society run by women would be different they argue – kinder, more caring and less likely to lead to conflict. But is this true? Some point to the few world leaders we have already had who were women. There seems to be no evidence that they were any more caring or less aggressive than male world leaders. Some point to the modern fashion of 'ladettes' – girls who are emulating the less attractive aspects of male behaviour – getting wildly drunk, having fights and driving like maniacs. Would a world where men were economically dependent upon women be any better than the world we have now? Some argue that it would not, and that the issue is economic dependence and not which gender is dependent.

Others disagree – arguing that we cannot keep things as they are today because the opposite *might* not be an improvement. They argue that the fact is that it is still mostly women who are economically dependent upon men in the 21st Century, and that this leads to all sorts of social ills and imbalance. We have to tackle this issue so that everyone has the same opportunities regardless of their gender. Maybe a world controlled by women won't be any better, but they should at least have the opportunity available to them to control it (or be better treated in it at least). Changes to economic dependence would get rid of many of the social ills which are attached to it.

Time Out 2

Are women behaving more like men these days? Is that good? Would a change in economic relationships change that?

Talk Point 2

What harm might it do a man or a woman to be completely economically dependent upon someone else?

Men might behave better towards women if they felt that women didn't need them – girls might have more positive role models to emulate as they grew up. No one might feel pressurised into a role they did not want. In short, making the world a fairer place for all is a desirable goal whether you are male or female. Some men might worry about their 'power' being taken from them – and they might not give it up easily. On the other hand, perhaps a fairer world is better for us all in the long run. The Utilitarian might argue that economic fairness between men and women benefits the majority in the long run and so should be a desired goal. Kantian ethics might argue that it is simply right that men and women are treated equally in all aspects of life. It's not to do with the consequences, it's because such fairness is right in itself. To move the world in the direction of increased economic equality between men and women, the UK government has put into place many laws designed to make the world a fairer place no matter what your gender.

UK Laws on Equal Pay

The main piece of legislation here is the Equal Pay Act (1970). This states quite clearly that it is unlawful to pay men or women differently for doing the same job – no matter what the job is. It also provides laws about how employers treat issues like maternity leave. In the UK, a woman is entitled to paid maternity leave and should not be penalised in any way for this. For example, she should not find that it hinders her promotion opportunities, nor that she returns from maternity leave to discover that she has lost out on something through being on maternity leave. A woman should also not suffer in the workplace because she might, at some time in the future, possibly become pregnant. Also in the UK, men are entitled to a period of paid paternity leave – though this is far shorter than maternity leave – based on the argument that women must physically recover from the demands of pregnancy whereas men do not need to.

Other laws refer to the amount people can be paid. In Britain, there is now a minimum wage which employers must offer – this wage should apply equally to men and women. In addition to these legal restrictions, many employers nowadays provide benefits for their employees which should further reduce the possibility of unfair treatment according to your gender. Many employers, for example:

- Provide workplace childcare facilities so that workers can work while raising a family.
- Provide periods of paid leave (sometimes referred to as 'Family Care') where employees can attend to family issues (it could be taking a child to the doctor or looking after an elderly relative).
- Have positive discrimination policies which aim to even out gender imbalance, for example, ensuring that a percentage of candidates for a job are male/female or keeping the gender of the applicant confidential right up to the point of interview.
- Constantly review their policies with respect to gender to ensure equality of treatment.

All of these are designed to put right the gender economic imbalances from the past. Some will still argue that they do not go far enough – pensionable age is still an area of disagreement. Others argue that positive discrimination is wrong because it is just another form of discrimination. On the other hand, others might claim that such laws and policies are an economic burden to employers and society. Some of course argue that in making men and women more economically equal we have altered the 'natural' roles of men and women in society and that this is not good for society as a whole.

The Equal Opportunities Commission

This monitors all possible forms of sex discrimination in the UK. One major focus is closing the pay gap between men and women. Recently it commented that this gap was still big and amounted to a staggering amount over a woman's lifetime...

Source 1

On the 26th October 2006, the new ONS pay statistics were released, showing the pay gap remains a shocking 17.2 per cent, the Equal Opportunities Commission (EOC) has used these figures to estimate that the average woman working full-time will lose out on around £330,000 over the course of her working life.

That's a hefty loss she might have other plans for, both big and small. It translates into:

- 19 house down payments
- Paying off a student debt 21 times over
- 29 years of childcare
- 15 new cars
- 525 extra holidays
- 10,500 nights out, including dinner and drinks, with friends

www.eoc.org.uk/Default.aspx?page=19724

The EOC is currently running a pensions campaign. It argues that this is still one significant area where men and women do not achieve equal treatment – with the balance in favour of men. However, the EOC does argue that if pensions for women are sorted out then this will also lead to a fairer pensions system for all…

Source 2

'If we get it right for women, we'll get it right for everyone'

- 1 in 5 single women pensioners risk being in poverty in retirement.
- 2.2 million women are not accruing rights to even the Basic State Pension. Retired men on average have between £50 to £100 per week more private pension income than women of the same age.
- The numbers of women who are saving for retirement halves when they have a baby. The figure for men remains unchanged when they become new fathers.
- 95% of people agree that women should have their own individual pension rights and should not rely on a husband or partner.
- Nearly 6 out of 10 people agree that NI contributions should rise by 1 per cent to give parents and those caring for others the same state pension rights as those who have been in paid work.

www.eoc.org.uk/Default.aspx?page=19748

Talk Point 3

Do you think fairer treatment for the world's women would benefit everyone?

UN Declarations

Throughout the UN Declaration on human rights, it is continually stressed that all the rights which are due to human beings – from the right to an education to the right to fair treatment at work – apply equally to men and women. However, the UN seems to recognise that globally the human rights of women are under greater pressure than those of men. For this reason, the UN has made specific attempts to secure economic equality for women. In September 1995, the UN's fourth world conference on women was held in Beijing in China. A 'platform for action' on women's rights was developed here:

> The Platform for Action is an agenda for women's empowerment. It aims at… removing all the obstacles to women's active participation in all spheres of public and private life through a full and equal share in economic, social, cultural and political decision-making. This means that the principle of shared power and responsibility should be established between women and men at home, in the workplace and in the wider national and international

communities. Equality between women and men is a matter of human rights and a condition for social justice and is also a necessary and fundamental prerequisite for equality, development and peace. A transformed partnership based on equality between women and men is a condition for people-centred sustainable development. A sustained and long-term commitment is essential, so that women and men can work together for themselves, for their children and for society to meet the challenges of the 21st century.

www.un.org/womenwatch/daw/beijing/platform/plat1.htm#statement

The Beijing Platform recommended that there were certain areas which it saw as areas of critical concern with respect to fair and equal treatment for the women of the world:

- The persistent and increasing burden of poverty on women.
- Inequalities and inadequacies in and unequal access to education and training.
- Inequalities and inadequacies in and unequal access to health care and related services.
- Violence against women.
- The effects of armed or other kinds of conflict on women, including those living under foreign occupation.
- Inequality in economic structures and policies, in all forms of productive activities and in access to resources.
- Inequality between men and women in the sharing of power and decision-making at all levels.
- Insufficient mechanisms at all levels to promote the advancement of women.
- Lack of respect for and inadequate promotion and protection of the human rights of women.
- Stereotyping of women and inequality in women's access to and participation in all communication systems, especially in the media.
- Gender inequalities in the management of natural resources and in the safeguarding of the environment.
- Persistent discrimination against and violation of the rights of the girl child.

www.un.org/womenwatch.daw.beijing/platform/plat1.htm#concern

In 2005, the UN got together again in the Beijing + 5 process to further the aims of the Beijing Platform declarations from five years before. Among other things, this conference looked at the Role of Men and Boys in Ending Gender-Based Violence (6 June 2000). Notable achievements in this area, according to the UN, are:

- In 1997, the United States granted more than 10,000 loans, totalling 67 billion dollars, to women business-owners.
- Cameroon, Madagascar and Niger have identified women as a specific target group in their national poverty eradication programmes.
- Senegal has conducted gender training for senior decision-makers to mainstream a gender perspective into sectoral development planning.

www.un.org/womenwatch/daw/followup/session/presskit/fs1.htm

The Global Dimension: Women and the World Economy

The United Nations Organisation, the United Nations Development Fund for Women (UNIFEM) argues that *feminised poverty* is one of the major issues facing the world today. Feminised poverty is the idea that women become and remain poor as a result of their gender. It states:

> Since poverty traps women in multiple layers of discrimination and hinders their ability to claim their rights, ending feminised poverty has always been a core UNIFEM priority. Not only do women bear a disproportionate burden of the world's poverty, but in some cases, globalisation has widened the gap, with women losing more than their share of jobs, benefits and labour rights. From tax systems to trade regimes, however, economic policies and institutions still mostly fail to take gender disparities into account. With too few seats at the tables where economic decisions are made, women themselves have little chance of rectifying the deepening of existing inequalities.
>
> www.unifem.org/gender_issues/women_poverty_economics/at_a_glance.php

It is often argued that the world's women do badly out of the world's economy:

- Women are often paid less for the same work as men.
- Women do not receive the same kind of social benefits as men, for example, pensions, and paid sick leave.
- Women often end up in the lowest paid and most poorly regulated jobs in society and experience poor working conditions.
- Women are often more likely than men to be exploited in the workplace – from working in sweatshops to being involved in the sex trade.
- Women are under-represented in the political systems of the world – from local government to worldwide institutions, women don't hold the reins of power in the same way that men do. Many argue that this means their situation gets worse because they don't have the political power to change it.
- Many women still have to combine often hard working lives with running a home and raising a family.
- Because of their economic lack of power, many women probably suffer at home too – through physical and emotional abuse by their partners. The economic

situation probably doesn't cause this, but will mean that many women feel that they have to stay in such abusive relationships because having no means of support they don't see that there is any alternative.

Elsewhere, the UN expands upon its ideas of what the feminisation of poverty means that the majority of the 1.5 billion people living on 1 dollar a day or less are women. In addition, the gap between women and men caught in the cycle of poverty has continued to widen in the past decade, a phenomenon commonly referred to as 'the feminisation of poverty'. Worldwide, women earn on average slightly more than 50 per cent of what men earn.

Women living in poverty are often denied access to critical resources such as credit, land and inheritance. Their labour goes unrewarded and unrecognised. Their health care and nutritional needs are not given priority, they lack sufficient access to education and support services, and their participation in decision-making at home and in the community are minimal. Caught in the cycle of poverty, women lack access to resources and services to change their situation

www.un.org/womenwatch/daw/followup/session/presskit/fs1.htm

Check Your Learning

1. Would more female leaders make the world a better place for women?
2. Why might some men worry about their economic 'power' being taken from them?
3. Is economic dependence still an issue about women in the 21st Century?
4. Describe what UK law says about equal pay for men and women.
5. What changes to the UK pensions situation does the EOC want to see?
6. Explain what the major recommendations of the Beijing Platform for Action are.
7. What is meant by feminised poverty?
8. What evidence does the UN give for the existence of feminised poverty?

Time Out 3

Do you think organisations like the UN are right to focus so much on the rights of women? Are they paying enough attention to the rights of men?

Advantages and Disadvantages of Different Economic Relationships

The 'Traditional Relationship': Man as Breadwinner and Woman as Homemaker

Advantages

It is more 'natural', allowing men to support the 'natural' female role of mothering and home-making.

It allows both men and woman to be equal yet different.

It provides stability for society and positive role models for children.

Disadvantages

It keeps women economically dependent upon men, which can lead to many abuses, both personal and social ones.

It denies men and women the opportunity to express themselves the way they want to and not as they think society expects them to (especially true where a woman stays at home simply because her partner earns more).

It does not provide a good role model for children as suggests only one possible form of male/female relationship.

Both Man and Woman in a Relationship Working in Equally Well-Paid Jobs

Advantages

It brings a good level of income into the home where both man and woman are economically independent – this personal independence being a good thing.

It allows both man and women to express themselves and develop their work skills as much as they want and so leading to a more creative and rewarding life (and so society).

It provides good role models of successful people for both male and female children.

Disadvantages

Home and family life outside work may suffer – as this may take second place to work-related issues.

It may just lead to a more pressurised society for everyone as competition overtakes cooperation – too many people chasing too few jobs may make work harder to get and hold on to.

It may provide the wrong kind of role models for children – suggesting that personal fulfilment can only be achieved through work.

The 'Modern Relationship': Woman as Breadwinner and Man as Homemaker

Advantages

It gives women both economic independence as well as the economic 'upper hand' in a relationship.

It is more likely to lead to women being empowered in many other aspects of modern life.

It provides good role models for children as they can see that gender does not need to determine role in the world.

It allows men and women to choose how to live their lives rather than following society's unwritten 'rules'.

Disadvantages

It makes men economically dependent upon women which could lead to the same kinds of abuses as where women are dependent upon men.

It may not be a good role model for children as it just suggests a different form of inequality at home and work.

It may deny the man the chance to express himself in his work, especially if his staying at home is because his partner's earning powers are greater.

Talk Point 

4

Which of these three relationships do you think is 'best'? Why?

Moral Implications

The economic relationship between men and women is mostly to do with the balance of power in society.

Can it ever be right to pay people for their work differently according to their gender? Most people would argue that it wouldn't be right. However, some might argue that people should be paid according to their need – so if a family had only one breadwinner then she or he would be paid more than someone doing the same job who was not the only breadwinner in a family.

Does economic imbalance between the sexes lead to an unjust society? Again, most would probably argue that it does and that the sexism this demonstrates is just as wrong as racism and any other kind of discrimination. Some would say that economic imbalance harms society as it keeps some people 'beneath' others and so splits society into 'haves' and 'have-nots'. This is especially wrong because it depends upon your gender – over which you have no control – rather than anything you have control over (such as how hard you work). This has all sorts of related effects on a society – from making girls less likely to push themselves at school because they don't see the point if they're going to earn far less than men to men thinking that they are more valuable members of society than women because they're paid more.

Christianity

As you know by now, Christians have quite mixed views about the role of women in society in general. However, most Christians would be concerned if a woman felt powerless or devalued because she was economically dependent on a man. Christians believe that all people are created in the image of God and as such all have equal worth. That doesn't mean to say that they have the same roles in society, but they do all have the right to be treated with love. Some Christians talk about a concept called *complementarity*. This is the idea that men and women complement each other – each provides something that the other does not and they are equal but different. There is very little in the Bible which might suggest to Christians that women have to stay at home and depend for their survival on their men.

Also, there is certainly nothing which would suggest that a man should feel that he is more important than a woman and can lord it over her because he is the breadwinner. In fact, even in modern Christian communities where women do stay at home and men work this is not seen as making the man something better than the woman, but in fact as an added responsibility for the man who must provide for his wife. It is therefore more of a responsibility than a right. Although some Christians remain convinced that a woman's place is in the home – even more conservative Christians argue that the role of women is as varied today as men's and should be that way.

Source 3

RISK-FREE TRIAL ISSUE!

From cover to cover, Today's Christian Woman magazine is written with you in mind. Each issue is brimming with lively and trustworthy articles, stories, and regular features that cover meaningful areas in your life – family, career, children, health, and friendships. Each article provides fresh inspiration and biblical insight to help you meet the pressures of life with greater confidence.

The organisation, Christians for Biblical Equality states:

In the Christian home, husband and wife are to defer to each other in seeking to fulfil each other's preferences, desires and aspirations. Neither spouse should seek to dominate the other but each
is to act as servant of the other... In so doing, husband and wife will help the Christian home stand against improper use of power and authority by spouses and will protect the home from wife and child abuse that sometimes tragically follows a hierarchical interpretation of the husband's 'headship'.

www.christianitytoday.com/women/features/conversations.html
www.cbeinternational.org

Buddhism

In some forms of Buddhism, ordained monks and nuns are completely economically dependent upon the lay Buddhist community, without whom they would not survive. Buddhism stresses that all life on earth is interdependent – we all depend on each other. Buddhists would not mind whether the male or female in any relationship was the breadwinner – it wouldn't make any difference. What would be wrong would be if the breadwinner made the supported person feel less valuable as a person because they were not earning. This would be selfish and hurtful. Buddhism would oppose any discrimination based on income or lack of it. Some Buddhist businesses, for example, are unusual in that they pay people according to their need not their qualifications or job. In such businesses it would be possible for the Chief Executive to earn less than a 'factory floor worker' if the latter's need was greater. With this kind of approach to economic equality – it would be fairly unlikely for Buddhists to support economic differences based on gender alone.

Obviously if economic dependence led to either men or women being abused or exploited in any way then Buddhists would oppose this. All beings should be happy according to Buddhists, and exploitation and abuse as a result of economic imbalance could lead to people being unhappy. According to the female Buddhist teacher, Swarna de Silva, the Buddha was 'not interested in establishing and perpetuating a particular world order, for whatever actual regime that would be put in place would in a Buddhist sense be unsatisfactory'. However, obviously the

Buddha would have preferred a fair "world order" rather than an unfair one. The Hindu world in which the Buddha lived had very strict roles for men and women at home as well as boys and girls – the Buddha's approach to women was therefore very enlightened – no pun intended.

Source 4

The Buddha lived in an ancient religious culture where, for most people, one's position remained defined for life. Though the Buddha was unable to dispense totally with gender discrimination, he still launched women's spirituality as a collective force... The Buddha's willingness to accept women into the... sangha... radically challenged the conventional role for women, thus sparking a liberation movement in [his] culture.

If one were to get a general principle on the question of the relation between the sexes it is the principle of reciprocity and non-dominance that emerges in the Buddhist writing. Even in the later Jatakas it is sometimes stated that women who live in fear of their husbands are not true wives

The Green Buddha, Titmuss C, Insight books 1995 p251
www.enabling.org

Viewpoints Independent of Religious Belief

The British Humanist Association argues that:

Source 5

'...discrimination becomes something unfair and harmful when it stops people flourishing by making a big issue out of unimportant or irrelevant differences... if we are all to be happy and prosper, every individual needs the chance to flourish and play a part in society. Society loses out if we prevent some of its members from contributing for no good reason, and it is in everyone's interest to oppose prejudice and discrimination, not just those on the receiving end of it. If we treated people of all kinds with respect, the world would be a more peaceful and happy place'

www.humanism.org.uk

This viewpoint represents a Utilitarian approach to gender equality. It suggests that a fairer world will benefit us all in the long run. The issue for a utilitarian would not be whether a woman stayed at home or went to work, it would be whether she had the choice about which one to do, and about how she was treated once she had made that choice. A society where everyone can have free choice about their role in life and be fairly treated in whatever role they choose is obviously one which would maximise happiness and minimise unhappiness.

Check Your Learning

1. Explain ONE advantage and ONE disadvantage of a 'traditional' relationship where the man works and the woman stays at home.
2. Do you think economic imbalance between the sexes is unfair?
3. What do Christians mean by complementarity? What do you think of this idea?
4. What does the organisation Christians for Biblical Equality teach about the role of men and women?
5. What might the fact that the Buddha welcomed women into the sangha tell us about what he would think of economic inequality between men and women today?
6. Explain how the British Humanist Association's argument about gender equality represents a Utilitarian viewpoint.
7. What are the similarities and differences between the three viewpoints you have studied in relation to the economic relationship between men and women?

Extension Activities

Knowledge, Understanding and Evaluation through Practical Activities

1. You are the leader of a feminist group. You have just read Lady Cynthia's diary. Write a letter to Lord Harris-Fforde.
2. Work out how much you think it might cost to run your own house for a week. If your parents are happy to discuss it, you could simply ask them. It would also be interesting for you to find out what percentage this is of the money coming into your house – perhaps you'll be a bit more sensitive to your family financial situation!
3. Carry out an anonymous written survey into gender economic relationships. You should aim to find out what proportion of couples both work, or where the man or woman only works.
4. Carry out further research into the facts and figures behind the issues in this topic. These figures are constantly changing so haven't been included in the book. Just how much more than women do men earn on average?
5. Have a class debate: 'Supporting women is a man's role – it's not domination but protection'.
6. You are a man who believes that paternity leave should be just as long as maternity leave. Write a letter to your employer outlining your views.
7. In groups, choose a number of developing world countries. For each one, make up a fact sheet about the economic position of women in that country.

Extension Activities continued

8 Make up an illustrated poster entitled 'Feminised Poverty'.

9 Make up a poster which encourages employers to pay men and women equally.

10 Using information in this section and the previous section do a 'Frequently Asked Questions' item for an imaginary Christian website focusing on Christian views of women and their economic status.

11 Look into the Jataka tales. Which tales have messages about the treatment of women? (see: www.thebuddhistsociety.org)

12 Make a list of things you think would improve in society if women and men were paid equally and neither had to be economically dependent upon the other.

Unit Assessment Question

Intermediate 1: Jim doesn't want his wife to go out to work. What reasons might he give for this? **4KU**

Intermediate 2: 'Women should be treated as the equals of men in all respects'. Would a religious person agree? **4AE**

Higher: 'Religions have unfortunately done a good job in keeping women under the control of men.' How might someone who bases their morality on a viewpoint independent of religious belief support this statement? **4KU 6AE**

Sample Exam Question

Intermediate 1: What is meant by the economic dependence of women? **2KU**

Intermediate 2: How has the economic relationship between men and women changed in the recent past? **6KU**

Higher: 'The economic equality of women will lead to a far more just society.' Do you agree? **4KU 8AE**

Homework

Interview a couple about their working life choices. Keep their personal information confidential, but present a short report of your findings to your class and note down the variety of types of economic relationship you hear about.

Personal Reflection

Would you be happy being economically dependent on someone who is the opposite gender to you?

CHAPTER 4 Crime and Punishment: The Purpose of Punishment

On What Grounds Can Punishment Be Morally Justified?

Timothy is four years old. He sometimes gets into trouble. He thinks through the reasons for his various punishments. Although he's only four he hits on the four main reasons for punishment which moral philosophers have long debated. . .

When you have done something very, very bad something even bigger and more very bad will happen to you. You should always be good. You might get a smack – but the Primed Minister who works in a cabinet thinks this is bad too and so maybe you won't get a smack. But your mummy and daddy might have had a bad day and just get you back for the rotten thing you done. But they should not do this because this is just getting REVENGES and mummies and daddies should teach you that hitting back is not good and you should just tell them and they will fix it all and you should not hit back. But if your mummy and daddy give you a smack you won't smile at them any more and you will just think they are grumpy old people who drink wine. Even if they don't give you a smack they might shout very loud in your face and you will have to smell old people breath. Or they might just hide your toys.

You might also get a row to teach you A LESSON. Then you will know what you done wrong and you will watch out next time and you will be a nicer person who does good things not bad things. This will turn you into a fine upstanding citizen and you will vote and sing the song about saving the Queen who is grace.

➜

If you get bad trouble from mummy and daddy you will be good from now on but other people will see that you got trouble and this will scare them. This will make them be PUT OFF doing bad because they don't want to catch your trouble which they might get if you sneeze or don't wash your hands after loo-loo or something. When you are bad you might be told to be groundinged. This means that you don't get out to play in case you be bad somewhere mummy and daddy can't see and hurt other children (my big brother is always groundinged but that's because he's a teen-aged-er and it's not fair because they get picked on). This means that all the nicey nicey boys and girls get PROTECTING from the nasty you – even though they might just be big cry-babies. You might have to stay in your room and not get jelly or ice cream and you might only get to watch TV like Question Time and things where people wearing ties talk about things which make you sleepy.

But mummies and daddies punish you when you are very bad and they think this is their job and people will talk about them if they are scared of you and you will grow up to be a delinkwent or even worse.

Talk Point 1

When you've done something wrong at home, what kinds of punishments do you get? Which are the most and least effective?

What is Punishment For?

When you have done something wrong, you get punished. Obviously the seriousness of the punishment is linked to the seriousness of the crime. The greater the crime, the harder the punishment. This is for a number of reasons.

You have to know that society thinks that certain crimes are more serious than others. The level of punishment gives you an idea of this. Hopefully this will lead to fewer people doing the really nasty stuff.

If the punishment for one crime is too harsh then what's to stop you doing something even worse – it's not like it's going to matter any more is it? For example, if the punishment for scratching someone was the same as for murdering someone then there's no real incentive for you not to murder them too. But if the punishment for murder is worse than for scratching then you're less likely to go on to commit murder aren't you?

No matter what level of punishment you get for a particular crime, the reasons why you are being punished are the same whether it's for a serious criminal offence or being nippy to your very nice parents. The answer to the question 'what is punishment for?' should obviously be 'to punish someone'. The real question is about why we punish people. What are the reasons behind punishment? Are some reasons for punishment morally justifiable and others not?

Time Out 1

Can you think of any situation where it might be wrong to punish someone for something they have done wrong?

Retribution

'I'll get you back for that pal'

Your RMPS Teacher asks wee Tony why he has just thumped Stuart. Tony replies, 'Sorry Sir, I was simply exacting some degree of retribution for an offence previously committed to me by said Tony.' Yeah, right. In school you've probably heard the defence from pupil to teacher about something they've done wrong: 'Aye, but he did it tae me'. This is an example of revenge or getting someone back for something they've done. There's probably a little of this in all punishments. It's a kind of balancing act: 'You've done X so X should be done to you'. It is almost as though your punishment evens things up somehow, bringing some kind of balance back to an imbalanced situation. There's maybe also a bit of anger release going on too in some cases, though this varies, but it can be hurting someone back because they've hurt you – all even now, ah that's better.

Talk Point 2

Is Tony's defence of his actions acceptable?

Retribution has two obvious meanings:
Revenge – getting back at someone for what they have done. This might even just be to make you feel better.
Restoration – Making the offender pay back for what's been done – in some way restoring things to right.

Benefits of Retribution

Some people believe that **revenge** is a perfectly good reason for punishing. In some countries, revenge is closely tied to the idea of honour. It is thought to be honourable to take revenge when you, or someone in your family, has been wronged. This shows that you have courage and are proud enough of yourself or your family to defend yourself. This maybe makes people realise that your family is not to be messed with and that if it is, the person who does it will have to pay for it.

Revenge also makes it quite clear that you, your family, or the society in which you live won't take assaults lying down. It sends a clear message that there will be consequences for whatever action is taken against you. In fact, you may have in your pocket an example of this... On a Scottish pound coin you will find the phrase '*Nemo me impune lacessit*', which is the motto of Scotland. It means, 'No one shall provoke me with impunity' or, in other words, 'Dinnae mess wi me pal'. This suggests that any such provocation will attract some kind of retribution. Maybe someone should tell Tony that all he's done is to rephrase the motto of his own nation and apply it in his defence.

Revenge can also be a way to make people who have been wronged feel better – and what's so bad about that? It's probably a perfectly natural human response which has developed to ensure our mental health – or maybe even our survival.

Talk Point **3**

Some people say that criminals should be handed over to their victims who should decide how they should be punished. What do you think of this suggestion?

Retribution is also sometimes seen as restoring an imbalance back to balance. In many societies, laws based on **restorative retribution** aim to make the wrongdoer pay something back for the wrong done. In the UK this is part of the reason for Community Service sentences – someone does wrong and they try to make up for it by doing something useful for the community to make amends. The trouble here of course is that this can only work for certain crimes. What could you do to make up for having killed someone? In some countries this can mean that offenders have to pay back an amount of money to the victims (or their family) to make up for what has been done – or maybe even work for them in some way. In the UK it might mean a burglar would have to paint an old lady's house...

Drawbacks of Retribution

The big trouble with revenge is... when does it end? If you have to take revenge for every wrong done, then revenge won't ever end. Imagine that Luigi kills a member of Malky's family, so in revenge Malky kills a member of Luigi's family. In revenge Luigi kills another member of Malky's family and so it goes on and on... To make sure that revenge does end somewhere, someone has to stop it permanently. For a society to take revenge against its people would just mean that people would continue to take revenge against society in some way or another. Tit for tat wrongdoing would therefore just go on. Also, why should anyone suffer for someone else's wrongdoing? Should you be blamed for something wrong done by your brother or your parents?

It is also very odd for a society to accept a method of punishment which is based on the schoolboy excuse that 'he did it to me first' – not exactly a grown up way to live is it? Not much of an example for young people to follow. In fact, revenge as a reason for punishing people seems pretty strange altogether. Also, for a society, revenge just doesn't seem like the right response to solving problems at all – many crimes are committed by people in the heat of the moment. Society's revenge, in whatever form of punishment it may take, is cold, calculated and clinical – doesn't really match up does it? So getting people back for what they have done by doing it to them sends out a confusing message. It would seem as if society taking revenge is saying that it's not okay for you to do whatever you did and we'll prove that to you by doing it to you too...

And what about making the wronged person feel good? Does getting revenge really make you feel better? That's hard to say. It might just do in the short term, but what about the long term? Anyway, even if it did make the wronged person feel good is that a good enough reason to excuse it? After all the act of revenge will have consequences too: you will cause hurt and maybe pain to others, and not just the person who wronged you – it will also be their family – who are just as innocent of any wrongdoing as you were when first wronged!

What about the 'dinnae mess with me' argument? Again, it seems an odd way for a society to work to be based on the idea of getting people back for the things they have done – or even just threatening to. Do we really want a world where we have to think twice about everything we do because it might lead to someone getting us back for it? Would we really want to live in a society where the government thought that was a perfectly grown up way to respond to problems? People shouldn't live in constant fear of acts of revenge should they? Revenge might be a perfectly natural human emotion – but does that make it right? Just because it's natural doesn't make it good.

Time Out 2

Have you ever wanted to get revenge on someone? Did you? If you did, was it a good way to deal with the situation? If not, why didn't you take revenge?

Retribution as restoration is also not easy to work out. Someone has to decide how much should be paid back, in time or money, for certain crimes. But is this possible? Can you put a price on the pain and suffering which crime causes its victims? And isn't it just an easy way out? You commit a crime and all the punishment you get is having to tidy up a public park? Big deal.

One last wee but important point. Retribution, like all forms of punishment, needs to be based on the correct facts if it is going to be an accepted way to punish. If you get revenge by getting back at the wrong person or you made a mistake about who committed the wrong in the first place then you don't just have a chain of revenge – you have a very complicated and nasty web of revenge and revenge for revenge and so on.

The Moral Implications of Retribution

The conversation between your RMPS teacher and wee Tony above probably involved, at some point, your teacher explaining to Tony that thumping Stuart makes Tony just as bad as Stuart! The major problem with revenge as a form of retribution is that it makes the person taking revenge do something equally wrong to the person who did the bad thing in the first place. How can that be right? If someone steals from you and so you steal something back from them is that right? Does that make you a thief too? Taking revenge could have serious psychological consequences for the person doing it – and might not always be possible anyway. Imagine that you have been beaten up: could you really be put into a room with the person who did it to you, and beat them up back? Even if you were helped to do this (if the person was stronger than you) what would you feel afterwards? Joy? Satisfaction? Some people might – but what kind of person would that make them? Getting people back for wrongs they have done might actually make your situation worse instead of better. Take Malky and Luigi above – would they really be happy with each additional death? Surely not. So retribution as revenge might seem like what we'd like to do to an offender, but in reality what would it do to us?

And what about restorative retribution? Could we really draw up a table of wrongs and give them a score? Who would decide this and based on what? What about the situation itself? Is all killing equally bad? Should we treat all murderers or burglars in the same way? It all seems just a little too simplistic to work doesn't it?

A Christian View of Retribution

There are two clear responses from Christianity about revenge. One based on the Old Testament and one on the New Testament. Most Christians would probably agree that Jesus' teaching cancels out the Old Testament one and replaces it – but of course some Christians don't think so and would still use the Old Testament teaching as something to support their acceptance of retribution as a good reason for punishment.

The Old Testament view probably has to be seen in its context. It was given as part of a law which was designed to keep society stable in difficult times. Maybe they thought it was enough to say it without actually having to do it too.

Source 1

'Eye for eye, tooth for tooth, hand for hand, foot for foot, burn for burn, bruise for bruise...'

Exodus 21:24-25

This law was part of a typical way to make laws at the time – by making it obvious what would happen if you didn't stick to your side of the bargain. So, if you sliced off someone's ear in a drunken argument, then your ear had to go too. The distinction between deterrence (see below) and retribution is a bit fuzzy here because obviously the aim was for you to be so afraid of something being done to you that you'd avoid ever doing it to anyone else.

By the time of Jesus, this law was mostly applied in monetary form – with set penalties having to be paid by wrongdoers according to the crime they'd committed. Jesus was being quite clear when he said:

Source 2

'You have heard that it was said 'an eye for an eye, and a tooth for a tooth'. But now I tell you: do not take revenge on someone who wrongs you. If anyone slaps you on the right cheek, let him slap you on the left cheek too...'

Matthew 5:38-39

Most Christians today think that this teaching rules out retribution as a way of punishing in the form of revenge. It doesn't need to rule out restorative retribution though and doesn't obviously mean that Christians should just accept anything or avoid seeing that justice is done. This teaching fits in with a lot of the other teachings of Jesus which stress that we should be positive and creative in our response to wrongs done. We can hate the wrong done but love the wrongdoer at the same time. One of the advantages of this is that it's more likely to avoid acts of revenge spiralling out of control. It's part of Jesus' teachings about meeting hate with love and demonstrating forgiveness no matter what. In turning the other cheek, you attempt to turn a negative destructive reaction into a positive and creative one.

A good example of turning the other cheek comes from South Africa. South Africa used to be run by a minority of whites. The treatment of the majority blacks was not good at all. However, there were also many cases of people being rotten to others no matter what their colour was. After the end of apartheid, Archbishop Desmond Tutu was given the job of setting up the **truth and reconciliation committee**. He knew that after apartheid ended people might want to get revenge on those who had wronged them. He brought together wrongdoers and the people they had wronged and let them listen to each other and ask for forgiveness. This was very public and often very emotionally charged – some of it was even on TV. But it worked. A lot of bloodshed was probably avoided by this unique approach to dealing with the possibility of endless revenge. There was retribution happening though – people made up for what they had done by saying they were sorry for it and promising to change for the better.

Source 3

'It is not enough to say let bygones be bygones,' Archbishop Desmond Tutu said, speaking with great conviction. 'Indeed, just saying that ensures it will not be so. Reconciliation does not come easy. Believing it does will ensure that it will never be. We have to work and look the beast firmly in the eyes. Ultimately you discover that without forgiveness, there is no future.'

www.forgivenessday.org/tutu.htm (the Worldwide Forgiveness Alliance)

Christians also believe that retribution goes on beyond your death. Whatever you have done will be judged by God and you will have to pay back for it – perhaps for all eternity! Christians believe in Heaven and Hell and one of the reasons you might end up in hell is as a punishment for your sins during life.

A Buddhist View of Retribution

Buddhists would definitely not support revenge. However, the idea of retribution for wrongs committed is central to the faith. No one gets you back as such, instead, your actions produce their own consequences. Whatever you do in life, good or bad, results in consequences where you may have to pay back for the wrong that you've done. This is in the form of kamma. As you go through life, all of your moral choices have kammic consequences – good or bad. This kamma constantly sets the pattern for the next you and so you go through life being constantly reborn based on what you have done in your life to that point. Your next rebirth, from moment to moment, is based on your actions which are based on your beliefs. Whatever choices you make will result in you having to pay back for the consequences of these choices. Even when your physical body ceases to exist at death something carries over into the next rebirth based on what you have done in this life. There's no heaven or hell, but you constantly shape the new you based on the actions of the old you, paying back right enough!

Source 4

Kamma is not Punishment

According to Buddhism, neither punishment nor reward is meted out by some 'Higher Power'.

However, we are subject to **the consequences of our actions, a situation called *kamma*.** Because our constant wants and needs are ever-changing, that fact initiates yet more activity with consequences. Therefore, we should try to act judiciously, or mindfully.

The **impermanent nature of reality** complicates the situation, as it is influenced by the sum total of all the consequences of the ever-changing inter-activity of all beings. To help the situation, we should avoid actions that are un-virtuous (or perhaps a better expression is *unskilful*) such as those that are motivated through anger, lust, greed, confusion or ignorance.

www.khandro.net/buddhism_paths_tibetan.htm

Time Out 3

In what way(s) is the you of today based on the things you did yesterday?

A Viewpoint Independent of Religious Belief on Retribution

The British Humanist Association recognises that there is no single Humanist view on punishment and retribution. It distances itself from the Christian view of meeting hatred with love however. Humanists suggest that the best form of punishment is the one that works to reduce or get rid of crime. So, perhaps if retribution could be clearly shown to be a solution, Humanists would accept it as a good way of punishing. However, Humanists also stress that humans are very complex beings and no two situations can be treated in the same way, nor two different individuals. Obviously this is tricky when you're looking at the same crime committed by two different people. How much do you take into account each person's circumstances in deciding how to punish them? Not easy.

Humanists in practice would almost certainly not support revenge because decisions about punishment should be neutral and unbiased. The strong emotions associated with revenge would interfere with this.

Source 5

Humanists generally find 'Do as you would be done by', the 'golden rule', a useful ethical principle, based on our knowledge of human nature and on our need to be treated well by others and to live harmoniously with others. But when dealing with crime and criminals, it has to be admitted that the 'golden rule' doesn't work very well – trying to apply the golden rule by imagining what we would want if we were burglars, would probably result in extreme leniency. But perhaps a burglar has forfeited his right to be treated according to the golden rule of reciprocity by not following it himself – when he steals he is not treating others as he would like to be treated. The Christian ethic of forgiveness and turning the other cheek also seems inadequate in the face of crime, and would, quite literally, allow people to get away with murder.

The Chinese philosopher Confucius seems to have got it right when asked what he thought of the principle of repaying injury with kindness. He replied, 'With what then will you recompense kindness? Recompense injury with justice, and recompense kindness with kindness'.

www.humanism.org.uk

This quote simply says that you can't just apply the same rules about punishment to everyone in every situation. You also definitely can't apply rules about how you treat the person next door to how you treat Alex the Axe Murderer (unless Alex lives next door that is...). Humanists aim for a solution to the causes of crime. They would be unlikely to support revenge as retribution because of the possibility of a mistake being made about the offender and so an act of revenge being carried out on the wrong person. They could support retribution as making amends for what you have done in the form of some kind of community service.

Retribution Scottish-Style

What forms of punishment in Scotland are examples of retribution? Probably all of them:

- When you get a **fine**, you have to pay something back for breaking the law. This money might be used by the government to help the victims of crime. Recently, money seized from drug pushers in Scotland has been used to set up drug education projects with young people.
- **Community service** is obviously retribution – you have to give up

your time and energy to work for others in the community. This pays the community something back.

- Finally, **imprisonment** takes away your freedom – maybe you paying back for taking away someone's life or making them prisoners in their homes because of the fear which they have following your crime. For many people, prison is seen as something which should be a really grotty experience, as a way of society getting its revenge on you. Obviously the more serious your crime the larger the fine or the longer the sentence – this 'balances up' what you've done – it 'takes' something from you just like you've taken something from someone else.

Talk Point

4

Should prison be a horrible experience for prisoners?

Check Your Learning

1. In what TWO ways can retribution be understood?
2. Explain ONE benefit of retribution: for society; for the victims of crime.
3. State ONE possible drawback of retribution.
4. Do you think it is right to take revenge?
5. Can retribution really make up for a crime committed?
6. What do Buddhists Think of retribution?
7. What are the similarities and differences about retribution between religious viewpoints and viewpoints independent of religious belief?

Deterrence

'The last person who did that to me now has to eat only soft food – cos he's got no teeth left!'

Once again, when you're young, one of the ways you might try to stop others harming you is by warning them of the consequences if they do. Sometimes you might even give them an example of what happened to the last person who did what they're about to! Deterrence is just where we try to put people off doing things, very often by giving them examples of what might happen if they do their dirty deed. In the olden days some teachers said that the belt was a good deterrent – if you saw someone writhing in agony after 'six of the best' then you wouldn't be very likely to cause any trouble in your class would you? Deterrence as a punishment therefore gives us an example of what might happen (usually a negative one) in the hope that we'll avoid doing wrong to avoid suffering the same negative consequences.

Talk Point 5

Has witnessing somebody being 'made an example of' ever affected your behaviour?

Benefits of Deterrence

The benefits are quite simple. People will avoid doing wrong because they will have been put off (deterred) by knowing what will happen to them if they do. Sometimes it's quite difficult to work out what the consequences of any action will be, especially if you're not thinking straight, as people who are committing offences often aren't. But if a deterrent is strong enough and clear enough then it might just leap to the front of your mind at the crucial moment and cause you to think again about your actions.

So the good thing about deterrence is that it doesn't come after the crime but before it, and so stops the crime from ever taking place. In this way it is way much better than retribution because by the time retribution takes place the damage has been done. Deterrence stops the damage being done in the first place. If deterrence works then crimes will be greatly reduced, the world will be a nicer place and you won't ever have to come face to face with the long arm of the law.

Drawbacks of Deterrence

There's a story about a commanding officer who was in charge of an occupied town during the war. The people around him were starving and he had a huge pile of potatoes which he wanted to give them because he felt sorry for them. However, as he was the enemy, no one would have taken them – they'd rather die than take the

enemy's food. So, in a clever move, he left the potatoes at the back of his headquarters and informed the local people that anyone who stole a potato would be shot. Before long, every potato was gone. He had no intention of punishing anyone for stealing a potato – but they didn't know that. His order, which should have been a deterrent, worked in exactly the opposite way!

Talk Point

6

What does this story tell us about deterrence?

There are a number of drawbacks with deterrence. The first is just whether it works or not. There's no good way of checking just how much crime *would have* happened if people hadn't been put off by the deterrence value of punishments or seeing what happened to others. Maybe we would all be criminals if we weren't put off by seeing what happens to people who are criminals – we'll never know. Part of the problem here is that many crimes are committed 'in the heat of the moment'. Offenders don't usually stop to carefully think through the rights and wrongs of what they're already doing and what all the possible consequences might be. Besides, some say that the average criminal mind works on the basis that he'll never be caught anyway – so the consequences of his action won't matter. Others argue that deterrence just doesn't work on 'hardened' criminals anyway because for them punishment is sometimes just part of the job and certainly wouldn't ever stop them committing crimes. Others might think that deterrence isn't linked to their crime because the circumstances of it are quite different to the ones which have already happened and been punished. One piece of evidence which questions the effectiveness of deterrence, is that where punishments for crimes are long and harsh there doesn't seem to be any less crime in those countries than in others where punishments are less severe.

Another problem with deterrence is whether or not it's right to use someone as an example. It's probably true that teachers in Scottish schools used to give more of the belt than was sometimes necessary in the hope that it would act as a deterrent for others. Is that fair? Should a society use some people to set an example to others and maybe punish them more harshly than they deserve just to warn others off?

The Moral Implications of Deterrence

All of this means that the moral implications of deterrence are pretty obvious:

- Using punishment as a deterrent only makes sense and can only be right where it works.
- There have to be good ways of finding out if it works or not and it has to be clear that it does.
- Using punishment to deter others isn't easy because every situation is different and crimes are committed for all sorts of reasons.

- Deterrence in itself is morally suspect – the punishment should match the crime, not be more harsh than it needs to be just to set an example. Even criminals have the right to some amount of fairness, and it would probably be unfair to use them as examples in this kind of way – especially if it meant that their punishment went far beyond what it really should be.

A Christian View of Deterrence

Christians would be wary of using anyone as a scapegoat to warn others off. Christians believe that everyone is entitled to fair treatment – even the criminal, and so it would be wrong to use them as an example of what might happen to others. Punishing someone as a deterrent to others might mean that you're not taking into account their own individual circumstances. Of course there are criminals who choose to live that way, but crimes happen for all sorts of reasons. For example, you can steal because you are greedy or you can steal because you are starving. The deterrent value of punishment might work to stop you stealing in one of these situations but not the other – so what's the use of it? Also, as many crimes are committed without the offender really thinking about it too much what use will any deterrent value be – all the examples of deterrence in the world will fail miserably where the crime is committed in a moment of madness. Christians would oppose using someone as an example to warn others off – the correct response to a crime is to 'turn the other cheek'.

Source 6

But you see, what people often miss – Christians and, indeed, society at large that scorns this law: 'An eye for an eye and a tooth for a tooth' – is that not only is it a command to punish, but it is a limitation on punishment. What God is saying in the Old Testament is: 'The penalty must not exceed the crime'. So in order to command to punish, it also says you mustn't punish too hard, over and above the crime that has been committed.

www.preachtheword.co.uk/sermon/sotm10.shtml

A Buddhist View of Deterrence

A Buddhist might be quite comfortable with the idea of deterrence in one way. Buddhism is based on the relationship between your actions and the consequences of those actions. Everything you do has implications for your kamma. So, yes, knowing what the result of a crime will be for your own well-being should act to stop you doing wrong. In fact, for the Buddhist, knowing that all your actions have kammic consequences should act as a deterrent in itself – even without the threat of fines and prison! Buddhists would not like the idea of society using people as an example if it meant treating them too harshly. However, other people can serve as an example of deterrence because if you know what the kammic consequences of their action is likely to be you might want to avoid that for yourself.

A Viewpoint Independent of Religious Belief on Deterrence

Humanists do see the value in punishment as a form of deterrence. However, it has to be clear that the deterrent value of any punishment is balanced. You can't punish someone too harshly just so that their punishment is a deterrent to others. All punishments need to be fair and related to the crime committed. A Utilitarian would argue that if deterrence works then it's a good reason for punishment because it will protect the majority by putting the minority (of criminals) off crime because they don't want to suffer the consequences. However we shouldn't go too far in our uses of punishment.

Source 7

But this still begs the question of the moral propriety of acting on our retributive impulses, even in the measured, judicially restrained compass of a courtroom. The desire to inflict suffering and death on those who knowingly take the life of someone we love may be natural, but that alone doesn't make acting on it just.

www.secularhumanism.org/index/php?section=library&page=clark_25_2

Deterrence Scottish-Style

Again, most major forms of punishment in Scotland can be thought of as deterrents. When a **fine** is attached to an offence it should deter you from carrying out the offence because you want to keep your money for yourself. The only trouble with this is that as fines are not related to how well-off you are (maybe they should be of course) a £100 fine for speeding might mean one thing to a big businessman and another to an unemployed person. In this case it will be more of a deterrent to one than another. **Community service** should also be an effective deterrent – as you have to give up your time and maybe suffer the shame of being identified as an offender – but of course many will see this as an easy option and not harsh enough to put them off committing a crime in the first place.

Imprisonment is probably the best deterrent – though again it can mean different things to different people. For your average law-abiding citizen the threat of prison might be enough to turn their stomach so much that they avoid any law-breaking of any kind. But for people who are 'used to' prison it might be less of a deterrent and just something you have to put up with. Also, if prison is too 'cushy' then its deterrence value is much weaker, taking us back to the issue of how harsh prison should be.

Talk Point 7

What would the threat of prison put you off doing?

Check Your Learning

1. Explain what is meant by deterrence.
2. How effective do you think deterrence is?
3. Explain ONE benefit and ONE drawback of deterrence.
4. What evidence would you need to show that deterrence does/does not work?
5. Is there any evidence of this kind already available?
6. Is it right to use someone as an example for others?
7. Would a Christian support the idea of punishment as a deterrent? Explain your answer.
8. What actual punishments exist in Scotland which might have a deterrent effect?
9. Would one form of punishment be more likely to act as a deterrent for you than another? Explain why/why not.

Protection

'Stick them in prison and make the streets safer...'

In Scotland there's something called a dispersal order – this is where the police have the power to break up groups of three or more people who might be causing distress to others. There have been all sorts of arguments about this – mainly because dispersal orders have mostly been to do with teenagers hanging about. The point of this law is to protect people from potential harm. This is another of the purposes of punishment: to protect people from crime and wrongdoing. When a pupil is put outside the class by a teacher part of the reason is deterrence, part of the reason might be retribution (well it would be if the teacher secretly hopes that the Head comes along and catches the offender outside and obviously in trouble) another reason is protection. The teacher's job is to help the whole class learn. If one pupil's stopping this happening, then the class should be protected from that by removing the offender. That's really all protection is about, stopping the offender committing another offence so that people are protected from further harm.

Benefits of Protection

So the benefits are obvious: if an offender is in prison he can't commit the crime again, and if he has been punished in some other way this might make him less likely to repeat the offence and so society is protected. Everyone is happy, except for the offender. That's the point of course – the purpose of this kind of punishment is nothing to do with the offender and everything to do with everyone else. It doesn't really matter what the consequences are for the offender, as long as everyone else is now protected from him then that's all right, and there of course is the problem...

Drawbacks of Protection

The major drawback is probably to do with just how long this protection lasts. Unless a prisoner is locked away for ever he's going to come back out again and the protection bit of his punishment will be over. In fact, some say that the problem will be even worse because of all the new tricks the criminal has learned from fellow criminals in prison. Once he gets out, then he'll be an even more skilled criminal and so society will be even less protected than it was before he went to prison!

Also, some argue that prison just makes offenders angry about being there – long years of brooding about the horrors of prison life don't make for a very happy person once released. So, the offender comes out of prison and is ready to take revenge on the society which put him there. He was a danger before he went to prison and on release he's even more dangerous. Punishment as protection might work, but it probably doesn't last long. Remember too that when someone is imprisoned, although society is protected, the others in prison aren't. Tough, you might argue – they shouldn't be there in the first place – but that's not the point. Even though they have committed crimes most reasonable people would agree that they have rights of some kind, and surely one should be that they have a right to protection from harm just like everyone else? So although protection of society does occur when someone is punished it only works with certain punishments and even then it might just be a short-term response.

The Moral Implications of Protection

A society has a duty to protect the weak and vulnerable from harm. But who are the weak and vulnerable? Perhaps those who commit crimes are exactly that and they have only done wrong because society has let them down in the first place. Do we then lock them up and throw away the key to protect others because we failed to protect the offenders in the first place? Seems a bit mixed up. Also, who are we protecting from what? Robin Hood stole from the rich to give to the poor – should those rich people have been protected? Some would argue that the protection argument is just sweeping the whole problem of crime under the carpet. A great many people who have committed crimes have done so for all sorts of reasons. Some have had harsh upbringings: poverty, abuse and all sorts of social problems as they were growing up. Now this doesn't excuse their wrongdoing, but it does make you wonder if it's fair that they're being punished because they weren't protected in their lives and ended up living the life of a criminal. Some argue that punishment as protection deals with the symptoms of crime but not the causes, and so is a poor reason for punishing.

A Christian View of Protection

A central idea in Christianity is the idea that the strong should protect the weak, but of course that cuts both ways. Obviously, we need to protect innocent people from harm, but maybe we also have a duty to protect criminals from themselves – maybe those who end up in a life of crime are the neediest of all. Jesus once said that he associated with society's outcasts because a doctor is not needed where people are well, but only where people are sick. Perhaps if we protect the vulnerable from harm and make sure life is fair and just for everyone, then there will be no need to punish anyone for anything, because no one will feel the need to do wrong. Christians would agree that one of the purposes of punishment is to protect people from further harm, but punishment needs to be more than that if it's to be a proper solution rather than just a temporary sticking plaster.

A Buddhist View of Protection

Buddhists too would think that protecting people from further harm is good. This would obviously help the people who are being protected because Buddhism seeks the happiness of all beings, but it would also help the kamma of criminals – who wouldn't be able to make their situation any worse if society was protected from them! So society and the criminal both receive protection.

A Viewpoint Independent of Religious Belief on Protection

A Utilitarian view on protection is that it is probably a valid purpose of punishment. If punishment of one person results in protection for many then that would be acceptable. There should still be an element of fairness in the punishment for the individual, but in order to protect society, the individual may have to suffer. In particular, if the offender is highly likely to re-offend on release from prison, then perhaps his sentence should be very long indeed – in order to protect the majority.

Protection Scottish-Style

- **Fines** obviously protect people from harm if they work in stopping someone repeating an offence – but it's not always the case that they do stop re-offending. Also, if someone has committed a crime because they are experiencing poverty, then fining them is just going to make it worse – how are they likely to pay a fine if they didn't have enough money in the first place?
- Community service might help protect people from re-offenders, but only when the person's doing their community service. Of course, doing **community service** might make you see things differently and so stop you re-offending, but then again it might not.

- **Imprisonment** obviously keeps you off the streets but it might just build up resentment in you during your sentence and might show you what's wrong but do nothing to teach you what's right. It might also just be a great way to learn how to be a better criminal and make society even less safe once you're out again – so in the long-term, society ends up being less protected.

Check Your Learning

1. When punishment is being used as protection, who is being protected?
2. Give an example of punishment as protection from your school life.
3. Explain a benefit and a drawback of protection as a reason for punishment.
4. Why might a Christian think of punishment as protection as just a 'temporary sticking plaster'? Would you agree?
5. How would a Utilitarian argue that protection is an important part of punishment? Would you agree?
6. Is protection just dealing with the symptoms of crime rather than the causes?
7. Are the short-term and long-term benefits of protection as a reason for punishment always going to be the same?
8. Do you agree that a fine doesn't protect anyone?

Reformation

'No point in prison unless you come out a better person than you went in'

Reformation is where part of the 'punishment' for wrongdoing involves learning what you have done wrong and persuading you not to do it again. This might be done in loads of ways, for example, teaching you about the harm your actions did to others – maybe by you meeting victims of crimes like yours. It might also help you with your behaviour, so if you are an aggressive person you might get some psychological help. It might also be practical help which tries to give you an alternative to going back to crime once you're released, for example, you might learn a new skill while in prison which could get you a job on 'the outside' which might make you better off and so less likely to commit a crime again. It might just be having someone to listen to you or help you to understand yourself so that you become a different person, the kind of person who won't commit a crime ever again.

Benefits of Reformation

The obvious benefit of reformation is that if it works it will mean you won't re-offend again. Even more than that, on your release you might work to stop others committing the kind of crimes which got you into jail in the first place. All of this

turns your wrong action into something from which good can come. You won't leave prison wanting to get revenge on society, and in fact you might come out grateful for the help you've had and become a model citizen – an example for others to follow – the right kind this time. All of this means that society is protected from you committing any more crime – sounds just about perfect eh?

Drawbacks of Reformation

Some say that reformation's not very likely – the 'leopard doesn't change its spots' kind of argument, and that all the time and energy spent on criminals to try to reform them is wasted. In fact, some feel that all this time and energy could be put to better use by maybe helping the victims of crime or paying an old lady's heating bills, for example. Also, if prison is all about reformation, then it might become a nice cushy place: somewhere you can learn a skill for free with three square meals a day and your washing done for you. People might be queuing up to get *into* prison if it's too nice! Prison would no longer be a deterrent, it could hardly be called retribution and it wouldn't protect society if after all the reforming which goes on in it, you come out just the same as you went in.

The Moral Implications of Reformation

So the main point with reformation is: does it work and is it worth it? All prisons today try some kind of reformation of offenders and it works with some and it doesn't with others. Perhaps part of the problem is that people on the outside often don't trust ex-offenders – finding it hard to believe that they really can change. If people on the outside don't accept your change then all the efforts to reform you might end up being wasted – so everyone has a part to play here. Of course, the money spent reforming you could be used for other things – but maybe if it stops people re-offending then its money well-spent (cheaper than the costs of you re-offending). Also, it is true that if all prison meant was a chance to learn a new skill then it wouldn't be seen as much of a punishment, however, even the most open and kindly prisons are still prisons – your freedom is still taken away and they can still be harsh places to live no matter what kindnesses you're being shown in them. Society has to decide if the costs are worth it and if we're prepared to accept that ex-offenders can change

A Christian View of Reformation

Christians would support reformation because they believe that everyone can change for the better – no matter what you have done – there's no such thing as a lost cause in Christianity. There have been in fact, a few Church of Scotland Ministers who are ex-offenders of one kind or another and who are now good-living people making a difference in people's lives. Christians believe that everyone is capable of change, no matter what the crime was. Once you have changed, the new you should be accepted because, apart from anything else, this new you could use the experience of life you've had to help others.

A Buddhist View of Reformation

Buddhists also accept the idea that anyone can change. The kammic consequences of your actions cause you to be reborn moment by moment – you can make good choices or bad ones. All of your choices are within your control and so you make your own future. There's nothing to say that someone might not completely change through reflecting on their lives and go on to live a life of kindness and service to others. The Buddha himself went from a selfish partying dude to a selfless being who put his own attainment of Nibbana to the side so that he could help others – you don't get much more of a change than that!

Source 8

The wicked man is an ignorant man. He doesn't need punishment and condemnation so much as he needs instruction. [reformation]

Buddhism rejects not only the death penalty, but also the repressive forms of punishment and internment that still characterize many modern states, including many democracies. It calls for a legal-penal system guided not by the quest for revenge, but by the desire to rehabilitate the offender

John Waltem, 'Mind unshaken' at www.buddhanet.net/budintel/othrelig/budidsin.htm www.thezensite.com

A Viewpoint Independent of Religious Belief on Reformation

Humanists would support the reformation part of any punishment, in fact they might even argue that this is the most important purpose of punishment. Humanists believe that humans are capable of good and evil – but that education and fairness in the world will lead to people being more likely to do good rather than bad. If you change someone's life for the better, then they'll be less likely to re-offend and the world will be a safer place. However, this doesn't mean forgiving people no matter what – the person has to change and the change has to be of benefit to others. A Utilitarian argument would be that punishment deals rightly with the minority in order to maximise the happiness of the majority. This would mean that a Utilitarian would support punishment as a way to protect society through deterring criminals, but in the long-term, protection of society is going to be more likely if the criminal has been reformed while in prison.

Source 9

...if he spoils his life by mismanagement, we shall not, for that reason, desire to spoil it still further: instead of wishing to punish him, we shall rather endeavour to alleviate his punishment, by showing him how he may avoid or cure the evils his conduct tends to bring upon him.

J S Mill, On Liberty

Reformation Scottish-Style

- **Fines** might make you change your ways – if only to avoid getting another one – but they still might cause you to be a better person.
- **Community service** might help reform you as while on it you might start to see things from someone else's point of view and come to realise that you've not been the nicest person.
- **Imprisonment** can obviously have a role in reforming you. It can give your life a new direction which leads away from the old offending you. One famous example of this is the one-time criminal Jimmy Boyle. Once described as Scotland's most violent man, he had a string of prison sentences. Eventually in Barlinnie's Special Unit his creative side was awakened, discovering a talent for art. He changed. On release he started up a series of youth organisations to help young people avoid the kinds of things that got him into prison – and he's still doing that having left his life of crime far behind him.

Check Your Learning

1. How might a prison sentence help reform a criminal?
2. Do you think the possible benefits of reformation outweigh the possible drawbacks? Explain your answer.
3. Is reformation worth the time, effort and money?
4. What example might a Buddhist use to show that reformation and change for the better is possible?
5. In what ways are the religious viewpoints and the viewpoint independent of religious belief similar/different in their approaches to reformation as a purpose of punishment?
6. How might a spell of community service reform a criminal?
7. Some people argue that reformation is the most important function of any punishment. Do you agree?

Extension Activities

Knowledge, Understanding and Evaluation through Practical Activities

1. Think of a number of crimes from not very serious upwards. Allocate them a seriousness score. Decide which ones you think should result in fines, community service or imprisonment. Decide too, how much the fine should be or how long the sentence should be for each crime. Also, think through what lawyers call 'mitigating factors': what individual circumstances might lead to your fine or sentence being reduced?
2. With this list of crimes, now decide which of the purposes of punishment most closely applies to this crime. Discuss this in class and make sure you're clear about the reasons why you have reached your decision.
3. Imagine it has been agreed by the Scottish Parliament that life imprisonment is to mean exactly that – life. In your class, allocate different groups to represent one of the purposes of punishment you've studied. Each group is to write a short speech explaining how this new life sentence fits with their view of punishment. Is it actually a good idea?
4. Think through some school punishments. Which fall into the categories you've studied? Draw up a table linking purpose of punishment with punishments in your school.
5. You read the following letter in a newspaper. Reply to it, pointing out why some people might agree and disagree with it.

Extension Activities continued

Dear Sir!

Again, another good-for-nothing walks from a courtroom with a pathetically light punishment – I mean to say, a fine for causing death by dangerous driving? How ridiculous. Isn't it time that we got tough with these people? Lock them up and throw away the key. . .

6 Find out about one organisation (e.g. Scottish Association for the Care and Resettlement of Offenders) which supports the idea of the reformation of offenders. Devise a fact sheet on this organisation explaining what it does and why.

7 Find out about prison conditions in Scotland today. Are they harsh, easy or just right? You could display your findings on a display board.

8 Draw up a table summarising the two religious viewpoints and viewpoints independent of religious belief you have looked at in this section in relation to the purposes of punishment. Highlight in green similarities between them all and in red, major differences. Write a paragraph or two summarising what you find.

Unit Assessment Question

Intermediate 2: State one example of how someone might be punished for a crime in Scotland today. **2KU**

Higher: 'The punishment should fit the crime' Do you agree? **10AE**

Sample Exam Question

Intermediate 2: How might a religious person support the idea of punishment? **4KU**

Higher: 'Retribution is one of the weakest reasons for punishing someone.' Would someone who held a viewpoint independent of religious belief agree? **2KU 6AE**

Homework

Find a newspaper article about a crime committed and a sentence passed. Cut it out and put it in your workbook. Explain which of the reasons for punishment this represents.

Personal Reflection

What do you think about the idea of 'loving your enemies'?

CHAPTER 5 Crime and Punishment: Capital Punishment

Is Capital Punishment Morally Justifiable?

The Case of Timothy Evans

They sent Tim Evans to the drop

For a crime he did not do.

It was Christie was the murderer

And the judge and jury too.

The Ballad of Tim Evans by Ewan MacColl at www.traditionalmusic.co.uk/folk-song-lyrics/Ballad_of_Tim_Evans.htm

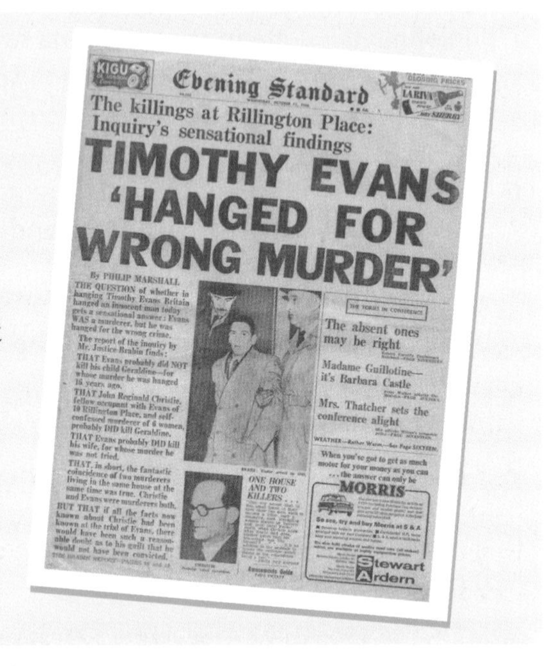

Evening Standard

The killings at Rillington Place: Inquiry's sensational findings

TIMOTHY EVANS 'HANGED FOR WRONG MURDER'

By PHILIP MARSHALL

THE QUESTION of whether in hanging Timothy Evans Britain hanged an innocent man today gets a sensational answer: Evans WAS a murderer, but he was hanged for the wrong crime.

The report of the inquiry by Mr. Justice Brabin finds:

THAT Evans probably did NOT kill his child Geraldine—for whose murder he was hanged 16 years ago.

THAT John Reginald Christie, fellow occupant with Evans of 10 Rillington Place, and self-confessed murderer of 6 women, probably DID kill Geraldine.

THAT Evans probably DID kill his wife, for whose murder he was not tried.

THAT, in short, the fantastic coincidence of two murderers living in the same house at the same time was true. Christie and Evans were murderers both.

BUT THAT if all the facts now known about Christie had been known at the trial of Evans, there would have been such a reasonable doubt as to his guilt that he would not have been convicted.

ONE HOUSE AND TWO KILLERS

The absent ones may be right

Madame Guillotine—it's Barbara Castle

Mrs. Thatcher sets the conference alight

When you've got to get as much motor for your money as you can ... the answer can only be MORRIS

So see, try and buy Morris at S & A

Stewart Ardern

On 9 March 1950, Timothy Evans was hanged for the murder of his wife, Beryl and one year old daughter Geraldine. He had originally claimed that he had committed the murders, but when the police could find no bodies, he changed his story, saying that the man downstairs at 10 Rillington Place, Reginald Christie, had tried to give his wife a backstreet abortion and that she had died during this. Evans helped to hide her body – odd you might think – but it is claimed that Evans was mentally retarded, with a very low IQ. Eventually the police found the bodies and Evans now changed his story again, claiming to be guilty of their murders after all, and he was executed as a result.

However, in March 1953 a new tenant moved into 10 Rillington Place, and in Christie's room, hidden behind a walled-up alcove, he found the bodies of three women. The Police returned to the house and discovered more bodies. Christie was found and confessed to eight murders – one of them Beryl Evans. Much discussion followed in the courts, even in the House of Parliament it seemed as if the execution of Evans had been a miscarriage of justice. Christie was executed for murder and after much legal and political wrangling, and a major review of the case by Mr Justice Brabin, Evans received a posthumous royal pardon in 1966. But, a free pardon doesn't mean that conviction is squashed and Evans' remaining family applied to have his case referred to the criminal cases review commission which could send the case back to the court of appeal. It agreed that there was a real possibility that Evans would be cleared, but decided that there was no real benefit to anyone in doing so. So, the legal system seems to agree that Evans probably did not commit murder but won't clear his name, and the only two people who could ever have cleared up what was and wasn't true, Christie and Evans, were both executed. The case of Timothy Evans paved the way for the abolition of the death penalty in the UK.

(For a more detailed account of the circumstances surrounding the trial and execution of Timothy Evans see: www.innocent.org.uk/cases/timothyevans.)

Source 1

November 17 2004: Cleared Evans can 'rest in peace'

Timothy Evans, who was wrongly hanged for one of the notorious Rillington Place murders, can at last 'rest in peace' after two High Court judges today made an unprecedented declaration of his innocence.

In an extraordinary twist in one of the most infamous of all miscarriage of justice cases, his family lost their legal battle to get the case referred back to the Court of Appeal.

But there was 'heartfelt thanks' from the family when, for the first time ever, a senior judge stated definitively in a courtroom that Mr Evans should be regarded as innocent of murdering either his wife Beryl or his 14-month-old daughter Geraldine.

http://icwales.icnetwork.co.uk/0100news/0200wales/tm_objectid=14883433&method=full&siteid=50082&headline=cleared-evans-can—rest-in-peace—name_page.html

Confused, Confusing and Final

The case of Timothy Evans was one of the final nails in the coffin of the death penalty in the UK. It was surrounded by argument and debate, political as well as legal. No one was really quite sure what actually happened at 10 Rillington Place, and no one will ever know, as the execution of Christie and Evans means that the past has been silenced. Evans' case was confused in so many ways and, even today, it is more or less agreed that he wasn't a murderer, but the legal system doesn't seem to want to open it all up again. For many opponents of capital punishment, cases like Evans' suggest that because capital punishment is so final it is wrong – you can't put the mistakes right later, you can't open up the case with those involved in it able to put their case again. With capital punishment you get one go at a conviction and, if you do convict, there's no turning back later when you find out that you made a mistake.

As well as this, society changes, and what was plain black and white murder in the past might now be looked at more sympathetically.

The Case of Ruth Ellis

Source 2

Daily Mirror

FORWARD WITH THE PEOPLE

EXECUTION EVE

Crowd break police cordon round gaol

DAILY MIRROR REPORTER

CASSANDRA talks to YOU about—

THE WOMAN WHO HANGS THIS MORNING

By CASSANDRA

Dregs of Shame

Our Guilt . . .

MILLIONS

MORRIS MINOR

THE TENT OF BLUE SHOULD BE DARK AND SAD AT THE THING WE HAVE DONE THIS DAY.

Ruth Ellis is being portrayed as a victim of a cruel boyfriend who abused her, and a cruel legal system that hanged her. Ellis's sister, Muriel Jakubait, 77, wants her conviction reduced to manslaughter.

She says the jury was never told that David Blakely treated Ellis violently and caused her to miscarry by punching her in the stomach.

The jury was also not told that she had been raped by her father as a child, and was addicted to anti-depressants. Ms Jakubait believes that her mental state at the time meant she should never have been convicted of murder. If found guilty of manslaughter, Ellis would probably have received a prison sentence totalling a few years, instead of the capital punishment of hanging. Ellis, 28, was hanged after killing her lover Mr Blakely outside a pub in Hampstead, north London, in 1955. Mr Blakely and Ellis formed a passionate and tempestuous relationship after they met in a London night club which Ellis managed. Ellis suspected Mr Blakely was having an affair with a friend's nanny and in a pique of jealousy and rejection, she went to Hampstead where she lay in wait outside the Magdala public house in South Hill Park. Mr Blakely came out of the pub with a friend and Ellis shot him five times, the last shot from point blank range, as he lay wounded on the ground.

http://news.bbc.co.uk/1/hi/uk/542186.stm
See also: www.guardian.co.uk/crime/article/0,2763,1040438,00.html

Source 3

Ellis was properly convicted of lover's murder, rule appeal judges

ANGUS HOWARTH

THREE senior judges yesterday threw out an appeal on behalf of Ruth Ellis, the last woman to be hanged in Britain, saying it was without merit. They said that Ellis was properly convicted of murder according to the laws at the time she shot her lover in 1955.

http://news.scotsman.com/topics.cfm?tid=1011&id=1349422003

Modern Views on an Old Crime?

Ruth Ellis has not been pardoned for her crime even though her supporters claim that had she committed the crime today she would probably have been found guilty of manslaughter. They argue that she was suffering from what today would be called 'battered wife syndrome' (where a person's mental state is put out of balance through being abused by a partner) and that because of this, she would not have been in her right mind when she murdered Blakely. It's claimed that Ellis had been on tranquilisers and that these might have reacted badly with the alcohol she drank on the day of the shooting. It's also claimed that she was in a frenzy when she shot Blakely. She'd found him with another woman and, for someone in her fragile and abused mental state, this was the last straw. Was Ellis a villain or victim?

Supporters say victim and that she should be cleared of the murder – having committed it during a period of diminished responsibility (an idea which didn't even legally exist at the time). After discussion however, in 2003, the courts didn't agree – stating that you can't simply apply modern ideas to an old case. Others disagree, claiming that Ellis was completely aware of what she did and was therefore a cold-blooded killer. Of course, just as in the case of Timothy Evans, the truth will never be known because Ruth Ellis was executed. Had she been imprisoned and today's theories of 'battered wife syndrome' applied to her case, then perhaps eventually she might have been released – who knows?

Time Out 2

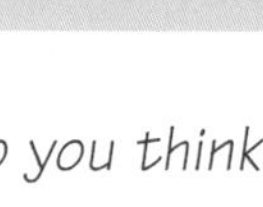

If Ellis' crime had happened today what do you think her sentence would be?

Check Your Learning

1. What is a 'miscarriage of justice'?
2. Why might the case of Timothy Evans be an example of one of these?
3. In what way might a miscarriage of justice make people question capital punishment?
4. Why do some people think that Ruth Ellis was a villain and others a victim?
5. Should we look at crimes committed in the past through 'modern eyes'?
6. What is 'battered wife syndrome' and how does it relate to the case of Ruth Ellis?
7. Why do you think these two cases led to the eventual abolition of capital punishment in the UK?

The History of Capital Punishment in the UK

273 people were publicly hanged in Scotland between 1800 and 1868. After this date, hanging tended to take place privately in prisons, though with invited witnesses to the executions. Of these 273 people, 55 were executed for housebreaking and 2 for sheep stealing. Scotland's last execution took place in 1963 and only one woman, Susan Newell has been executed in Scotland's recent history.

However, throughout the UK, capital punishment has been around for a long time. Mostly it has been used for criminals, but often for political opponents, people accused of witchcraft – or even just as an easy way to get rid of troublesome enemies. The Scottish hero William Wallace was hanged, drawn and quartered in London for fighting for what he thought were the rights of his country to be governed by Scots and not by a King in a 'foreign' land. Protestants have burned Catholics and vice-versa and enemies of the state have all been executed in gruesome ways. Capital punishment in the UK could mean beheading, hanging, burning at the stake or many other forms of execution, for example, by a firing squad in military situations. In recent history it was always done in private – the last public hanging in the UK was in 1875 on the island of Jersey. Ruth Ellis was the last woman to hang in the UK in 1955 and the last ever hanging in the UK took place in August 1964.

Although capital punishment was no longer available for almost all crimes after this date, strangely enough, it was not until halfway through 1998 that the death penalty was finally abolished in the UK for the crimes of high treason and piracy with violence. The death penalty was eventually abolished in the UK mainly as a result of the concern that miscarriages of justice could take place and innocent people ended up being executed.

Talk Point 1

Before you go on any further in this section, discuss whether you think capital punishment is an acceptable sentence for crime in today's world. Are there any situations where it would be more acceptable than others?

Capital Punishment in the World Today

Get someone to time you for seven seconds. During this seven seconds look around you and see how much you take in – or think about things which have happened to you in the past. How much could you do in seven seconds? It is said that the brain stores enough oxygen in its blood supply for seven seconds of consciousness after its blood supply is removed. In beheading, still used as a form of execution in the world today, the blood supply to your brain is removed immediately... but perhaps you still have seven seconds when your head is no longer attached to your body when you are aware and conscious. Some say the shock probably makes you lose consciousness right away... but maybe not.

Capital punishment is still carried out in the world today. It is present in some states of the USA, as well as some Middle Eastern, African and Asian countries. It still exists as a possible sentence in many countries of the world for crimes like treason and piracy, for example, but is almost never applied in these situations. Most countries carry out capital punishment for murder only, though some countries carry it out for political crimes too. In some Middle Eastern countries it may still be carried out for many other crimes which do not involve murder.

A summary of the major forms follows. In general, the major issues associated with its modern use are:

- How traumatic is it for the condemned person? Its aim is to take their life, but does this need to be done in a humiliating or degrading way?
- Should it be publicly or privately carried out? Should the victim still be allowed as dignified a death as possible.
- Although the aim is to kill the person, should this not be done as quickly and humanely as possible?

Capital punishment today takes many forms:

Form of capital punishment	Method	How death occurs	Advantages	Disadvantages	Issues
Beheading	The head is removed from the neck by the use of a sword or an axe – the guillotine is a machine which drops a heavy blade onto the neck.	Probably through shock and/or loss of blood supply to the brain.	Death is probably instantaneous if the blow is quick and efficient – pain may be minimal.	Often a number of blows are required which prolongs death and may result in severe pain. Depends very much of the 'skill' of the executioner.	Still used in many Arab countries and often still a public event. The rituals leading to the beheading may be traumatic. Probably an inhumane way to execute because it is degrading, traumatic and possibly painful.
Hanging	A rope noose is put around a person's neck and then they are dropped quickly – often through a trapdoor.	Either through the breaking of the neck on the drop or through strangulation.	If done correctly the neck should break on the drop. Careful calculations of body weight and height are usually carried out to achieve this.	Often the neck does not break on the drop and death is by strangulation which may take some minutes and be very painful.	Still used in many countries – rarely public, though can be. Major issue is with how humane it is as witnesses often describe the victim thrashing about in obvious distress during strangulation where the neck has not broken.
Stoning	Either large rocks are thrown at the person or they are laid in a pit and huge blocks of concrete are dropped on them one by one from the feet upwards. Sometimes, victims are wrapped in a white shroud and then buried up to their waists or chest before the stoning begins.	If stones are thrown then probably due to major head injury. In the pit version probably through shock or major trauma to the vital organs.	Very little associated cost with stone throwing. Pit version efficient if horrific.	May take a long time to die using either method and will be extremely painful.	Still used in many countries – most often now the pit version. Has attracted a lot of attention because often a form of capital punishment reserved only for women. Is also most often associated with sexual/moral 'crimes'.

Form of capital punishment	Method	How death occurs	Advantages	Disadvantages	Issues
Electrocution	Person is strapped to a chair and a massive electric current is passed through the body.	Probably heart/vital organ failure.	Technologically efficient and should end life relatively quickly.	Witnesses often report that victims take a long time to die and thrash around trying to free themselves. Flesh may catch fire. Probably very traumatic and painful for the victim.	Used mainly in the USA – descriptions of executions suggest that they are very inhumane.
Gas Chamber	Person is secured inside a sealed chamber and hydrocyanide gas is introduced to the chamber caused by a chemical reaction.	A combination of asphyxiation and damage to the cells caused by the cyanide gas.	Compared to some of the other methods, this is 'clean'.	Death can be quite slow and painful as the person slowly chokes and runs out of oxygen – witnesses often refer to the death as a very violent one indeed.	Like electrocution, death often comes after a struggle and clear distress. There is also the danger of the deadly gas leaking from the chamber and causing potential harm to those outside the chamber.
Lethal Injection	Person is strapped to a hospital bed and then administered a tranquiliser followed by an injection of a lethal (deadly) chemical.	Usually through respiratory and heart failure.	Should be painless as the person should be unconscious by the time the poison is injected. Also carried out by medically qualified people who can react quickly if anything 'goes wrong'.	Requires medically qualified staff, who are trained to save lives, to take a life. It is claimed by some that this method of execution takes the longest and it is possible that some people remain aware of their dying for a fair amount of time.	Seen by some as the most humane form of execution.

Talk Point 2

If you had the responsibility of choosing which kind of capital punishment to apply from this table, which would you choose and why?

A United Nations View on Capital Punishment

In the preamble to the UN Declaration of Human Rights, the UN states: 'disregard and contempt for human rights have resulted in barbarous acts which have outraged the conscience of mankind'. The UN argues that while countries have the right to exercise their own systems of justice and treat crime as their culture sees fit, there are some 'inalienable rights of all members of the human family'. This means, for example, that all human beings have the right to life – and that would include murderers. Taking human rights into consideration should mean that countries consider whether their punishments fit into the category of 'barbaric' or 'degrading'. The UN declaration encourages governments throughout the world to act humanely and fairly towards their citizens. This applies to criminals who have been found guilty after due process of law. People have responsibilities too:

'In the exercise of his rights and freedoms, everyone shall be subject only to such limitations as are determined by law solely for the purpose of securing due recognition and respect for the rights and freedoms of others and of meeting the just requirements of morality, public order and the general welfare in a democratic society.'

This means that if you act against the law or the principles enshrined in the UN Declaration then you may well be punished. However, it is the form of punishment which is the issue of debate. If capital punishment is degrading or barbaric, then the UN is against it. Of course, opponents of capital punishment say that it is and that therefore it goes against the principles set out by the UN. The UN itself does not decide a country's law however. Even so, the UN has continually fought against execution in specific situations, for example, when carried out against children or someone suffering from a 'mental disorder'. The document: United Nations High Commissioner For Human Rights Resolution Supporting Worldwide Moratorium on Executions April 1999 [Preliminary unedited version] Question of the death penalty Commission on Human Rights resolution 1999/61 quoted at: www.deathpenaltyinfo.org/article.php?scid=18&did=226 sets out in detail the UN position on capital punishment.

The UN Declaration should make a government ask these questions about capital punishment:

- Is it degrading? Cruel? Inhumane?
- Does it respect the dignity of the person being executed?
- The answer to these questions should help a government decide whether to apply capital punishment or not.

Source 4

United Nations Universal Declaration of Human Rights

Article 5

No one shall be subjected to torture or to cruel, inhuman or degrading treatment or punishment.

www.un.org/Overview.rights.html

The General Assembly

Bearing in mind the principles embodied in articles 3, 5, 8, 9 and 10 of the Universal Declaration of Human Rights Resolution 217 A (III) and the relevant provisions of the International Covenant on Civil and Political Rights and the Optional Protocols thereto, See resolution 2200 A (XXI), annex, and resolution 44/128, annex. in particular article 6 of the Covenant, which states, inter alia, that no one shall be arbitrarily deprived of his life and prohibits the imposition of the death penalty for crimes committed by persons below 18 years of age, and article 10, which provides that all persons deprived of their liberty shall be treated with humanity and with respect for the inherent dignity of the human person, www.unhchr.ch/Huridocda/Huridoca/nsf/TestFrame/7a49b79a7e0f423bc1256b82005d4aae?Opendocument

Talk Point

3

Do you think that the UN's views about capital punishment are clear enough?

Check Your Learning

1. When and why was capital punishment eventually abolished in the UK?
2. What major practical and moral issues are associated with capital punishment in the world today?
3. Choose TWO forms of capital punishment. In your own words, explain what each involves and their 'advantages' and 'disadvantages'.
4. From what you have learned, is there any form of capital punishment which is much better or worse than all the others?
5. Explain why the UN is opposed to capital punishment.
6. Why might some say that the UN isn't clear enough in its guidance about capital punishment?

What Might the Benefits of Capital Punishment Be?

Capital punishment puts people off committing crime. If they have seen others executed for a crime then the chances of them doing the same crime are reduced. People usually imitate behaviours which are rewarded – they usually don't copy behaviours which are punished – especially if the punishments are as severe as capital punishment. So, capital punishment is an example of deterrence. Where it exists it should deter people from committing crimes because they know what will happen to them if they do.

It protects. Once a criminal is executed they can obviously no longer commit crimes, so people are protected from them. Prison isn't enough because people can escape or be let out on parole. Also, while in prison, perhaps a criminal is a danger to prison officers or even other prisoners. An executed criminal is a danger to no one.

It saves money as prisons are expensive. Capital punishment with its one-off cost means you don't have to support a criminal for the rest of his life. Why should law-abiding people pay to keep a murderer well-fed and protected for the rest of his days?

It sends an important message out that human life is valued by society (because nowadays capital punishment is almost always in response to murder). If you take someone's life then yours will be taken from you. This shows that society means business with those who take life.

What Might the Drawbacks of Capital Punishment Be?

It doesn't deter. Countries with capital punishment don't seem to have any fewer murders than countries who don't have it. People don't always think about the consequences of their crime. Murders are often committed in a moment of madness and, at that point, the thought of the consequences will probably not even enter the murderer's head. Even if it does, some criminals still think they'll get away with it and so carry on anyway. Also, what about murders committed by people who aren't in their 'right minds' for one reason or another? Is capital punishment acceptable for them too? And what about children and the mentally ill and so on?

Source 5

'I do not now believe that any one of the hundreds of executions I carried out has in any way acted as a deterrent against future murder. Capital punishment, in my view, achieved nothing except revenge.' He should know. Albert Pierrepoint was, by far, Britain's most prolific hangman. Between 1934 and 1956, he executed more than 400 men and women, among them Ruth Ellis, the last woman to be hanged in Britain, Derek Bentley... He put to death Timothy Evans, wrongly convicted of murdering his daughter, and subsequently John Christie, the real killer

http://film.guardian.co.uk/features/featurepages/0,,1743973,00.html

Capital punishment is final – if you make a mistake you can't put it right. The case of Timothy Evans is an example of this. Also, how we view crime and those who commit it changes with time. Perhaps it would be wrong if someone was executed because they lived at the wrong time in the wrong place (think of those who were executed in Britain's dark past for crimes which nowadays would lead to little more than a fine).

Albert Pierrepoint

If society thinks killing is wrong, it's a funny old way to show that by killing a killer. The message is obviously that some lives are worth more than others. Now you might think that's true because criminals are bad people, but nowadays, all sorts of explanations are given for why people commit crimes. Some say that most crimes are committed by people who are poor and disadvantaged in some way and so capital punishment just deals with the symptoms of crime and not the causes. Criminals are not bad people, they are people who have done bad things.

Capital punishment doesn't protect: it makes martyrs out of people and martyrs might have followers, dangerous followers. Many people today say that terrorists should be executed to protect others, but perhaps every time you execute a terrorist you make him a hero to his followers – who then want to be like him and who all then go on to commit crimes like he did. So who's protected now?

Capital punishment treats all murders as being the same, but killings are carried out for many different reasons and the way you were when you killed might not be the same way you are now. People change: maybe some murderers really do regret their actions and would never do anything like it again, so they wouldn't be a threat to society if they were eventually released. In fact, maybe they could help others avoid their choices by sharing their experience with people, reducing the number of murders. They can't do that if they've been executed.

Capital punishment makes the world more violent, not less. It sends the message that the taking of life is sometimes morally justifiable – which might make murderers think that their own crimes were in some way equally 'right'.

Time Out

3

In your opinion, do you think the 'benefits' of capital punishment outweigh the 'drawbacks'?

The Moral Implications of Capital Punishment

The central issue is: is killing right or not? If it is wrong then that means that capital punishment is just as wrong as any other kind of murder. Some might say it is worse, because it's cold-blooded and follows a chilling 'ritual'. Capital punishment is murder by the state, making killing seem like something a society should accept. If society thinks it's wrong to kill, then it's wrong no matter who does it or what the reason is, and that would include capital punishment.

Also, capital punishment *makes* people killers. Albert Pierrepoint, Britain's hangman for 18 years, killed more than 400 people. Does this make him a murderer? Throughout his career as a hangman, very few people knew his identity. In fact, he ran a pub, and most of the people in his life knew nothing of his 'other job'. What did being a hangman do to Albert? Is it right for a society to give anyone this job? And what about the prison officers who sometimes got to know the condemned men and women and then had to escort them to their deaths? Is it ever morally right to put anyone in such a situation?

What about the judgements which lead to capital punishment? Different countries put people to death for different reasons – are all reasons equally justifiable? These reasons can also change with time. Even if capital punishment still existed in Britain today, maybe people like Ruth Ellis would escape it because of the circumstances of her killing. Perhaps she was suffering from abuse and so her crime was a form of self-defence – or at least understandable in her circumstances.

So, the main issue is this: either it's wrong to kill in every circumstance or some reasons for ending a person's life are morally justifiable.

Talk Point

4

Do you think it is ever right to take a human life?

Check Your Learning

1. Choose ONE of the 'benefits' of capital punishment you agree or disagree with and explain your position.
2. Why might some think that Albert Pierrepoint's argument is quite powerful?
3. Choose ONE of the 'drawbacks' of capital punishment you agree or disagree with and explain your position.
4. Thinking through the 'drawbacks' and 'benefits' which set of arguments do you find most convincing? Explain your answer.
5. What do you think is the most important moral implication of capital punishment?

Christianity and Capital Punishment

Christians are split very clearly into two camps when responding to capital punishment. Some stick to the Old Testament principle of *lex talionis* (Exodus 21:24-25). This means an eye for an eye and is the idea that whatever crime you commit you should have that same thing done to you. So if you take a life then yours should also be taken. The Old Testament was written at a time when laws were often stated this way. This tried to serve two purposes: *deterring* people from crime because they wouldn't want the same thing happening to them and getting *retribution* for a crime committed. This was a society where, if someone was killed, revenge killings carried out by family members could go on indefinitely afterwards – so the swift execution of a criminal could nip this in the bud. The Old Testament does allow execution for all sorts of other, sometimes odd, things too. But modern Christians who support the death penalty usually only support it in the case of murder, basing their argument on the 'eye for eye' principle.

However, many modern Christians oppose capital punishment, some for the same practical reasons as non-Christians might oppose it (e.g. that it doesn't deter crime), and others for specifically Christian reasons. For example, the concept of forgiveness, not revenge is central to Christianity, so capital punishment is wrong because it does not give society a chance to forgive the criminal. Also, it means that reformation of the criminal isn't possible, yet even a criminal is someone who is made in the image of God and so is a person with the 'potential' to change for the better. Many Christians think that reformation is one of the main points of punishment: the expression of love towards a criminal and the hope that even murderers can change. Some Christians also oppose capital punishment because they believe that only God has the right to take a life. Jesus specifically taught that his followers were not to take revenge on someone who wrongs you (Matthew 5:38-39).

Source 6

In 2004, the Catholic Bishops of England and Wales issued a document, 'Cherishing Life' which covered the issue of capital punishment.

194) Accepting the need to maintain peace in society, the Church has allowed the possibility that capital punishment may be used as a last resort in extreme situations. However, Pope John Paul II has stated that 'as a result of steady improvements in the organisation of the penal system, such cases are very rare, if not practically non-existent.' ...We welcome the fact that the United Kingdom has completely abolished the death penalty and made an international commitment to its permanent abolition... The abolition of capital punishment bears witness to the sanctity of life and helps a society to become more consistent in cherishing every human life.

www.catholicchurch.org.uk/cherishinglife/c141.htm

Talk Point 5

Should a Christian support capital punishment?

Buddhism and Capital Punishment

The central Buddhist concept is compassion for all beings. This includes criminals. You can hardly call capital punishment compassion in any form. Buddhists would also argue that the kammic consequences of your actions will stay with you – and the kammic consequences for killers of taking a life are very bad indeed. Killing a killer would only result in the creation of *even more* bad kamma and so can't be

right. However, many Buddhist countries do still have capital punishment, and there are Buddhists who support its use because it is a form of obeying the law of a country.

Source 7

> **Buddhism does not subscribe to the taking of a life, human or animal, under any circumstances but if someone chooses to transgress the established laws of a country he or she has to pay the penalty – even if the penalty is a death sentence.**
>
> ***What Buddhists Believe, Dr. K. Sri Dhammanada, p292, expanded 4th Edition at www.buddhanet.net***

However, as capital punishment entails killing and therefore requires breaking the first Precept [avoid taking life] it is incompatible with Buddhist ethics and Buddhist social and legal philosophy. The Buddha described the judges of his own time as practicing wrong livelihood as they often handed down cruel or lethal punishments (www.buddhanet.net/e-learning/dharmadata/fdd20.htm).

A Viewpoint Independent of Religious Belief and Capital Punishment

John Stuart Mill argued that life imprisonment was even worse than capital punishment because it was a long form of suffering whereas capital punishment was mercifully quick. Mill did think that capital punishment was right because murder was so much against the idea of the greatest good for the greatest number. He didn't think much of it as a deterrent – arguing that hardened criminals just looked on it as one of the 'dangers of the job'. However, it would put some off crime and for that it was valuable.

Time Out 4

What do you think of Mill's ideas here?

The British Humanist Association opposes capital punishment because it argues that it doesn't work as a deterrent and is open to making mistakes. Also because it's unreasonable to show that killing is wrong by carrying out another killing.

Source 8

Capital punishment, which is not used in Europe, is generally opposed by Humanists because they think premeditated killing is wrong, even when carried out by the state, and because of the possibility of error and an irrevocable failure of justice. Treating criminals fairly also helps to ensure that innocent suspects are treated fairly... Capital punishment does not seem to deter murder: the US, which is one of the few democracies to retain capital punishment, has one of the highest murder rates in the world, at around 1 per 10,000 of the population (in Britain it is 1 per 100,000). Numbers of murders do not rise when capital punishment is abolished. US states with the death penalty have 50% more murders than those without.

www.humanism.org.uk

Check Your Learning

1. What TWO views might Christians have about capital punishment and why is there a possible difference of opinion within Christianity?
2. Is it right to say that the thing most Christians should be concerned about is that capital punishment doesn't allow criminals to reform?
3. What do the Roman Catholic Bishops say about capital punishment?
4. For Buddhists, how is compassion linked to capital punishment?
5. How might a Buddhist support capital punishment?
6. Why did John Stuart Mill think that capital punishment was a rubbish deterrent?
7. Explain why a Humanist might oppose capital punishment.
8. In your opinion, should capital punishment be brought back in the UK?

Should Capital Punishment Be Brought Back?

Every time there's an act of terrorism or some gruesome murder, there's a call for the return of capital punishment in the UK and many arguments for and against. It's neither a pleasant nor an easy topic but perhaps one simple way to look at it is this: If capital punishment was brought back in the UK would it *save* any innocent lives by deterring people from killing or would it result in the *taking* of innocent lives – the lives of those wrongly found guilty of crime? Difficult one to call. Alternatively, you might simply take the view that no one has the right to kill anyone for any reason, even as a punishment for killing. What do you think?

Extension Activities

Knowledge, Understanding and Evaluation through Practical Activities

1 Write your own report on the case of Timothy Evans as if you were a newspaper reporter at the time. Include details of the circumstances as well as an 'editorial' which expresses 'your newspaper's views on the trial and conviction.

2 Write a short speech which might be given by a supporter of Ruth Ellis today who was trying to get her conviction overturned. How would you present the events of Ellis's day in a modern light?

3 Design an illustrated poster about the history of capital punishment in the world today.

4 The organisation Amnesty International is strongly opposed to capital punishment. Go to its website and design a guide for others about what this website contains. You should also include a review of the website – explaining how helpful it is in covering the issues associated with capital punishment. Perhaps you could also contact the organisation and express your views on the topic – or maybe even become involved in its work if you agree with it.

5 Debate in class 'capital punishment should be brought back in the UK, but only for terrorists and mass murderers'. You should prepare for this in groups by researching further the arguments for and against and representing the views you have studied in this section.

6 Look through the UN Declaration of Human Rights and decide which of the Articles in it might directly or indirectly be against capital punishment. Write each Article out (or at least a summary of it) and explain how it could be used to oppose capital punishment. Are there any other UN documents which might give you further ideas about UN views?

7 Ewan MacColl's song criticised the execution of Timothy Evans. Make up the words for a song about the Ruth Ellis case, where you express your view on her conviction and execution. It's up to you what view you take of it.

8 Make up a graffiti board in your class where everyone writes a statement about their views on capital punishment. You could follow this up with a whole school survey – perhaps you could even involve parents by giving them the questionnaire you devise at a parents' night.

9 Look again at the purposes of punishment chapter. For each of the major purposes of punishment you found there apply it to capital punishment. Explain for each one how you think capital punishment relates to this purpose, for example, *'Deterrence – capital punishment is a good/bad deterrent because. . .'*

Unit Assessment Question

Intermediate 2: Should a Christian support capital punishment? Give reasons for your answer. **2KU 4AE**

Higher: How might a viewpoint independent of religious belief argue against the return of capital punishment in the UK today? **4KU 4AE**

Sample Exam Question

Intermediate 2: 'The case of Timothy Evans proves that capital punishment is wrong.' Do you agree with this statement? **4KU 4AE**

Higher: 'Capital punishment is an appropriate response to crime.' How might one religious viewpoint you have studied respond to this statement? **4KU 2AE**

Homework

Using the Internet, find out about the statistics of capital punishment.

- Worldwide – What's the difference in crime rates between those countries where capital punishment exists today and those countries where it has been abolished?
- UK – What has happened to crime rates in the UK since capital punishment was abolished?

Be prepared to share your results with others in your class so you can build up a dossier of information which will help everyone.

Personal Reflection

Can capital punishment ever be morally justified?

CHAPTER 6 International Issues: Globalisation

Is the Process of Globalisation Morally Justifiable?

Matt wants to check the times of the local bus from Livingston to Fauldhouse. In the Yellow pages he finds a phone number for 'Davey's Directions' which promises 'complete mastery of travel issues anywhere anyhow'. So Matt dials the number and listens to a series of very peculiar electronic bleeps and gurgles until he hears eventually what he assumes is a ringing tone...

Matt: Hello... hello... is that 'Davey's Directions'?

Operator: Yes Sir, indeed it is. May I be able to help you?

Matt: Hope so. I'm trying to find out the times of the bus from Livingston to Fauldhouse.

Operator: Most certainly Sir, [*click of computer keys*] would that be Livingstone in Springfield Massachusetts?

Matt: Eh? No, I think you're thinking about the Simpsons there. [*laughs*]

Operator: [*very serious*] You want to go to Simpsons?

Matt: No, Springfield... where the Simpsons live.

Operator: Sir, is this the Livingstone you want, or is it the one in Zambia?

Matt: I'm not likely to hop on the bus here and ask for a single to the Victoria Falls via Marrakech am I?

➜

Operator: Is that where you want to go, Sir?

Matt: [not quite as patient as he was at the start] No... Fauldhouse from Livingston.

Operator: Can you spell Livingstone for me please?

Matt: L...i...v...i...n...g...s...t...o...n.

Operator: Ah yes Sir. It is clear now. Livingston Avenue New South Wales?

Matt: No... Livingston... the town of Livingston.

Operator: I have a Livingston Alabama...

Matt: Livingston, West Lothian. Shale bings, Almondvale, roundabouts...

Operator: Ah yes – and Auldhouse was where you wanted to be getting to?

Matt: Fauldhouse, there's an 'F' in Fauldhouse.

Operator: Yes Sir. You can get a bus to Glasgow and then from there to Fauldhouse.

Matt: But that's insane – I'd have to pass Fauldhouse on the way to Glasgow and it would take hours.

Operator: Have you considered flying, Sir?

Matt: [*in a state of disbelief*] From Livingston to Fauldhouse? It's only about ten miles.

Operator: I see. Perhaps you could use a bicycle.

Matt: Have you any idea what the roads are like around here?

Operator: Many busy roads, Sir, with much traffic?

Matt: No, many quiet roads with much semi-suicidal boy racer.

Operator: You wish to race to Auldhouse?

Matt: [*irate now*] Fauldhouse! And no I don't want to race – I just want to know when the bus leaves Livingston and how long it takes. Have you even got the slightest clue where any of these places are?

Operator: Sir, I have the latest AMSTRAD microcomputer in front of me.

Matt: Where exactly is 'Davey's Directions'?

Operator: Our Chief Executive, Sir, lives in Broxburn.

Matt: And where are you?

Operator: [*mumbles*]... Phra Pradaeng, Thailand, Sir.

Matt: Thanks, I'll just go round and stand at the bus stop I think.

(Note – 'Davey's Directions' – calls charged at £2 for every unit of 30 seconds)

What is Globalisation?

It is said that we live in a shrinking world. You are just as likely to get your 'local' travel directions or discuss your bank account details with someone on the other side of the world as you are with someone in your own hometown. New technology, easier travel, changes to working patterns have all led to the modern issue of globalisation. Globalisation is the idea that the world is one big village. You buy stuff in far away lands and sell it halfway around the world, or you employ people in foreign countries to do the work you want done, or you take advantage of the natural resources a country has to offer or its rules about employing people or you relocate your entire business somewhere else. Why? Pure economics. Globalisation means that you can increase the profits of your business in many ways:

- by lowering your production costs through the use of resources wherever you can find them cheaper
- by lowering your production costs by taking advantage of cheaper labour or land for your factories or more relaxed rules about health and safety or environmental controls
- by getting access to whole new markets for your products – growing markets where you can make and sell your product in the same faraway land – much cheaper than you could do at home.

Globalisation is also the idea that the world is 'shrinking' – we can all travel around more easily and people are moving around in search of work. Global satellite media means you can watch TV from almost every country no matter where you live, this all leads to the world becoming a 'smaller place'.

Talk Point 1

What evidence is there that the world is becoming a 'global village'?

An Economic World

It is important to understand some key terms here:

- *Industrialisation*: the process where a country moves from mostly agriculture to mostly industry. This can be 'heavy, dirty industry' like shipbuilding or 'light industry' like making computers and electronics.
- *Liberalisation*: opening up world markets to free trade and competition.
- *Free trade*: trading between countries with no rules or regulations attached.
- *Developed world*: those industrialised countries where economic stability is the case. They are wealthy and most people have a very good standard of living (sometimes called the 'first world' or 'north').
- *Developing world*: those countries which are industrialising – and economic stability is improving. They have some wealth and many have a good standard of

living – though many do not (sometimes referred to as newly developed countries or industrialising countries).

- *Underdeveloped world*: those countries which are not industrialising and where there is little economic stability. They are generally poor and most have a very low standard of living – some being so poor that it seriously affects their life chances (sometimes called the 'third world').
- The split between these 'three worlds' is sometimes called 'The North-South Divide' with the developed world in the 'north' and the other two in the 'south'. These are economic terms rather than geographical ones. It is also important to note that the vast majority of the world's population lives in the 'south' while the vast majority of the world's wealth is in the 'north'.

Economic Globalisation

Chasing cheaper production costs makes economic sense. For example, the Clyde used to be world-famous for its construction of ocean-going ships. Now shipbuilding is all but dead on the Clyde. Now part of this is because people use shipping far less for travel and the transport of goods, but part of it is also because the companies who make ships and the buyers of the ships found that ships were far cheaper to make in the developing world. So many contracts for shipbuilding moved away from the expensive Clyde to far cheaper places in Asia. This was good for the developing countries but a death sentence for the Clyde. Of course trade between countries of the world is nothing new – but many people argue that modern globalisation is different because it treats people and places just as 'commodities' to be used and discarded once they have fulfilled their purpose. Companies taking advantage of globalisation are generally based in the developed world and the products made in the developing world. So the true power is still held by the big companies (usually multi-national corporations) who can pull the strings and eventually pull the plug on their foreign workforce with little consideration for them.

Advantages

Globalisation definitely makes products cheaper. This means that we can buy more for less and have a better quality of life. Usually this is mostly the case in the developed world, but there are economic advantages for the developing world too.

When a company relocates in the developing world it brings jobs, money and some economic security. Developing world workers are not paid anything like as much as developed world workers for doing the same job – but at least they have a job. Perhaps without globalisation they would still be struggling through poverty – with all the linked miseries that poverty brings.

This can have long term benefits too. Perhaps, even although the country is being 'used' by wealthy outsiders at first – the investment kick-starts the country's own economy. It now has skilled workers and money in the economy. This could lead to the country shaking off outside control and standing on its own feet economically.

So, globalisation has economic benefits for everyone – and the economies who initially suffer (like the Clyde) eventually recover by changing working practices and diversifying. This stops people being complacent and is therefore better in the long run.

Economic globalisation leads to a more stable world. The more countries are interdependent (rely on each other for all sorts of things), the less likely it will be that those countries will end up at war with each other.

Disadvantages

Some argue that taking advantage of a workforce abroad is just pure exploitation. They are paid less than the workforce in the developed world – how can this be right? Some argue that it is wrong for anyone to be able to buy something more cheaply if it's cheaper because someone's been paid less to make it.

Relocating in the developing world has negative effects on a country's economy because the country may do all sorts of things to 'woo' foreign investment (like 'turning a blind eye' to dodgy health and safety practices, for example). This works against locals who might be earning money but who might be taking all sorts of personal risks to do so – risks which workers in the developed world would not be prepared to take. Have we the right to apply one set of standards in one country and another in another?

The governments in such countries may also cut back on education and welfare spending to make their country more attractive to 'big business'. Also, with the kind of money involved, corruption is always a risk.

The power is still with the multi-national corporation, not with the developing world country. Multi-nationals are powerful organisations and control things from the developed world. The bulk of the profits therefore make their way back to the few in the developed world at the expense of the many in the developing world. This is unfair exploitation.

Economic globalisation makes the world a less stable place. People don't like to feel exploited and so local unrest can be targeted at multi-national operations, resulting in conflict which can escalate (for example, local attacks on oil installations in Nigeria).

Although a country's economy might be 'kick-started', the price paid for goods and services can still be dictated by the international markets controlled by the developed world.

Some argue that the economic benefits of globalisation aren't worth the cost, others that it's all a price worth paying for making everyone's lives better.

Time Out

1

Does a business 'owe' anything to its workforce or the community in which it is located?

Check Your Learning

1. Why did the operator have so much trouble with Matt's request?
2. What is globalisation?
3. Explain what is meant by 'the North-South Divide'.
4. Why would a multinational company move production to the developing world?
5. Explain ONE economic advantage of globalisation.
6. Explain ONE economic disadvantage of globalisation.

Globalisation and Social and Cultural Change

When the shipbuilding days on the Clyde died out it wasn't just economic changes that took place. Whole communities were affected. People had to move in search of work, families were separated and communities broken apart. People not directly involved in shipbuilding were affected too, for example, shopkeepers and pub owners, as there was less money around. Even teachers would have been affected as pupils moved with their families to new places in search of work, changing the nature of schools and even the numbers of pupils in a school. This changed society in quite a drastic way. With economic depression comes a whole load of other social problems like increased violence, alcoholism, family problems and so on. The social make-up of a place changes and not always for the better. Of course, it could be argued that in the countries where the work did go the opposite happened and so you had winners and losers. Some also say that people shouldn't expect jobs for life – and certainly not jobs that they can just hand on to their children.

Advantages

Social change is a good thing. Even when people are wealthy and in work it doesn't mean that life is always going to be rosy. Maybe it does people good to have to change every now and again, otherwise society just gets stale. Perhaps we all need to change things around sometimes – it keeps us fresh and alive and stops us getting into a rut. Perhaps we might even discover a better, more rewarding way to live.

Social change makes the world a more interesting place: people move around and mingle with different people, they learn new languages and new ways of living. The mixing up of the people of the world is far better than every little social group hiding forever in its own small world. The crossing over of different people in the world will lead to better understanding between the peoples of the world – or even between different communities in one part of the world. Recently, Scotland has seen an influx of people from Poland. This is great because it helps Scottish people to learn about other cultures and ways of life – it means that many unfilled jobs are being filled (many Polish dentists are now practising in places where before their arrival it was impossible to get a dentist's appointment!). This kind of intermingling of peoples of the world can only be a good thing.

Social change is inevitable nowadays. With global media, the Internet and the movement of people around the world – the 'differences' between cultures are becoming less and less important. People are thinking of themselves more as world citizens than Scots or English. For example, how many people in your class support teams like Barcelona and Real Madrid as well as the local teams?

Social and cultural mixing makes the world a more stable place. One of the main reasons for tensions and conflicts in the world is misunderstanding. As people throughout the world mix more often this makes misunderstandings less common. People will learn to understand and value each others' cultures and so tensions and possible conflicts will become far less likely.

Big multi-nationals moving into a country means that the social and cultural benefits of one country might end up in another – maybe some receiving countries actually have to *improve* their treatment of workers to match up with the laws applying in the multi-national's home nation. Also, it might lead to a country which was once very isolated becoming much more aware of the rest of the world. Many multi-nationals have set up operations in China, for example, which means more interaction between China and the rest of the world (in the past China was very much 'cut-off' from the rest of the world – through its own choice). This could mean that positive things like democracy, trades unions and welfare benefits might become an increased feature of Chinese life where they were not in the past.

Ideologies and cultural belief systems often go hand-in-hand with globalisation. This means that better ways of looking at life, better beliefs or social practices might go with the culture which is mixing with another culture – maybe Capitalism is an improvement on Communism?

Disadvantages

Social and cultural mixing is all very well when it's your choice – but not when it's enforced. Communities take time to build up and their quick destruction can have all sorts of negative social consequences for an individual or the community in which they live.

Social and cultural mixing could lead to tension rather than understanding. People could feel that 'incomers' are 'taking their jobs' and tensions could arise through misunderstandings between different cultures and customs suddenly thrown together and expected to get along without problem. People could resent the arrival of new cultural groups and feel that their own 'way of life' is under threat. This could lead to the rise of some very dodgy groups and all the nasty stuff which goes with them.

So this might make the world a less stable place. Maybe people in one country will resent losing their jobs to people in another. This might make them react negatively towards the people of that country and maybe even more ready to go to war with them.

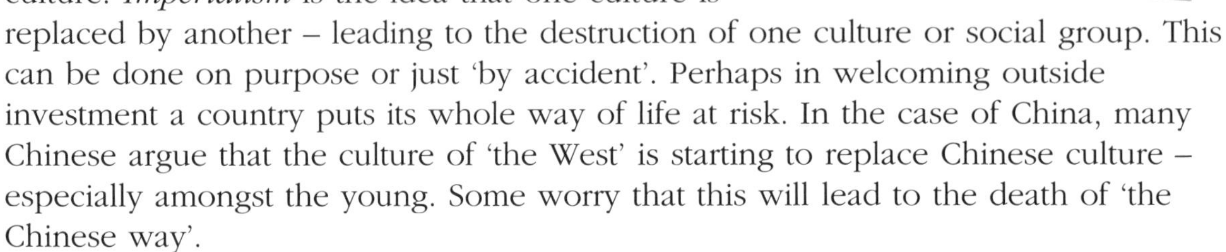

When one culture moves into another sometimes it overwhelms the home culture. *Imperialism* is the idea that one culture is replaced by another – leading to the destruction of one culture or social group. This can be done on purpose or just 'by accident'. Perhaps in welcoming outside investment a country puts its whole way of life at risk. In the case of China, many Chinese argue that the culture of 'the West' is starting to replace Chinese culture – especially amongst the young. Some worry that this will lead to the death of 'the Chinese way'.

Social change makes the world a far less varied and interesting place. Local ways of life are replaced with global as the world becomes one village – hobbies, interests even eating styles can be affected. For example, there's almost nowhere in the world now where you can't eat at a McDonald's. Some see this as progress, others as the enforcement of one way of life over another. This can also extend to religious beliefs, cultural practices and many other central features of a country's culture. For example, it is becoming more common for Chinese brides to 'marry in white' as in the west as opposed to the traditional Chinese red.

Opponents of globalisation argue that it is very rare for a multi-national to support and preserve a local culture once it has moved into a country – all that matters are the economic issues.

Talk Point **2**

What evidence is there of cultural changes because of globalisation where you live?

The Influence of Globalisation on International Trade

Developing and underdeveloped countries often have the natural resources which the developing world wants, but not the infrastructure to make use of them. This can mean that powerful multi-nationals from the developed world move in and take control with all the problems you've learned about already. However, sometimes this is not the case – but the developed world controls the markets for the products coming from the third world. This means that the developed world can pay third world producers whatever it wants, and will probably always do deals which benefit us in the developed world far more than those who are producing the goods. Such people are often in a 'no win' situation. If they don't trade with us, then they make nothing from their product (as often the home market isn't worth very much). If they do trade with us they have to accept the price we're paying or it's no deal.

This is made even more complicated because of the nature of the international commodities market. For example, the price paid for coffee or cocoa (and many other things) can go up or down wildly even in one day. Such products can't be stored forever and so you need to sell them soon after you've harvested them – you might just be ready to sell on a day where the price is very low. There's nothing you can do about it, you are powerless. All the power is in the hands of the wealthy buyers. If you don't sell them your coffee then they'll just get it from someone else who is prepared to sell it more cheaply. This is particularly important where your crop is a cash crop. If you produce coffee you have to sell it – you can't survive by eating it.

All of these issues are even further complicated by the issue of international debt. To put it simply, the third world owes the developed world a lot of money. To pay this back it needs to sell its goods – to the developed world. It has no choice. Not nice eh? World trade is monitored by the World Trade Organisation (WTO). However, many argue that this is completely controlled by the developed world and acts in its favour and against countries which are not in the developed world club.

Advantages

There has always been international trade. Without it many countries might be even poorer than they are – they would have no home market for their products and so go out of business and starve.

It means that a country doesn't have to depend on its own produce for its needs (imagine a Scotland where we could only eat oats, turnips and herring – we'd be okay for water though) because it can get products from all over the world. This is

good for everyone. This also increases our interdependence in the world, meaning that we need other countries. This could lead to a more stable world where we all live more peacefully because we want to trade freely

There are agreements about trade in the world which are set out by international organisations like the UN and international laws. These stop the poor being exploited by the rich.

International trade can benefit some countries greatly. Many Middle Eastern countries were pretty poor until they started exploiting their only resource – oil. Now they are fabulously wealthy which they wouldn't be if the only market for their oil had been their own country.

Disadvantages

The balance of power in international trade always favours the wealthy countries. They can call the tune and the poor country just has to do what it's told if it wants to survive. The international markets work for the wealthy and against the poor who are held to ransom by the mighty purchasing power of the developed world. Funnily enough it could work the other way too, countries who have vital resources needed by the developed world might hold it to ransom. Although, if history teaches us anything it's that the powerful are more likely just to take what they need from the powerless.

Again, this can lead to local hardship and the build-up of resentment. It is argued that international terrorism gets its recruits in countries where the people feel that they are being exploited by the developed world. So, this can lead to a far less stable world.

International trade can harm producers in the developed world too. If a product can be bought more cheaply abroad than 'at home' then it will. This affects the home country's economy. For example, huge Russian floating fish factories operate in the North Sea. Many Scottish fishermen argue that these are putting them out of business as the Russians can provide fish much more cheaply than the 'home' producers. Again, this doesn't do much to improve international relations.

The international laws and agreements on trade still favour the rich developed world at the expense of the third world. International trade agreements are usually drawn up and monitored by the developed world and the developing world has little power or control over them.

Some argue that even though some countries do very well out of international trade – the wealth which comes from it isn't equally shared among all the people. The wealth of some of those wealthy Middle Eastern oil-rich countries is in the hands of a few. Also, it is important to remember

that world leader countries like the UK and the USA also contain some very poor people indeed who, it is argued, get no benefits at all from the international trade of their countries.

Time Out

What do you think of completely free trade?

Check Your Learning

1. In what ways can globalisation cause social changes?
2. Explain ONE way in which this kind of social change is a good thing.
3. How could these social changes make the world a 'less stable place'?
4. If you produce coffee, how might globalisation help you or harm you?
5. Do you think international trade is good for us all? Give reasons for your answer.
6. How can international trade benefit some and harm others in a developing world country?

The Influence of Globalisation on the Environment

So far we have really only thought about the human 'costs' of globalisation. Humans are a part of the environment and so what happens to us can ultimately affect what happens to 'nature'. But all human activities affect nature, so what's so special about what globalisation might lead to?

Globalisation goes hand in hand with industrialisation. Countries which want to improve their standard of living usually think this will happen through the development of technology. This can result in the environmental harm caused by industry becoming more widespread.

The more land which is taken up by industry, the less there is available for agriculture. So marginal land is used (and lots more artificial chemicals applied). All of this exhausts the environment. Also agricultural practices change – usually towards being less environmentally friendly.

Connected to all this is the increased need for energy, which harms the environment through its creation and use.

If globalisation's aim is to make life better, then ultimately it might lead to increases in population. If it does lead to increases in population then that puts a great strain on nature's resources.

Some argue that the biggest problem with globalisation is that it is leading to *rapid* environmental change and most of it would not be for the better. The speed of this change doesn't let nature adjust to it properly. Also, political boundaries are a human invention – nature doesn't recognise them. This means that environmental damage (fast or slow) caused in one country can lead to environmental damage in another, sometimes far away from the source of the environmental harm. How might this happen?

Talk Point  3

What recent environmental changes are you aware of?

Resource Depletion

The earth has a limited set of natural resources. Once they're used up that's it. The drive towards industrialisation is using up natural resources at quite a pace. This could be coal, gas and oil for energy use, or it could be the raw materials needed to create goods. It could even be the destruction of natural habitats for some other kind of use (like clearing forests for grazing cows... for burgers). Part of the problem is the pace at which these are being used up and the other part is what is being used where. Some resources come from environmentally sensitive areas – like wood from the rainforests. The issue here is important but simple. The countries where these resources come from are struggling to industrialise and improve their quality of living. They want to use their natural resources to help them do this, even if that regrettably means some environmental harm. They don't think that the developed countries of the world have the right to stop them doing this, after all, they've done the same kind of thing in the past. Anyway, what right do they have to interfere? Some argue that some areas of the world are so environmentally important for the whole world (like the Amazon rainforest, for example) that they should be protected from exploitation, even by their own governments.

This issue is further complicated because the process of globalisation can involve powerful countries exploiting the natural resources of weaker ones. So, the weak country's resources get used up and its own people don't even get the benefits. Also, resource depletion reminds us of the interconnectedness of all things in the environment. Once a resource is used up it could lead to all kinds of other changes. For example, in the case of over-fishing, as fish stocks become seriously depleted this can affect all other marine organisms – and maybe have effects that we can't even imagine. The world's oceans are two-thirds of the planet after all!

Pollution

With the extraction and use of resources comes an environmental cost in terms of pollution. This is a problem because pollution knows no national boundaries. With industrialisation and more intensive agricultural practices comes the increased risk of pollution. Also, with globalisation, goods are being moved around the world far more often, with all the added pollution this brings. Some argue, in fact, that this is the major mistake in globalisation: globalisation is where companies relocate around the world to make their products more cheaply, but the environmental cost of all of this is so high that the product isn't actually cheaper at all because we'll all 'pay' the environmental cost in one way or another. In fact, making a product in the cheapest way maybe means making it as close as possible to the point where you sell it and use it. Newly industrialising countries have a fairly poor environmental record – perhaps environmental concerns are put to the side in the struggle to industrialise. This can actually attract multi-national corporations because they can make their products in a country where they don't have to spend loads of money on environmental safeguards (as they would in the developed world).

Also, some countries in the third world have very dodgy laws about the use of certain chemicals and environmentally harmful products. Multinational corporations can take advantage of this to make their product more cheaply because they wouldn't be able to use these at home. All of this can lead to serious pollution of the country where the product is made (to all its natural systems, including its people). But it can also spread beyond that country through water and air pollution. This can spread downriver or downwind to neighbouring countries, countries which might have very good environmental records. Add to this the problem that pollution can actually spread right around the world and you have, arguably, the biggest danger of the environmental impact of globalisation...

Climate Change

Destroying or changing natural habitats and the effects of pollution on land, air and water can all lead to a change in global climate. The problem with this is that no one is exactly sure what might lead to what and how quickly, or what the effects will be. It's all very complicated. However, it is clear that the more we abuse nature, the more likely it is that nature will strike back. The earth is a very finely balanced system. When it is put into a state of imbalance it seems to try to get back into balance again. This process will take place without any 'concern' for its effects on humans – we're only one part of nature after all. It is now very clear that human activities have global environmental impact. Some years ago a hole in the earth's protective ozone layer was discovered in the northern hemisphere. As a result, many new laws were put into place in the developed world to reduce the amount of ozone-depleting substances released into the atmosphere. It seems to have worked, with recent reports suggesting that the ozone layer is showing some recovery.

However, many of these ozone-protecting laws don't exist in the developing world yet. Climate change could be caused by the effects of pollution (the release of too much $C0_2$ into the atmosphere too quickly) or the exhaustion of natural resources leading to imbalances in ecosystems. All of this could lead to global climate change which would affect us all. It might lead to the Greenhouse Effect or a new ice age or sea-level rise and so on. Each of these could have devastating effects on everyone in the world. They could lead to poverty, hunger, increases in disease, social unrest, wars. In fact, if world climate change becomes a reality, it could undo every single benefit which was brought by globalisation in the first place! Now the trouble is that developing world countries want to improve their lives and don't want to be held back by environmental rules based on preventing what might happen. Add to this the dodgy multinationals who are more interested in profits now than what the climate will be like in ten years and you've got a real recipe for environmental disaster, one which will affect everyone.

Advantages of Globalisation for the Environment

Humans are part of the environment – if globalisation works in our interest then eventually it might be good for nature. The world's developed countries have really cleaned up their environmental act recently – but that's maybe because they can afford to... now. Once we get over the difficult stage at the beginning maybe the whole planet will be able to be more environmentally friendly, because the developing countries will be able to practice sustainable development rather than the unsustainable scrabble for improvement at the beginning.

Co-operation between the different countries of the world might lead to more effective approaches to protecting the environment. Countries can share scientific expertise and good practices.

If globalisation leads to us all being more interdependent then the effects of our actions on the whole world become far more important to us. Maybe one country will start to worry about the environmental impact of its activities on another country because it needs that country's resources.

Maybe globalisation will lead to a reduction in population and not an increase. If people's life-chances are improved they may not feel the need to have so many children as there's a greater chance that their children will survive into adulthood. A reduced population will put far less strain on nature's resources.

Maybe we'll all become world citizens. Already the developed countries are looking at helping the developing world to industrialise while still protecting their natural resources. Some have suggested making places like the Amazon rainforest protected world parks and compensating the Brazilian government for not using the rainforests in an unsustainable way. This means that the world community pays to protect the world's special places. Not all multinationals are environmental villains – some do try to make profit while applying good ethical principles.

Disadvantages of Globalisation for the Environment

The main issue is how far the environment can withstand the effects of globalisation. Some argue that it's all just too much too quickly. If we don't live in an environmentally sustainable way then we'll pay the price.

Globalisation puts wealth creation first – environmental issues come a poor second. Multinationals just want to make as much profit as possible and developing world countries want to become developed ones. Environmental concerns are therefore not the highest priority.

We don't exactly know what actions will lead to what environmental effects. The science is complex and there are disagreements about cause and effect. It's not likely that countries will spend a lot of time and energy (and money) solving a problem which might never arise.

Sadly, we're not world citizens yet. A government looks out for its own people. Not many countries would want to pay to fix an environmental problem which doesn't directly affect their country. There's always a balance of cost and benefit to be struck. Yes, some developing world countries do have very poor environmental laws, but maybe they see the alternative (missing out on the benefits of industrialisation) as worse for their people in the long run.

Time Out 3

Is globalisation good or bad for the environment?

Check Your Learning

1. How are humans and nature linked?
2. Explain TWO ways in which globalisation can harm the environment.
3. Why does the 'speed' of environmental change matter?
4. Describe one possible cause and effect of resource depletion.
5. How might globalisation lead to more pollution?
6. Describe ONE possible effect of pollution.
7. Give ONE example of how human activities can affect the climate.
8. How might globalisation affect world population? How could this affect the environment?
9. Why might a government be prepared to ignore environmental issues?

Effect on Government Policy

There are three areas which play a part here:

- The policies of developing world counties where multinationals set up.
- The policies of those multinationals' home base.
- International agreements.

Developing World Policy

The important questions in this area are:

- How far will the developing world country have to adjust its own laws to fit in with the WTO and GATT?
- What relaxations in law might a country put in place to attract investment from the developed world?
- What laws might it change to make sure that the investment remains because it's economically an advantage to stay?

Many argue that because the developing world countries are the 'weaker partner' in the globalisation process, they will change their laws for all the wrong reasons, leading to them being exploited by the wealthy nations. Others say that this is not the case because every country makes its laws to benefit its own people either now or in the long-term.

UK Government Policy

In 2001, the WTO met in Doha to review its policies. The organisation Christian Aid called for the UK representative to 'call for fundamental change to the world trade system' because, Christian Aid argues, it does nothing to help the poor. The Department of Trade and Industry responded by saying that

> 'The creation of a free and fair trading system is at the heart of the Government's international trade policy... the lowering of trade barriers... should help to stimulate [the developing world's] economic growth... the European Union will continue to give preferential treatment to imports from African, Caribbean and Pacific countries... The United Kingdom has already committed £15million to [supporting] developing countries and... announced a further £20millon package of programmes to ensure that developing countries have the capacity to participate effectively in WTO negotiations... The Government will also continue with and build on the work currently in progress to encourage British companies to apply the highest possible standards of behaviour overseas...'
>
> (Source: www.christian-aid.org.uk/campaign/trade/dtireply.htm)

The government's own website for the Department of Transport and Industry (www.dti.gov.uk) sets out its international trade policies in full. It argues that the GATT has improved world trade greatly and that the benefits to the UK of free world trade have been significant. It argues that the developing world also benefits through opening up its markets, but that this doesn't just come automatically with free trade – it needs those countries to work on their social infrastructure too. It claims that 'research shows that trade liberalisation generally helps to alleviate poverty' and explains how on its website.

The UK government has a White Paper entitled: *Trade and investment white paper 2004: making globalisation a force for good [cm6278]*. The full text of this White Paper can be found at www.dti.gov.uk. In summary it says that the UK needs to:

- maintain sound economic policies
- invest in education and skills
- encourage the EU to lead in international negotiations
- make the case for structural economic reform.

Meanwhile, the EU needs to:

- develop more outward-looking policies
- push ahead with the liberalisation of markets
- lead the way in following the Doha Development Agenda (*see WTO website*)
- recognise the benefits of liberalisation
- end the trade distorting effects of its policies.

Finally, the international community needs to:

- reject the view that treats open markets as 'concessions'
- recognise that trade represents an opportunity for developing countries to lift themselves out of poverty
- help developing countries to access the benefits of export markets
- support developing countries in their efforts at reform
- help developing countries make the difficult transitions necessary.

Based on www.dti.gov.uk

International Agreements

The **World Trade Organisation (WTO)** was set up in 1995. The aim of this organisation is to regulate trade throughout the world. It monitors trade barriers and makes discussions between nations about trade issues possible. The WTO tries to ensure that trade is free and fair – with no one taking advantage of anyone else. It argues that it tries to help developing countries with their trade by protecting them against more powerful and wealthy countries. There are 149 member countries in the WTO. The WTO itself argues that there are ten benefits to the WTO trading system:

1. It promotes peace.
2. It handles disputes constructively.
3. Its rules make life easier for all.
4. Freer trade cuts the cost of living.

5 It leads to more choice about products and their quality.
6 Trade raises incomes.
7 Trade stimulates economic growth.
8 This makes life more efficient.
9 Governments are protected from powerful pressure.
10 This encourages good government.

Source: www.wto.org

It argues that this is all achieved through the *multilateral trading system* – a negotiated system

> '...guaranteeing member countries important trade rights. They also bind governments to keep their trade policies within agreed limits to everybody's benefit.'

It says that its 'goal is to improve the welfare of the peoples of the member countries. Over three-quarters of the members of the WTO are developing or least-developed countries. It argues therefore that WTO policy is to support these countries in whatever way possible to ensure their development.

Critics of the WTO argue that it is really run by the powerful few developed nations and that its decisions are made to favour them. The WTO rejects this suggesting that weaker countries would be even more helpless without the WTO. Other critics say that the WTO is for trade at any cost and that free trade benefits only the rich and powerful – not the ordinary people – especially if they live in a poor country. Again, the WTO rejects this saying that member countries still negotiate what they give and take and what they request and offer. So the 'power' is still in their hands.

The WTO is the successor of the previous world trade agreement known as the **General Agreement on Tariffs and Trade (GATT)**. This is a set of rules about international trade drawn up after WWII at the Bretton Woods Conference. It also established the International Monetary Fund (IMF). This conference aimed to open up world trade after the war while providing safeguards in an open market. The GATT documents were only made available to the public in May 2006, and they are not all available to look at yet. Of the 88,000 documents issued under GATT, 51,000 are available on the WTO website – so feel free to have a look at them if you must (www.wto.org/english/docs_e/gattdocs_e.htm). In short, the GATT governs international trade by trying to ensure fair play among nations. Some of course argue that the GATT is just a set of rules – and rules can be ignored or broken. The world's nations will always look after themselves no matter what agreements they have made – so the effectiveness of things like GATT and the WTO is a bit dubious.

Talk Point 4

Do you think all these laws and agreements help the poor?

The Moral Implications of Globalisation

Exploitation or Help?

If a global multinational corporation sets up in a developing world country, does it matter why it has done so? It might be after cheaper production costs but so what – it's a business after all. The people in the country who are employed by the company will have a good job, possibly better paid than local jobs. The economy of the country will benefit and so maybe education and welfare will too. The people may be being exploited when compared to workers in the developed world but they are still better off than they were before. The developed world gets cheaper goods and the developing world gets investment – what's the problem? Some argue that it is morally wrong to exploit people in this way, no matter what the benefits. It is using people for our own ends and therefore exploitation. Others argue that every worker is exploited by the capitalist system, so why does it matter where the worker lives? Some argue that the imbalance in economic power between the developed and developing world is unfair and means that the rich are taking advantage of the poor – either their labour or their natural resources. Others argue that this is just airy-fairy theoretical concern which we're wealthy enough to worry about. In the developing world, surviving comes first, not moral issues.

Equality and Fairness

Does globalisation lead to a world where there are different classes of person? Some say that the very principle means that some humans are more valuable than others. Dodgy work practices and lack of environmental concern means that globalisation treats people in the developing world as second class citizens compared to workers in the developed world. We're prepared to let developing world countries take risks – human and environmental – which we wouldn't accept for our own people. How can this be right? Supporters of globalisation might respond that we have some double standards about this. For example, many American multinational corporations relocated to Scotland (like the Singer sewing machine factory in Clydebank). No one complained about the effect this might have on workers in the USA. The UK government encouraged these companies to relocate here by creating all sorts of economic incentives. The only complaint was when they eventually relocated again – to the cheaper developing world! Globalisation isn't about equality, it's about economics.

However, the moral issue remains. Should a multinational have some commitment to its workers and to the country in which they live? Should a company have some moral obligations to the people who keep it alive? Or are they just drones to be used and discarded when the price is no longer right? Who should a multinational be accountable to: its home government, its shareholders, the whole human community? What responsibilities do we all have to each other? Perhaps we should all be concerned about the possible human and environmental effects of globalisation, because it's right to do so. If we want to live in a fair world where everyone has an equal chance of a good life then we probably have to have a view about globalisation. We can be selfish about it and still argue against globalisation: if it leads to unfairness and inequality it might eventually cause us all problems. The environment might strike back, but so too might the exploited and oppressed, making the world a much more dangerous place.

Talk Point

Can the world ever really be a 'fair' place?

Check Your Learning

1. Why might a developing country change its laws because of globalisation?
2. What, based on what you've learned, is the UK government's position on world trade?
3. What does the WTO do and why do some people criticise it?
4. Explain THREE of the benefits of the WTO trading system.
5. What does the GATT try to do?
6. Explain why some people think globalisation exploits people and others disagree.
7. In your opinion, is globalisation a moral issue? Give reasons for your answer.
8. How might globalisation make the world a safer or more dangerous place?

Christians on Globalisation

Christians would all agree that the strong should protect the weak. Perhaps globalisation is an example of this. If free and open trade means helping the poor to help themselves then it must be a good thing. On the other hand if it means the wealthy exploiting the poor then that's another thing altogether. So it really depends on what you think globalisation means. The charity Christian Aid is a bit doubtful about the benefits of globalisation because the poor are currently the weaker partners in international trade. The wealthy countries of the world may even mean well in their attempts to help the poorer ones, but sadly human nature means that too often they'll look out for themselves at the expense of the poor. Christian Aid argues that so-called 'free trade' works against the world's poor.

Source 1

The Economics of Failure (2005)

New research from Christian Aid shows that sub-Saharan Africa is a massive US $272 billion worse off because of 'free' trade policies forced on them as a condition of receiving aid and debt relief... 'we are not arguing that countries which liberalise do not grow, or that some people in them do not become less poor – but we are saying that without liberalisation, growth could have been higher and poverty reduction faster... following trade liberalisation, countries tend to buy more than they sell every year... as a result they have to live beyond their means... Trade liberalisation is not a good policy that has unfortunate consequences for a small minority... It is a policy imposed on developing countries... that has systematically deprived some of the poorest people in the world of opportunities to develop their own economies and end poverty.'

www.christianaid.org.uk

In its document: The climate of poverty: facts, fears and hope (May 2006), Christian Aid also argues that climate change and poverty are 'inextricably linked' because 'it is the poor of the world who are already suffering disproportionately from the effects of global warming'. It argues in fact that climate change could 'nullify efforts to secure meaningful and sustainable development in poor countries'. (www.christianaid.org.uk)

But do these views represent all Christians – that is hard to say. The two major Christian beliefs in question here are:

- *Stewardship*: humans were given the earth as a gift and should use it wisely for our benefit. But this means caring for nature as well as exploiting it. Globalisation might be an example of good stewardship – or the opposite!
- *Love for one another*: Christians should support the idea of the strong protecting the weak. They should work for a world where there is fairness and justice for all. Perhaps globalisation brings this – or the opposite!

Buddhists on Globalisation

If globalisation leads to people being more economically secure then it is good. The Buddha once refused to teach the dhamma to a man until the man had been fed. He believed that there was little point in trying to teach the finer points of Buddhism while the man's only thought would be on his hunger. If globalisation leads to greater prosperity for all and so greater world stability, then that is good. A person is far more likely to think about their spiritual life when they don't have to put all their energy into surviving. However, some believe that globalisation isn't based on the good of all, but the good of a few at the expense of the many. If this is so then the motivation for and the practices linked to globalisation will both attract very bad kamma. World trade is focused on material gain, which is selfish and greedy.

In Buddhism, such selfishness and greed are the roots of all bad kamma – tanha. The Second Noble Truth is that 'All suffering is caused by desire'. If globalisation is based on the desire for things and the improvement of our material lives then a Buddhist would be very wary of it. Also, many of the things which accompany globalisation would go against Buddhist ideals. If, for example, globalisation leads to environmental destruction then this would go against the Buddhist belief that all beings are worthy of kindness and compassion. Nature itself can be harmed and such harm could bring negative kamma upon us all. Globalisation might also be one group exploiting another which a Buddhist would reject. However, some features of globalisation might work in favour of Buddhism. Free travel around the world and the sharing of ideas and cultures has meant that the Buddha's ideas have reached every corner of the globe.

Source 2

In the new era marked by the triumph of the free-market economy the most pernicious delusion that hangs over us is the belief that the path to human fulfilment lies in the satisfaction of artificially induced desires. Such a project can only provoke more and more greed leading to more and more reckless degrees of selfishness, and from the clash of self-seeking factions, the result will necessarily be strife and violence

Bhikku Bodhi at www.buddhanet.net

The Dalai Lama argues that the modern world requires modern thinking, where the interconnectedness of all life is stressed:

> I think however, there is good news in that now we definitely will have to find new ways to survive together on this planet. In [the 20th] century we have seen enough war, poverty, pollution and suffering. According to Buddhist teaching, such things happen as the result of ignorance and selfish actions, because we often fail to see the common relation of all beings. The earth is showing us warnings and clear indications of the vast effects and negative potential of misdirected human behaviour. To counteract these harmful practices we can teach ourselves to be more aware of our mutual dependence
>
> www.dalailama.com/page.82.htm

A Viewpoint Independent of Religious Belief

Peter Singer, the modern Utilitarian, states:

> Consider the facts: by the most cautious estimates 400 million people lack the calories, protein, vitamins and minerals needed to sustain their bodies and

minds in a healthy state... According to one study, 14 million children under five die every year from the combined effects of malnutrition and infection. In some districts, half the children born can be expected to die before their fifth birthday.

Practical Ethics, Singer, CUP 1998 p 218.

Singer goes on to think about whether our allowing the poor to suffer and die in this way is the moral equivalent of murder. This murder is not something that only applies to the action of world governments,

'...it applies to each absolutely affluent individual, for each of us has the opportunity to do something about the situation' (p232). Singer argues: 'if it is in our power to prevent something very bad from happening, without thereby sacrificing anything of comparable moral significance, we ought to do it' (p229). He concludes that, for a Utilitarian, it would be right (and should be done) for those of us who are wealthy enough to have luxuries to give these up to help those who live in absolute poverty. Singer concludes his argument by stating that those on average or above average incomes in affluent societies should give 10% of their wealth to the poor: 'By any reasonable ethical standards this is the minimum we ought to do and we do wrong if we do less' (p246).

Singer clearly believes that it is a moral duty for the rich to help the poor. Where does this leave globalisation? Again, it depends upon your view of globalisation. Many of the negative elements of globalisation in this section would go against a utilitarian ethic. This is because they work in favour of the minority (rich) and against the interests of the majority (poor) – the opposite of Utilitarianism. But, if globalisation leads to a fairer, safer, more environmentally stable world then that would fit well with Utilitarianism because that kind of world would benefit everyone and so maximise everyone's happiness.

Check Your Learning

1. Explain how a Christian could support or oppose globalisation.
2. What do you think Christian Aid's view of globalisation is?
3. Why might the Buddha have thought globalisation was a good thing?
4. What view does Bikkhu Bodhi have of the free market economy?
5. What does Peter Singer think allowing the poor to die is? Do you agree?
6. What two views of globalisation could a utilitarian hold?

Extension Activities

Knowledge, Understanding and Evaluation through Practical Activities

1. You are in charge of a big call centre located in Scotland. Having looked at the figures you think you make more profit by relocating to the developing world. Prepare a speech for your shareholders where you explain your position.
2. You are a shareholder in the call centre – and you're also a Christian. Listen to the speech in task 1 and prepare your response.
3. On a world map, draw a line representing the North-South Divide. Pin information to the map – maybe linked to specific countries – showing the differences between developed, developing and underdeveloped countries.
4. Find out how one Scottish town or city recovered from the effects of an employer relocating abroad. Prepare an illustrated report.
5. Make a list of the benefits which cultural mixing brings.
6. Find out how Fair Trade works for the benefit of producers. Prepare a display board of its practices. Is this better than 'free trade'?
7. Make a short TV magazine item which explains one of the environmental consequences of globalisation.
8. Make a report on the websites of the WTO and the DTI. How well do they make their case for globalisation? From what you have learned what might a Christian, a Buddhist and a Utilitarian think of the claims of the WTO and the UK government about the effects of globalisation?
9. Have a class debate: 'Globalisation is good'.

Unit Assessment Question

Intermediate 1: Explain ONE way in which globalisation might harm the environment. **4KU**

Intermediate 2: Should a religious person oppose globalisation? Give TWO reasons for your answer. **4KU**

Sample Exam Question

Intermediate 1: State ONE advantage of globalisation. **2KU**

Intermediate 2: 'Globalisation will make the world a fairer place' Do you agree? Give TWO reasons for your answer. **2KU 4AE**

Homework

Using the Internet, find out about anti-globalisation events around the world. Are the people taking part in these right to protest or not?

Personal Reflection

What part are you playing in globalisation?

CHAPTER 7 International Issues: International Aid

Is International Aid an Appropriate Moral Response to World Poverty?

Ingledoink is from Betrapudlioian. He's (though the idea of he and she doesn't really amount to much on his planet) just been on a fact-finding mission to Earth. The Intergalactic Management Committee (QYX) has sent him to this small planet to find out if they're ready to be welcomed into the Intergalactic Club. If they find that we're ready, then all sorts of wonders will be coming the way of us blissfully unaware Earthlings (or Yoicks, as the aliens call us). For example, we'll be given the secrets of interstellar travel, the cure for cancer, the location of the Holy Grail and access to 47 zillion new TV channels (and best of all, the know-how to build our own Graglyx machines). Ingledoink's mission has been to find out if our society is advanced enough to cope with the wonders which lie waiting. For the last 10 years, he's been observing completely unseen by using the Betrapudlioian technique of temporarily inhabiting another body. Been dozing in class recently and didn't quite catch what the teacher said? You might well have been briefly borrowed by Ingledoink. Here's his report. (Did I mention that Betrapudlioians always speak to each other as if they were in an opera?)

Oh Great Chair and infected underlings of the QYX. I bring you greetings from the world of the Yoicks. I am sad to say that my report is not a happy one. For the Yoicks, or Earthlings as they call themselves – though why I do not know because most of their planet is water – are a most primitive bunch. They split the fortune of

➜

their planet in a most peculiar way: two-thirds of the people live in the top of the planet (which they call the south) and one third in the bottom (their north). Remember that this odd little world is upside down relative to everyone else in the Universe, and rightly so, as you'll see. The few keep the wealth to themselves. They make it through using and abusing the many – over long periods of history. They enslave people, and force them to work for them, sometimes because they are of a different gender (see note 1) and sometimes because they are a different race (see note 2). They also exploit other people because they live in a different part of their world. They draw imaginary lines on their world and call them countries. But even within these imaginary lines they don't treat everyone equally. The wealthy countries have starving people as well as the poor ones. But the poor ones... many... many die every day because they haven't got the simplest things: food and clean water. Some even die through silly diseases which could be stopped, even by these technologically hopeless Yoicks, quickly and simply. A young Yoick in the place called Africa – a swollen belly and stick thin legs – can be seen scrabbling in the dirt for a few grains of fallen wheat – a 'gift' from the UK (or YUK, as I prefer to think of it). At the same moment a young Yoick in the YUK will be tucking into burgers, fries and onion rings (the existence of these three would, in my opinion, be enough never to allow the Yoicks into membership of the QYX). This YUK Yoick would also be complaining about 'having nothing to do' while the African would have 'nothing to eat'.

To make themselves feel better, the rich Yoicks help the poor ones. But they do this in the strangest ways. They 'loan' money to the poor countries (not real money, just binary algorithms in a computer memory) and then make the poor pay for this money by giving them back more than they got in the first place (and this money is measured in time, energy and real products). The poor only get this helping money when they agree to do what the rich tell them.

Sometimes the rich give the poor food. This saves the rich storing it. But some of the rich Yoicks don't like this because it means the poor ones aren't buying their food – they'd rather feed it to their animals or have celebrations where they throw it at each other. Sometimes the rich help the poor with medicines. Even though these are very barbaric, there was a glimmer of hope here. Until I found that the rich spend almost as much on making their pets well and far more muddling their brain chemistry with the chemical alcohol. Sometimes the rich send their skilled and learned people to the poor to teach them the ways of the rich. They believe in 'teaching a man to fish' – even in the desert which did confuse me a little until I realised that it is a 'saying'. With all this confusion you'll be even more confused when you hear my discovery that sometimes the rich help the poor by giving them weapons. Perhaps the idea is that the poor all kill each other and so the problem goes away – and the rich can come along and steal what's left. This one I never quite got to the bottom of – but the rich seem to think it's very wise.

In short, the Yoicks are nowhere near ready for the wonders which we can offer, and so I must recommend that they are not granted membership of the QYX. They

→

would keep the benefits for the few and leave the many depending on them. The Yoicks have a long way to go before they realise that we're all in this universe together...

Note 1: Two genders – male and female – same species, different rights.

Note 2: Many races – all human but valued differently according to epidermal tone.

Talk Point 1

Is Ingledoink's report fair?

Why is International Aid Necessary?

Ingledoink paints a pretty bleak picture of our world. Is it really that bad? Are the attempts of the rich to help the poor really so feeble? Why is aid needed anyway?

It is a fact of economics that around five per cent of the world's population controls around 95 per cent of the world's wealth. Standards of living in the rich 'north' mean that most people who live there not only have more than enough to eat, they have spare wealth to enjoy luxury items. Along with this goes good quality healthcare and good quality education. Often these are completely free – and some are even so well-off that they can afford to ignore the free offers and pay for what they see as 'better' education or healthcare. In fact, many in the developed world are so wealthy that their wealth is causing them problems (!). Obesity is on the increase – with all the health problems which come with it. Social stresses are more common as people become even more aware of what they have compared with others – and are working longer and harder to keep up. Add to this our endless need for energy in the north and you have an Earth which, according to some environmentalists, is becoming clapped out and exhausted.

At the same time, the vast majority of the world's population lives well below this level of wealth – in poverty. Two terms are important here:

- *Relative poverty:* this means you are poor compared to others and depends on who you compare yourself with. You probably are wealthy enough to survive and even have some wealth left over for small luxuries.
- *Absolute Poverty:* This is being so poor that your life is threatened. You don't even have enough for your basic survival needs.

The world can be divided into three groups, the developed, developing and underdeveloped world (see Chapter 6). Most of the world's absolute poverty is in the underdeveloped world, but there's some even in the wealthiest countries on the planet.

Why is the idea of absolute poverty so important? Some people say that 'charity begins at home'. This argument means that we are under a greater moral responsibility to help people who live near us than those who live far away. There's nothing wrong with doing that of course. However, governments and aid agencies often argue that they help those in poverty abroad because their need is so much greater. International aid usually goes to those places where there is absolute poverty because this threatens people's very lives. Governments and aid agencies also help the poor 'at home', but give international aid where absolute poverty makes the aid vital. Why though do governments or aid agencies bother?

Time Out 1

What examples are there where you live of the 'problems associated with being wealthy'?

Why Give Aid?

Perhaps it makes the wealthy feel better about themselves. They can give some of their wealth away and not feel guilty about the stark facts of world poverty while they enjoy prosperity. On the other hand obviously it's better to give a little than to give nothing at all.

Governments might give aid because it wins them votes – or just shows that their country is wealthy enough to do it. Or maybe we give our world leaders a hard time. Many people get into politics because they want to make the world a better place and it gives them the power to do that. Giving aid might just be simple human generosity.

It is a moral duty to help our fellow humans – a categorical imperative. It should be done for no other reason than it is right – so it's an example of a Kantian ethic.

We'd like the same to be done to us if we were poor – so it's an example of the Golden Rule.

It benefits the majority in the long run – so it's an example of Utilitarian ethics. It might do this because it makes the world a safer place. People living in absolute poverty don't have a lot to lose and so might be easily persuaded to act against the wealthy countries who they could be told are the cause of their poverty. This leads to more instability in the world and the greater threat of wars and so on. Also, it might help poor countries to develop and prosper, which could eventually benefit us in some way.

Some argue more bleakly that international aid is often given so that poor countries are in our debt (either financially or 'emotionally'). If we give aid to the poor countries they feel they owe us something. Their governments might then be more likely to let us get at their natural resources or set up business cheaply in their country. It might just be that we want the poor country to think well of us and so be more likely to support our way of life (or support us against terrorists or in a war...). So aid is given so that we can eventually get something back.

Check Your Learning

1 Why won't earth be given membership of the QYX?
2 Explain the difference between relative and absolute poverty.
3 Explain TWO reasons why International aid is necessary.
4 Have you ever given to charity? Why? Why not?

The Effects of Absolute Poverty

Some say that it really doesn't matter why we give aid as long as we do. The effects of absolute poverty are so dire that we shouldn't need to think too much about responding to it however we can. The statistics of absolute poverty are mind-numbing. The World Bank's website has statistics for every imaginable development and poverty issue for every country in the world (see www.worldbank.org). Similar statistics are available at the United Nations' site at http://unstats.un.org. The aid organisation Oxfam probably sums all of these up by reminding us that *50,000 people die in the world every day from the effects of poverty – that means one child dies every three seconds* (see www.oxfam.org.uk).

What Does Absolute Poverty Lead To?

Death: This can be through a basic lack of nutrition, and in some cases sheer starvation. When your nutrition levels are low you are also more likely to get ill and not be able to fight the illness. Diarrhoea is one of the major killers of children in the developing world, even though it can be treated very easily at very little cost.

Illness of many kinds is sometimes more likely as people in absolute poverty will live in cramped conditions, with poor (or no) sanitation. Many will not have access to clean water and water-borne diseases are therefore very common. There can be little or no medical facilities to treat illness. Simple infections which could be treated by the same antibiotics we get when we have a sore throat can become killers.

All of this can lead to *poor social conditions*. In the struggle for survival, normal social rules can be ignored leading to a far more harsh society. This can take many forms, from violence to the neglect and abandonment of children.

The problem with absolute poverty is that it becomes a vicious circle. The poverty leads to poor living conditions which lead to more poverty and so on. Children living in absolute poverty are not likely to have much of an education and may be exploited for work or worse. It leads to a sense of hopelessness and a victim mentality which sometimes means people feel there's no way out of it all. This leads to a very grim life indeed.

These individual effects can lead to wider consequences. It can destabilise the world's economy and it can lead to the world being a more dangerous place politically. It can have negative impacts on the environment as people ignore environmental concerns in order to get what they need to exist. It robs the world of the creative powers of the poor – who knows, perhaps there's someone somewhere in the developing world who might have the brain-power to work out the cure for cancer – but will never be able to do so because she's too busy struggling just to survive.

The Causes of Absolute Poverty

If you live in a poor country it's going to be hard to break out of poverty. Many countries have long histories of being poor and so everyone born there is born into a situation which is already difficult.

Many such countries are poor because they don't have the capital to buy the means of production to lift themselves out of poverty.

Some borrowed money from the rich countries to do this, but now find themselves in great debt. This debt has to be repaid. This means that the people born in that country already have a burden of debt to repay before they even start looking after themselves. This might mean that the country has to engage in economic activities to pay off the debt it owes instead of feeding its own people. This can lead to ridiculous situations like in the 1980s before the first Band Aid fundraising campaign where Ethiopians were dying of starvation while their country was still exporting

vast amounts of food abroad. It had to do so to raise money to pay off its international debt.

All of this can lead to the rich world exploiting the poor world. Developed countries relocate in poor countries and get economic advantages from that while locals don't do very well. Big businesses encourage poor countries to buy products they probably don't need with the promise that it'll lead to prosperity. For example, many poor countries have been encouraged to engage in large-scale agriculture changes which are heavily dependent upon chemical herbicides and pesticides, or even seed stock. The supply of these is controlled by big multinational corporations and means that the poor country becomes dependent upon this and has to pay for it every year. This leads to unequal trade practices which favour the rich over the poor (see Chapter 6).

As if all this man-made misery wasn't enough, many developing countries unfortunately suffer from regular environmental disasters. Floods and droughts can lead to crop failure and famine. Poor countries don't have the means to withstand this and so it leads to even more poverty.

Also, poor countries are sometimes distracted in their efforts to improve their economies by conflict and war. Sometimes these are just the leftovers of history (sometimes the results of what the developed world colonists left behind when they left) and sometimes they're just the result of the human stresses of living so miserably. The country ends up spending money on war, not on poverty relief.

All of these combined mean a poor country can't pull itself out of poverty because healthcare, education and all the things which make life good in the developed world have to take a back seat to survival. Without these things beating the poverty becomes less likely, and so the vicious circle continues.

Talk Point 2

Do people in your class do enough to help the poor? What more could/should they do?

Check Your Learning

1 Describe fully TWO possible effects of absolute poverty.

2 Explain TWO possible causes of absolute poverty.

For these reasons, the developed world gives international aid to those countries struggling with the effects of poverty. This takes many forms each with their own advantages and disadvantages.

Aid Responses: Emergency Aid

This can be anything from food to medical help to warm clothing. It is usually in response to some unexpected natural disaster or where there is conflict. The UN World Food Programme has recently responded to man-made emergencies in war-torn Darfur in 2005 and the Indian Ocean tsunami in 2004/5. Emergency aid is just as likely to be given by charitable organisations like Oxfam as government ones.

Advantages

- It responds directly to a real need where the receiving country has been dealt a blow causing its normal activities to be interrupted.
- It can help a country recover from a temporary setback and maybe even start it on the road to recovery in the longer term.
- It is specific and focused – giving what is needed to those who need it without delay.
- It makes people in rich countries more aware of poverty issues. A natural disaster might make them think more about what poor countries have to suffer constantly and so it might spark off the will to do more – bringing good out of an otherwise bad situation. This is probably what happened in the 1980s following the Ethiopian famine and the Band Aid response. This resulted in a second Band Aid, as well as the founding of Sport Relief, Comic Relief and so on. Perhaps without this natural disaster such sustained action would never have developed.

Disadvantages

- It sometimes doesn't get to the people who need it. The receiving country's infrastructure may not be able to cope in the circumstances and in conflicts it may be diverted away from the needy to the military.
- It is short-term. Once the problem is over it will end and leave the poor back where they started. It's really just a temporary sticking plaster and doesn't cure the problem. In fact, it might make it worse because the rich nations might feel they have done their bit and feel able to walk away from the longer term issues the receiving country faces.
- It may not be appropriate – it may be what the rich think is needed but might not actually be what is needed. In such situations, communications can break down and supply and demand issues become confused.

Time Out

What emergency situations have there been in the world recently?

Aid Responses: Food Aid

Sometimes aid is in the form of direct food supplies. They can even be dropped by parachute into dangerous areas! The developed world spends a lot of money subsidising its own food producers so that they remain stable. In Britain, this began after World War II when it became clear that we had to look after home food supplies and not be too dependent upon other suppliers who would fail us in the event of war or conflict. Add to this, policies like the EU's Common Agricultural Policy (CAP) which resulted in the famous stocks of food (butter mountains and wine lakes!) which were stored away (often going to rot) so that they wouldn't be released onto the market where they would harm economies (all to do with supply and demand – ask your Business teacher!). This food could (and sometimes did) end up as food aid.

At other times, food aid is simply getting food to wherever it's needed quickly. It might even be bought in the receiving country for distribution there.

However, there is also a more sustained approach run by the United Nations World Food Programme (www.wfp.org). This provides free school food in the developing world to enable children to benefit from their education. It says that 34 US dollars a year is all it takes to feed a child at school... for a year. In 2004 this provided 16.6 million children with school meals, and overall fed 113 million people in 80 countries.

Advantages

- It uses developed world food surpluses for good reasons. Instead of throwing food away it saves lives. Good nutrition is vital to so many aspects of life.
- It encourages children to come to school and get an education instead of having to work to provide themselves with food. Without basic food supply a country is never going to pull itself out of poverty. It provides the strength to work and it means that energies can be directed in other ways than just the hand to mouth scrabble for a daily meal, helping to break the cycle of poverty.
- It can take the form of helping a poor country to make the most of its own food through agricultural training or the supply of seed stock and fertiliser. Many

developing world countries are actually very fertile and could supply the food needs of everyone in the country with much more to spare. What they don't always have is the technical expertise or the means to start the process off. So, aid in this way helps the poor to help themselves.

Disadvantages

- It still leaves developing countries dependent upon the developed world. It might make them less likely to work for themselves if they know that they will get free handouts anyway. So instead of empowering the poor it actually does the opposite.
- It can again be a short-term fix to a long-term problem. The wealthy give away some of their leftovers, feel good about themselves, and then forget about the poor until the next disaster (for example, are you still wearing your 'Make Poverty History' white bracelet?).
- It can only benefit some in a country, not all – and who decides which countries or who in those countries is most in need?
- Again, because of poverty, some poor countries can be troubled by official corruption. Food aid can often be redirected or abused for the benefits of the few. This makes it less effective.

Talk Point  3

How much food do you see wasted each day?

Aid Responses: Medical Aid

This can be the provision of medical supplies or medical staff. It can be as a response to a particular crisis or a more long term approach to improving healthcare for the poor. Organisations such as the International Red Cross (www.icrc.org) deal particularly with medical aid issues arising in places where there is or has been conflict. However, it responds to need wherever it arises – after the 2005 earthquake in Kashmir, for example, where it set up a field hospital, carried out medical evacuations and sent in teams of medical personnel to support the struggling local healthcare operations. It carried out similar work in Nigeria in 2006 in response to problems caused there by internal violence.

The UK government's aid work is controlled by the Department for International Development which oversees all UK government aid programmes (see www.dfid.gov.uk). It has recently been working with African nations on researching HIV/AIDS which is a major killer in the developing world. This has involved assisting with medical treatments as well as working together to find responses to this problem. Medical aid can also involve bringing people from the developing world to the developed world for specific treatments not available in their own land.

Advantages

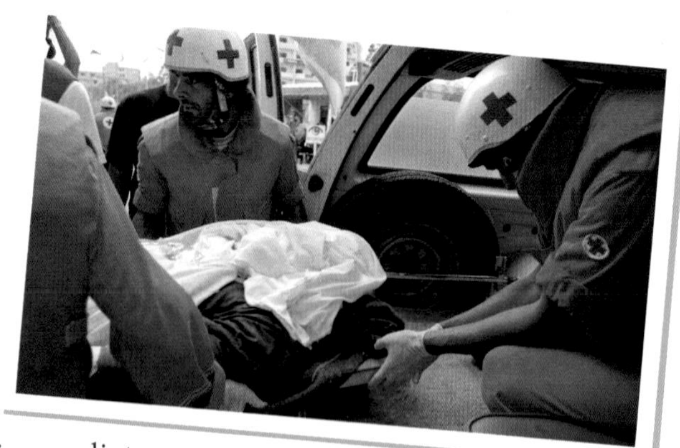

- For many in the developing world, poor health and lack of access to good healthcare is a major contributor to the vicious circle of poverty. Direct medical help either in the form of supplies or medical staff can relieve some of the suffering so that it doesn't add even more to the misery of the poor. This can be in response to an immediate problem like a disaster or a longer term issue like the spread of HIV/AIDS.
- Help with research into treatments and cures in the long-run might help alleviate the effects of poverty. Remember that much of the suffering of the poor in the developing world is not just economic but physical. Polluted water and even natural problems like malaria are things which the poor can't afford to fight back against. Medical aid helps them fight back. Often this is at very little cost to the rich, but of great benefit to the poor.
- All of this might help us in the developing world to be more aware of poverty issues. Doctors who spend time treating people in the developing world usually return home changed by it. This can widen out to others making us all more aware of the basic health issues faced by the poor. This might lead us to take more action.

Disadvantages

- Again, it can be only a temporary solution to a longer-term problem. It treats the symptoms of poverty but not the causes.
- It deals with only one dimension of the issue of poverty. Perhaps it's more important to spend time and energy working out why HIV/AIDS is so common in the developing world than in – perhaps pointlessly – trying to find a cure. It makes us all feel that we're 'doing something' when in fact we're not really doing very much at all – just sweeping the problem under the carpet.
- The scale of medical response can never match the scale of the problem. It's like bailing out a sinking ship with a teaspoon – bringing one sick child to the UK is great for that child and great publicity, but perhaps masks the sufferings of all the other children who are not so lucky.

Aid Responses: Expertise Aid

Many poor countries are poor because they haven't got the necessary skills to take advantage of their natural resources or to move towards industrialisation. Obviously better and more education is the answer in the long run, but in the short-term one solution is to send aid in the form of people who can get things started and running until local people build up the expertise to do it for themselves. This could be teachers, or engineers, or builders, or farmers – anyone who can teach local people

how to do it for themselves. This is a vital element to aid because it's not about waltzing in, doing your bit and running out again – it's about leaving only once you're no longer necessary. It links to the saying, 'give a man a fish and you feed him for a day. Teach him to fish and you feed him for life'. The Department for International Development recruits people at home and abroad to work in many capacities in the developing world. There are also many voluntary organisations which do this kind of work, as well as world organisations like the United Nations.

Advantages

- This does deal with some of the causes of poverty rather than the symptoms. It helps the poor to help themselves by giving them the expertise to do things for themselves instead of being dependent upon the experts in the developed world.
- This movement of people around the world will help to foster international understanding – the poor will learn that those who live in rich countries share the same human concerns that they do and the rich will get in insight into the problems faced by the poor – this can only be a good thing. It's not just about donating food or money – it's about sharing in the experience of the poor and giving them the know-how to end their own poverty.
- The benefits are also two-way in that an 'expert' sent to help in the developing world will have to confront problems in a different way. This might mean that they end up coming up with completely new ideas which can be developed for everyone's benefit. Approaching new problems will encourage creativity and maybe help find new solutions.

Disadvantages

- Contact with the developing world could lead to people in poorer countries becoming more, not less, aware of what they don't have and so lead to greater dissatisfaction and misery.
- Sometimes, when someone from a developing country is sent to the developed world for education and training, s/he never returns to their home country. This means that all the benefits gained never get back to the poor (other than that one person).
- Perhaps the education and training of people in the developing world is pointless if their country cannot deal with the other effects of poverty. No point in being a home-grown engineer if your country can't afford to buy the resources necessary for you to do your job.

Time Out 3

Thinking about what you want to do when you grow up – would you want to spend some time doing your job in the developing world? How could you help? How might it benefit you?

Aid responses: Armaments

Yes, you might not believe it, but aid is sometimes given in the form of armaments. This might seem strange, but it can be as the result of a request from developing world countries themselves. Efforts to lift your country out of poverty are probably going to be badly affected if you're also engaged in a war – either with another country or internally. Few things have the same power to throw everything else in a country out of order than armed conflict. The infrastructure suffers: the environment, agriculture, industry, education. In fact, all the things you need to get right to escape from poverty are held back by war. So, it is in your interests to get the war finished as quickly as possible so that life can return to normal. To do this, you might need help in supplying your troops with the necessary weapons, and so require armaments as aid. This sometimes takes the form of direct military assistance from another country, but can also be weapons and ammunition to let you fight your own battles. Once life returns to normal you can get back to the business of getting out of poverty – so maybe it's not such a strange idea after all.

Advantages

- We might not like it but conflict seems to be a fact of life. It does get in the way of economic development so if the rich can help the poor to end the conflict more quickly it should be done – even if this means giving armaments as aid.
- It is a moral duty for the strong to help the weak. Where a poor country has suffered aggression from a stronger country (rich or poor) – we have a duty to help the poor country. This might be by direct military intervention or through aid in the form of armaments.
- Doing this, even if we'd rather avoid it, is a necessary evil. It ends the conflict more quickly and helps life to return to normal – saving more lives in the long run.

Disadvantages

- People in rich countries might object to their money being spent on weapons for another country.

- It's sometimes hard to judge in such situations who to help. The 'goodies' and 'baddies' aren't always obvious and you might end up backing the wrong country – which could have negative implications for you eventually. Or you might end up backing a corrupt government against its own people – or corrupt rebels against a legitimate government. . .
- It might actually cause conflict to escalate – not to end. A small local conflict could end up drawing in neighbouring countries and leading to a wider war – or a world war, as other rich countries see you taking sides and decide to support the opposite side in the same way.
- How can it ever be right to give something which you know will lead to suffering and death? Maybe it's just plain wrong to give 'aid' in the form of armaments. Perhaps the same money should be used for some far more worthy kind of aid like healthcare or food. . .
- Many independent aid organisations are completely against armaments being given as aid, but some world governments still feel that there are times when it is necessary. It would be good if it was not so, but unfortunately human nature isn't like that.

Talk Point 4

Should weapons be given as aid?

Check Your Learning

1. Why is emergency aid so important?
2. Describe ONE possible disadvantage of emergency aid.
3. How is food aid often distributed?
4. What do you think is the most important advantage of food aid?
5. What forms can medical aid take?
6. Why might a country need aid in the form of expertise?
7. In you opinion, is aid in the form of armaments morally acceptable? Explain your answer.

The Tied Aid Issue

Some rich countries give aid because it's right, others for more selfish reasons. One issue of concern remains the question of 'tied aid', or, 'aid with strings attached'. Some aid comes with conditions attached. For many, there's nothing wrong with this because otherwise the aid might not help, as governments may misuse it or waste it. When you're giving aid in any form it seems perfectly reasonable to have some

conditions attached to it. On the other hand, some argue that these conditions usually favour the giver and not the receiver. They are usually in forms which keep the power in the hands of the wealthy and keep the poor dependent upon us.

Structural Adjustment Policies (SAPs)

When aid is given the provider may instruct the receiving country to make changes to the country's laws, economy or social infrastructure. Now this can be viewed in two ways – as a helpful bit of direction to a poor country, giving them useful guidance on how to make the most of their aid – or as a cynical way for the rich country to get more out than it puts in. Critics say that SAPs are usually intended to help the donating country in some way, for example, by opening up a new market (trade liberalisation) to its own producers or making it easier to exploit the resources of the receiving country. Structural adjustments are usually asked for when organisations like the International Monetary Find (IMF) or World Bank (www.worldbank.org) are giving loans to a developing country. They might ask the receiving country to:

- make financial changes to their economy – lower interest rates perhaps, or privatise public utilities
- make legal changes to their society – change employment law to make workers more attractive to outside investors
- open up trade to outside investment – trade liberalisation which should lead to economic growth.

All of these are designed to ensure that the aid does what it is meant to. It wouldn't make sense just to give aid willy-nilly, there have to be conditions, just like if you got a loan from a bank. Maybe this is especially true where the country has shown itself not to be able to stand on its own two feet – perhaps it needs some guidance about how to make the most of what it is being given – so that it makes a difference. Opponents of SAPs argue that they leave all the power in the hands of the donating country – which will end up getting more benefit from it than the receiving country. It leaves the poor country still dependent on the rich, as the aid can be stopped at any time if it doesn't stick to the SAP requirements. Also, the changes, especially at the beginning, may cause a great deal of hardship for local people until the economy adjusts (if it ever does) to the changes. This will actually make the situation worse instead of better.

International Debt

Lots of aid is in the form of loans. Loans have to be paid back. The scale of these loans means that developing countries end up paying back for a very long time – and sometimes paying back to the developed world more than they get in aid. Most of the developing world is repaying the debt of loans borrowed from the developed world, sometimes a long time ago. This means that every child born in such a country is born owing money to someone else.

According to the Jubilee 2000 campaign (www.jubileedebtcampaign.org.uk), which sought to cancel international debt, Comic Relief raised £26 million in 1997. This was paid back by Africa in the form of debt repayments in two days. It argues that although the original debts were paid off long ago, the interest repayments are still being made at the rate of US $100 million every day. For every US $1 received in grant aid, low-income countries pay US $2.30 back in debt. It cites ridiculous examples – like the fact that South Africa's government is still repaying US $21 billion in debt which was borrowed by the 'whites-only' apartheid government!

Many other equally dopey examples of debt facts and figures can be found on this website's information pages. It refers to promises made at the G8 summit at Gleaneagles in 2005, where G8 leaders promised 'full' cancellation of debts to the World Bank, The IMF and African Development Fund for countries which complete the Heavily Indebted Poor Countries (HIPC) Initiative. This is seen by critics as a series of conditions which leaves the poor countries still struggling and has led the organisation to engage in a 'Cut the Strings' campaign. This argues that debts should be cancelled with no strings attached.

What Issues Does This Raise?

- Should the wealthy countries just cancel debt? What changes to our lives might follow as a result of this money not coming in to our country's 'bank account' – will we all end up being poorer?
- Would it make poor countries more likely to borrow money – if they know they won't have to pay it back? Would this lead to them not making their own lives better for themselves but just putting their hand out for money?
- Should debt cancellation come with 'strings attached'? What is so wrong with that? Maybe without these, the poor countries will just carry on being poor through mismanagement of the money they are given?
- Don't we have a moral duty to cancel this debt? The rich don't need the money after all – and it might make the world a fairer, productive and more stable place if we just get rid of it and let the poor emerge out of their poverty.

Time Out 4

Should there be 'strings attached' to aid?

UK Government Policy on Aid

The UK government has already, to its credit, recently withheld £50 million of funds to the World Bank until there's evidence that the World Banks actions are actually helping the poor. The UK government has taken a lead among world leaders on the issues of international debt. It has a very well-developed international development organisation which is trying to fight poverty in the developing world. It reminds us that at the G8 summit of world leaders in Scotland in 2005, it was agreed to cancel US $50 billion of the debt of the world's poorest countries. The UK 'led the international campaign to write off US $18 billion of debt for Nigeria where 75 million people live in absolute poverty'. (www.dfid.gov.uk/wp2006intro/debt.html) It explains how international aid works in the UK:

- it is given to international organisations like the UN who support development
- it is given to international charities
- it is given direct to world governments
- it is given direct to projects based in poor countries
- it is given to charities working in poor countries.

(www.dfid.gov.uk/wp2006intro/how.html)

The government's reasons for doing this are clear – aid is given because:

> 'As a rich country, we have a moral obligation to fight poverty. And a safer, more equal, more prosperous world is in all our interests'.

On 13 July 2006, the government released its new White Paper 'Making governance work for the poor' where it claims that the UK government will:

- increase its development budget to 0.7 per cent of gross national income by 2013
- focus on helping countries to help themselves
- commit 50 per cent of all future bilateral aid to public services for poor people
- work internationally to tackle climate change
- help the world create an international system fit for the 21st Century.

This white paper sets out the government's latest policies on international aid and explains what it intends to do over the next five years. Clearly the government wants to tackle poverty. Let's hope it can.

Check Your Learning

1 What is tied aid?

2 Explain what Structural Adjustment Policies mean.

3 Do you think SAPs are fair?

4 Should the rich countries of the world cancel all international debt? Explain the arguments for and against this idea.

5 How does the UK government distribute aid?

6 How might someone argue that the UK government is doing: too little; enough; too much?

The Moral Implications of International Aid

Charity Begins at Home

Some argue that we should look after our own first before those abroad. This is linked to the question of absolute and relative poverty. Most of the world's absolute poverty is abroad and so perhaps we need to sort that out first. However, charities and aid workers will almost always argue that we should help those abroad *as well as* those at home.

A Moral Duty to Help

Can we really ignore the poor just because we might not see them? We certainly can't pretend that we 'didn't know'. In today's world we are not short of information – it would be hard to ignore the plight of the poor. Perhaps knowing that someone is dying through the effects of poverty and letting them die through our inaction is no different to killing them with our own hands.

One World

We share a planet, and perhaps what happens in one place will eventually lead to consequences in another. If we want to the world to be a stable and happy place, then maybe we've got to play our part in making it that way.

Consequences of Helping/Not Helping

The problem won't just go away – we have to make it. Perhaps it is in everyone's interest to make the world as fair and just a place as possible. If it isn't, who knows what the consequences for all of us might be.

Personal Involvement

Can we leave it up to our government, or charity organisations? What about our own actions? Every single purchasing choice you make throughout your whole life can make the world a fairer or less fair place...

Christians and Aid

Christians would all agree that we should help the poor – though they may disagree about how best to do it. Christian Aid states that it; 'believes in life before death'. Its review of its activities in 2005/2006 states; 'We didn't get everything we asked for. Not even close. But then you don't make poverty history in a year'. It helps the poor by working with them in partnership. It argues that the poor know best what they need and so this is the approach they take. It outlines its strategy for 2005–2010:

Source 1

'Our aims

Stronger communities – people don't ask for a hand-out but a hand-up

A better deal on trade – The huge potential of globalisation to create wealth should be closing the gap between rich and poor – not widening it

The right to share power – we support [the poor's] struggle to claim the right to decide their own futures

Halting the spread of HIV

Make poverty history

An effective organisation – we measure the impact of our work

www.christian-aid.org.uk

Christian Aid raises money in the developed world and uses it to support projects in the developing world. It works with partners there to ensure that the money is used effectively. Christian Aid is motivated by the desire to help because it believes that all people 'are created equal, with inherent dignity and infinite worth... poverty is created by an unjust society... so we take the side of the poor and marginalised... We have a duty to speak out and act... to challenge and change the systems that create poverty (see also www.cafod.org.uk for a Roman Catholic Aid organisation).

Why should Christians help the poor? The Evangelical Christian John Stott, in *New Issues Facing Christians Today* (Marshall Pickering 1999), suggests that the Christian's attitude to wealth and poverty has to be guided by the teaching of Jesus. But while the disciples were expected to give up everything they had and follow him, he had other followers such as Joseph of Arimathea who was both a rich man and became a disciple of Jesus. He points out that Jesus did say that it was impossible to serve God and have money at the same time. So, Stott argues that Christians are not literally expected to give up all their property, but are expected to 'put Jesus Christ first... above even our family and our property' (p275). Stott points out that the early Christian church shared all its wealth equally and gave to 'anyone as he had need'. Stott is critical of some fellow evangelical Christians who argue that being wealthy is a sign of God's blessing. He argues that Christians do not need to become poor to help the poor. He concludes: 'We cannot maintain a life (of extravagance) and a 'good conscience' simultaneously. One or other has to be sacrificed. Either we keep our conscience and reduce our affluence, or we keep our affluence and smother our conscience. We have to choose between God and mammon [money]' (p277). Stott argues that Christians should live between wealth and poverty and instead of wealth or poverty: 'we cultivate generosity on the one hand and simplicity with contentment on the other' (p280).

The Iona Community is another Christian group with a strong line on poverty. Members of this Community, who live normal lives in the community, believe 'that everyone should have the quality and dignity of a full life that requires adequate physical, social and political opportunity, without the oppression of poverty, injustice and fear'. The Community also requires that members give around 10 per cent of their disposable wealth away to support work aimed at making the world a more fair and just society. This organisation does not call upon its members to be poor but: 'to work for... a more just world. This means a redistribution of the world's resources in favour of the poor and hungry'

(www.iona.org.uk/community/justice.htm).

Talk Point 5

Should a Christian be rich?

Buddhists and Aid

The Buddha himself was once a rich prince with every material need satisfied. But he rejected this way of life because it was unsatisfactory. He believed that true happiness was to be found somewhere else. Before his enlightenment, he tried many ways – including living in poverty and starving himself. He didn't think this brought happiness either. So for Buddhists, the ideal is something between wealth and poverty. Buddhists believe that material wealth doesn't bring happiness, but nor does being extremely poor. Buddhists therefore believe that we need to work to get rid of poverty in the world. Being poor gets in the way of your journey towards enlightenment and so you must escape your poverty so that you can concentrate more fully on escaping the wheel of samsara. Added to this, the effects of poverty create an awful lot of bad kamma – both for the person in poverty and for those of us who cause it knowingly or not. Buddhists believe that there are three roots of all evil (the three poisons). Each one of these can be applied to the issue of poverty:

- Greed (raga) – one of the causes of poverty is the desire of some to have more than they need. This leads to many having far less than they need.
- Delusion (moha) – people fool themselves into thinking that happiness comes from having wealth. Perhaps we also fool ourselves into thinking that the poor are not our problem.
- Hatred (dosa) – perhaps seeing to our own needs first and ignoring the plight of the poor could be an example of hatred. The opposite of hatred is benevolence (adosa) – giving freely to others.

One Buddhist charity organisation is the Buddhist Relief Mission (www.brelief.org). It quotes a Buddhist text:

> 'If beings knew, as I know, the results of sharing gifts, they would not enjoy their gifts without sharing them with others, nor would the taint of stinginess obsess the heart and stay there. Even if it were their last and final bit of food, they would not enjoy its use without sharing it, if there were anyone to receive it' (Itivuttaka 18)

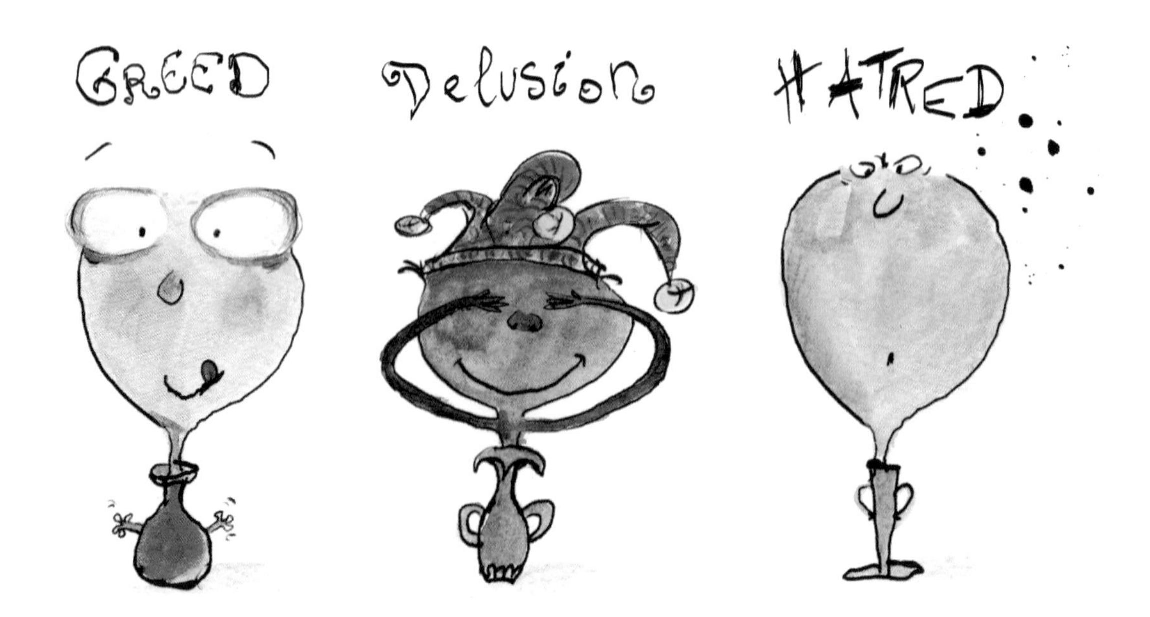

In the UK, the Karuna Trust (www.karunalanka.org) works with some of the poorest people in India. It states that its projects: 'aim to enable people to become self-sufficient. Instead of giving material help, which might give rise to an attitude of dependency, we try to create situations where people can come together to find common solutions to their own difficulties'. The organisation supports a number of self-help projects in India from karate clubs for kids to a medical clinic in Pune.

The Dalai Lama has said:

> '... despite the rapid advances made by civilisation in this century, the most immediate cause of our present dilemma is our undue emphasis on material development alone. We have become so engrossed in its pursuit that, without even knowing it, we have neglected to foster the most basic human needs of love, kindness, cooperation and caring... the development of human society is based entirely on people helping each other. Once we have lost the essential humanity that is our foundation, what is the point of pursuing only material improvement.' (www.dalailama.com/page.65.htm)

Viewpoints Independent of Religious Belief

Humanists argue that getting rid of world poverty is important in contributing to the sum of human happiness. The British Humanist Association (BHA) states that:

> '... as a result of human effort agriculture is more productive, there are more and better preventatives and treatments for disease, there are institutions that make international cooperation possible... These are all great achievements... but they are not shared equally across the globe and it is in everyone's interest to do something about it... It isn't chance or fate or destiny that brings people into the grinding poverty they suffer, or that keeps them there. It is man-made factors like a glaringly unjust global trade system, a debt burden so great that it suffocates any chance of recovery, and insufficient and ineffective aid that creates this poverty. The solutions will be man-made too... We can use what we know to help others, and in helping others we can contribute to the sum of human happiness, an important objective for humanists'
>
> (www.humanism.org.uk).

The BHA and the Humanist Society of Scotland (thss) joined the 'Make Poverty History' campaign in 2005.

The organisation Save the Children states that its aim is to 'Fight for the rights of children in the UK and around the world who suffer from poverty, disease, injustice and violence. We work with them to find lifelong answers to the problems they face'. The organisation carries out relief work as well as campaigning on wider issues. About international trade it says:

> 'Unfair trade rules mean that local economies are vulnerable to foreign competition, and poor countries face protective barriers when trading with richer countries. Foreign aid is inadequate, and it's often targeted in the wrong way, or comes with strings attached... Save the Children is lobbying for greater justice in world trade and we're pushing for trade agreements to benefit poor

people. We're calling on rich countries to increase their aid to poor nations and to use it to reduce child poverty. We're also campaigning for more generous debt relief that will benefit children'

(www.savethechildren.org.uk)

Time Out

5

What are the similarities and differences between these three viewpoints?

Check Your Learning

1. Should Christians help the poor? Explain your answer fully.
2. What does Christian Aid do and why?
3. Explain how Buddhism's three poisons are linked to the poverty debate.
4. Why do Humanists think it is important to help the poor?
5. What does Save the Children do and why does it do it?

Extension Activities

Knowledge, Understanding and Evaluation through Practical Activities

1. The QYX has contacted you secretly about Ingledoink's report. It wants a human response and has asked you to give it. Based on what you have studied in this section, write a response to Ingledoink's report.
2. Design an information leaflet: 'World Poverty: the Facts'.
3. Create a piece of artwork using any medium you want to illustrate the causes or effects of absolute poverty.
4. Make up a Powerpoint-based school assembly for younger pupils explaining why we should help the poor.
5. On a world map, label places in the world where there are currently aid activities going on. Try to show some of the different kinds of aid you have learned about in this section. The labels should include informative text as well as illustrations.
6. You are a (well-paid) doctor in the UK who has been asked to do a year's medical volunteering in the developing world. Write about the reasons why you should go and explain what you decide and why.
7. Have a class debate: 'Aid should never be given in the form of weapons'.

Extension Activities continued

8 Design an informative poster, or whole advertising campaign if you have the time, 'Drop the Debt!'

9 Look at some of the charity organisation websites which have been referred to in this section. What are their similarities and differences? Do you think they should all work together as one big charity?

10 Choose one of these charity websites. Write a review of the website for a young person's magazine feature: 'Ratemycharity'. Does this website make you want to help the charity? Could it be improved? Perhaps you could send your finished article to the charity!

11 Write a letter to your MP/MSP explaining your views on the UK government's current aid policies.

12 Choose one of the viewpoints you have studied in this section and write ten questions for a follower of Christianity, Buddhism or Humanism. These questions should be designed to find out more about their views.

Unit Assessment Question

Intermediate 1: Name ONE religion you have studied. Explain TWO reasons why a follower of this religion should help the poor. **2KU 2AE**

Intermediate 2: 'Giving weapons as aid is wrong.' How might a religious person **and** a viewpoint independent of religious belief respond to this statement? **4KU 4AE**

Sample Exam Question

Intermediate 1: 'Charity begins at home'. Do you agree? Give TWO reasons for your answer **4AE**

Intermediate 2: Describe TWO different kinds of international aid. **4KU**

Homework

Visit the websites of three aid organisations. For each one, explain how it suggests you can help its work.

Personal Reflection

Are the world's poor your responsibility?

CHAPTER 8 Medical Ethics: Genetic Engineering

Can Any Forms of Human Genetic Engineering Be Morally Justified?

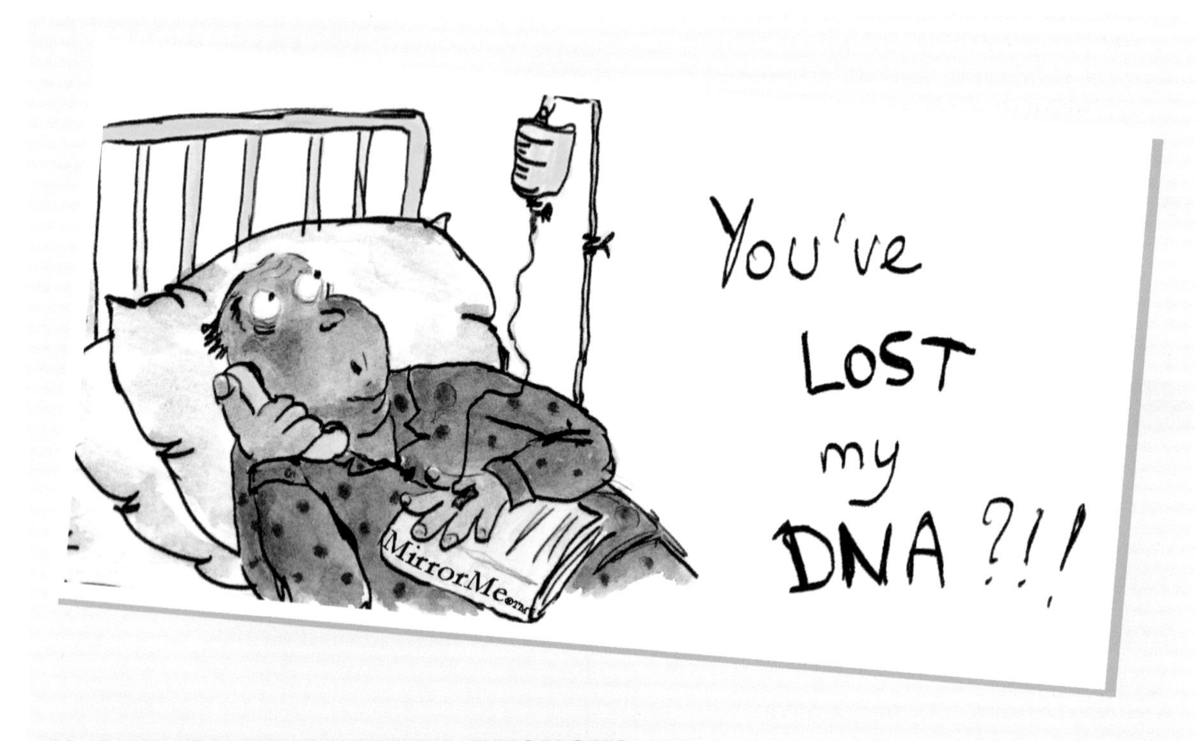

IS *ONE* YOU REALLY STILL ENOUGH?

In our hectic world, life isn't getting any easier. The stresses and strains of everyday life take their toll on even the toughest of us. You work hard. You live life to the max. You go to the gym, eat well and look after yourself. ILLNESS, DISEASE, ACCIDENTS can strike even the super-healthy. They can sneak up on us or stampede into our lives without warning, reducing us to crumbling wrecks, changing our lives for the worst IN AN INSTANT. It seems as if all the benefits of modern living still can't fight back against our old enemy – mother nature.

But is it really all so hopeless? Do we still have to be the slaves of our feeble human bodies?

NOT ANY MORE!

There is a solution! There is a different way! All is not lost! For, there is... MIRRORME®™!

Yes, MIRRORME®™, the answer to all your fears and worries. The reason why life can no longer outwit you! The one size fits all replacement for ANYTHING WHICH GOES WRONG!!!

→

Order your own unique MIRRORME®™ today, and all your troubles will be behind you. Instant replacement of any organ, temporary replacement of you in any situation, and with the incredible UPLOADYOURMEMORY^All rights reserved technique available as part of the price, the real chance to live forever by replacing one worn out body with a brand new one – IDENTICAL IN EVERY WAY! The creation of your own unique (or as many copies as you want!!) MIRRORME®™ couldn't be simpler. All that's needed are a few bits of your own DNA which are then cloned using our unique top-secret process to produce an identical you – a MIRRORME®™!!!

This identical version of you is kept in storage until you need it – either for that secret holiday from work or whenever you need a replacement organ. And if life deals you a fatal blow then all you need to do is use the UPLOADYOURMEMORY^All rights reserved technique to transfer all your personal life data into a brand new MIRRORME®™... which of course THEN BECOMES YOU!!!

For a free, no obligation chat about the incredible possibilities just waiting for you call free on; 0800 123 456 or visit www.you'vebeenhad.com

MIRRORME®™ – cloning your way to immortality!!!

Talk Point 1

Would you buy a MIRRORME®™?

Human Genetic Engineering

It's possibly true that people are more worried about what genetic engineering might be able to do in the future than what it can do at the moment. Fortunately MIRRORME®™ is just fantasy... at the moment. The film *The Island* gives us some idea of what such cloning possibilities in the future might lead to. Imagine an identical copy of you in storage somewhere, waiting for you to need a part of it to replace something which has gone wonky. Would that thing be a person? Would it be you? If so, should it have the same human rights as you? Complicated isn't it? At the moment, however, science fiction is still different from science fact – though some say that the gap between them is getting smaller. In February 1997 a sheep became a superstar. Dolly the sheep was the first ever cloned living thing, created at the Roslin Institute in Midlothian. In the book, 'Engineering Genesis' Ian Wilmut the 'creator' of Dolly explains how it was done:

Source 1

The nucleus of an unfertilised egg is removed by micromanipulation. The donor cell is made quiescent, so that the division process is temporarily halted. The donor cell is then placed next to the egg cell whose nucleus has been removed. By passing an electric current the two are fused and growth resumes. The resulting embryo is then transferred to the womb of a surrogate ewe and produces what is essentially a clone of the animal from which the cell nucleus was taken.

Engineering Genesis: Earthscan, Bruce D & Bruce A (Eds), 1998 p72

In the case of Dolly a mammary gland cell was used to provide the DNA element and then it all got much more scientifically complex, more than we need to know for this course anyway. In short, the cells which went on to divide and grow in the normal way were exact copies of the DNA of the donor sheep (a MIRROREWE perhaps?), making Dolly an identical copy of another living sheep. So, the usual process of combining DNA from two parents to result in offspring was bypassed resulting in the world's first clone.

Now, of course, Dolly was a sheep – but the same technique could be applied to humans – although the Roslin Institute has said that it is completely against this. So now we do have the scientific capability to make a cloned human being, and although no government in the world has sanctioned such a thing, that's not to say that someone, somewhere might not do it without permission... and for many this is the ultimate fear of the whole genetic engineering debate. If cloning is scientifically possible, then all sorts of complicated moral issues are raised. For this reason, many people are concerned about what is currently being done in the field of human genetic engineering, because each step takes us closer to the ultimate moral problems. However, many also have serious issues with what is currently being done even without worrying about what it might lead to. So let's examine more closely the current state of play before we worry about the future.

Time Out 1

Find out about DNA.

Source 2

What is Genetic Engineering?

Genetic engineering is a very broad term which covers a range of ways of manipulating the genetic material of an organism. It is also variously called gene manipulation, genetic manipulation, recombinant DNA technology, the new genetics, targeted genetics and, in humans only, gene therapy. In popular thinking it is frequently confused with cloning, which is not at all the same... it is the ability to identify one or more of these genes which underlies genetic engineering.

Engineering Genesis: Earthscan, Bruce D & Bruce A (Eds), 1998 pp2–3

Put simply, humans have always selectively bred crops and animals by allowing organisms with desirable qualities to reproduce and not allowing organisms with undesirable qualities to do so. The whole principle of evolution is that the organisms best adapted to the current environment are more likely to survive and reproduce. Humans have always given nature a hand in this respect by choosing which living things survive and which don't according to our needs. The power of genetic manipulation is, some argue, just the most recent version of this. It is the ability to select desirable genetic information and use it for reproductive purposes while screening out undesirable genetic properties, so selectively breeding 21st Century style.

Although many people oppose any form of genetic manipulation, some have mixed views about it. For example, many crops are now genetically modified (GMOs) so that they are more likely to survive (tomatoes containing 'fish anti-freeze' DNA which stops the tomatoes being destroyed by frost, for example), this could lead to cheaper food and possibly solving food supply problems in the developing world. Or, it could lead to DNA disasters where the outcome of the genetic manipulation takes unexpected and possibly dangerous twists with harmful effects for all. However, it is probably in the area of human genetic engineering that the most morally scary issues are raised. Bear in mind that this is a very emotive issue and that almost everything you read about the ethics of this issue might be biased in some way. For some, any cloned embryo is a potential life, for others, nothing more than a collection of biochemical material. This difference of view can lead to very heated debate in this area.

Therapeutic Cloning

Therapeutic cloning is the use of human embryonic stem cells (hES cells) to create identical human tissue of some description. Properly referred to as somatic cell nuclear transfer (SCNT), this does not create babies but stem cells for therapeutic use. A cell is taken from the patient who needs some kind of medical help. The nucleus of this cell is removed and fused with an 'empty' ovum. This is stimulated and normal growth begins. The stem cells are taken from the developing embryo

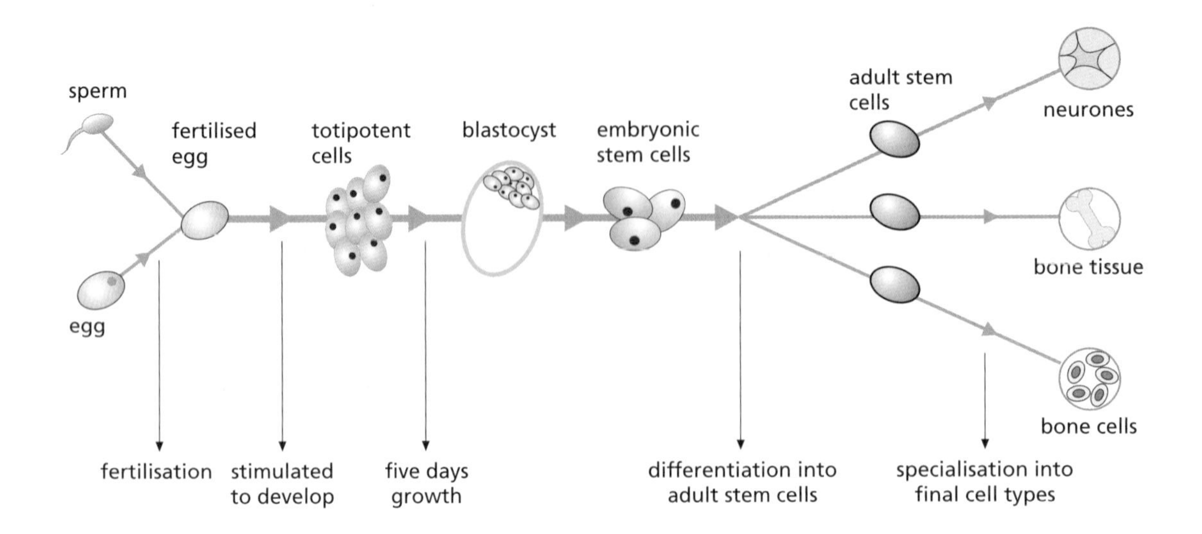

and the embryo destroyed. These stem cells can then be used to create any kind of tissue, from skin to brain cells. This could lead to the creation of a tissue bank for you with pretty much any kind of tissue available to replace your own if it goes wrong. Eventually such technology could perhaps lead to the creation of whole organs which are genetically identical to yours. The hES cells would be taken from a very close genetic match (ideally an identical twin) or, from the creation of a cloned embryonic you through the cloning process outlined above.

This is helpful because in the transplant process the biggest stumbling block is usually your body's rejection of the transplanted tissue. Your body sees it as an infection and fights it off. The closer the tissue is to your body's already existing tissue the less chance there will be of rejection. Obviously cloned tissue would work well in this situation (also getting over the problem of the lack of supply of donated tissues and organs). Stem cell cloning could benefit anyone where tissue replacement is required due to anything from burns to Alzheimer's disease. The Medical Research Council shows in diagrammatic form what stem cell therapy is (above).

In 2001, the HFEA made therapeutic cloning legal. This means that human embryos can be cloned and their material used for therapeutic cloning but the embryos can only be used up to the 14 day limit and must be destroyed afterwards.

Benefits

Therapeutic cloning might just be another medical technique which could save lives or make people's lives of a much better quality. It is therefore just something else which helps a doctor to treat his patient – not really any different from any other kind of treatment.

People have always interfered with nature in order to improve it, therapeutic cloning is another example of this. Many of the illnesses and diseases which we can currently do little about might benefit greatly from the advantages of therapeutic cloning. It is, therefore, an appropriate use of our human ability to counteract nature's errors with the benefits of therapeutic cloning.

Through therapeutic cloning research we might discover cures for all sorts of things, maybe even illnesses we weren't expecting to find cures for. Perhaps therapeutic cloning might lead to the end of cancer, for example.

Therapeutic cloning uses only stem cells. These are undifferentiated cells from an embryo. The embryo is destroyed before the 14–day limit of its development. It is therefore arguable that this embryo does not suffer and that the stem cells are no more morally important than any other cell in your body. So the benefits of this cloning are great and there is no real human cost.

The process might be complex and possibly costly. But these issues are both vastly outweighed by the possible benefits to people who currently suffer illness and disease – and, of course, for all the people to come who will also be spared misery through the benefits of therapeutic cloning.

Dangers

For many, the greatest danger is not what is happening but what could happen. The technology might lead to reproductive cloning and all the moral issues it raises. It might lead to the creation of designer babies and clone farms like in the MIRRORME®™ example.

The technology is still in its infancy. Dolly the sheep died much sooner than she should have. This leads some to doubt just how effective the process is. Maybe there are medical dangers attached to it that we haven't yet discovered. Perhaps the introduction of even your own cloned tissue might lead to the development of new viruses or infections which might mutate and turn into something very nasty for everyone.

Perhaps, like it or not, 'nature' has a reason for illness and disease (maybe 'nature's errors' are for a very good reason). Perhaps our messing around with this will lead to unexpected harmful consequences for all life. Maybe, for example, illness and disease is 'nature's way' of controlling the population. If we remove this possibility through the benefits of cloning then nature might just have to find another way.

Perhaps the costs of individual treatment are not justified. Perhaps vital medical resources would be better used in some other way and, besides, who would decide who would be the most suitable candidate for therapeutic cloning on a limited budget? The person who lost the use of his liver through disease or the one who lost the use of his liver through alcoholism? Perhaps we need to make sure that the moral thinking is keeping up with the scientific progress.

For many the most important issue is the cloned embryo. Is it really morally nothing? If it has all the potential to become a full human being then does anyone have the right to harvest its cells and then destroy it after 14 days? We would never use any other human in this way without its permission – we can't ask an embryo's permission – so even if it does benefit people, is it worth it?

Talk Point 2

Is therapeutic cloning just another form of medicine?

Reproductive Cloning

This uses all the same scientific techniques as therapeutic cloning with one pretty major difference. The cloned embryo would be implanted in a womb (or maybe an artificial one in the future) and allowed to grow and be born. Currently this is illegal everywhere in the world with respect to humans. It is covered in the UK in the *Reproductive Cloning Bill 2001* where it states quite clearly that it is an offence punishable by up to 10 years in prison, for any *'person who places in a woman a human embryo which has been created otherwise than by fertilisation'.* Reproductive cloning, in theory, could lead to identical copies of you being made which could grow to adulthood. Such a person could be a source of replacement tissue for you and harvested whenever you needed anything fixed. It has been argued that such beings could be developed as headless corpses which are kept stored until you need them. Therefore they would have no brain and not be thinking beings – just a replica of all your other bodily organs and tissues. Some have said that such beings could be complete but would be kept in a state of unconsciousness throughout their existence. This would mean that they would never think and therefore would not develop a 'self' (because what makes you who you are is a unique combination of your genetic inheritance and your experiences throughout life).

Of course, this is all futurology, and most people agree that creating such living things would be pretty morally horrific. However, there are some people who argue that reproductive cloning could avoid these horrors by allowing the products to grow and live perfectly normal lives.
Why? You might well ask. Perhaps such beings could be replacements for children who have died through accidents or perhaps they could be given to childless couples who can't have kids of their own. Perhaps even, through genetic screening, such clones could be genetically manipulated so that they didn't develop the deadly illness which killed the person they are a clone of. Or, they could be genetically enhanced so they would be clever or strong or whatever else was wanted: the so-called 'designer baby'. The possibilities are wide-ranging and each has its own moral

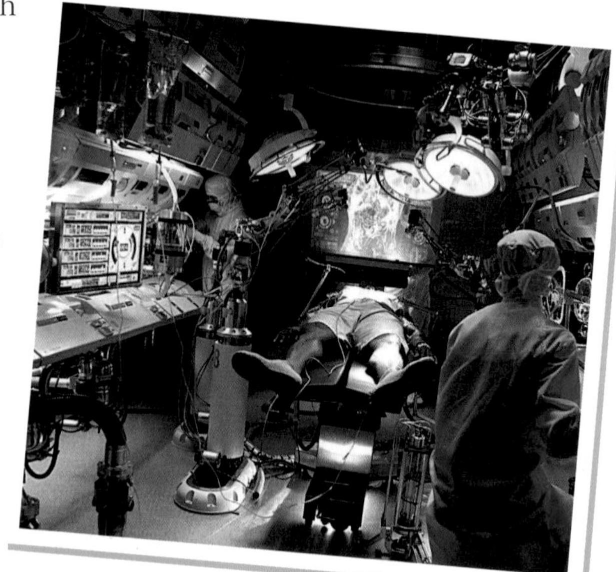

minefield attached to it. However, privately many scientists will admit that, even although the technology is primitive just now, and the dangers of trying this kind of thing are so vast, it is probable that someone, somewhere will do it one day... However, before you take a moral stand, could there be any benefits?

Benefits

Childless couples, infertile couples, gay couples, could all benefit by having a cloned child without the need for the normal process of sexual reproduction. This could improve their lives greatly.

People who have lost children through disease, illness or accident could all benefit – they could have a genetically-exact copy of the child.

You could have a permanent source of spare organs which could mean that you could live much longer, and who knows, perhaps one day it might be possible to transplant your brain (with all its memories and abilities) into a clone of your body, but 60 years younger, and you could live on – possibly forever.

Clones could be used for all sorts of things – to make up armies, do dangerous jobs and so on. We could think of them as expendable, especially if we didn't let them develop a sense of self.

Dangers

There would be two classes of people in society: 'originals' and 'clones'. Would it be right (or even possible) to have one set of rights for one and another for the other? How could these be decided?

What responsibilities would you have towards your clone – after all, in a sense it is you. Would it be entitled to your property if you died?

Could it ever be right to 'harvest' material from such creatures?

Does a couple's need for a child really justify the creation of one for them using cloning?

If you created a clone child replacement for a child who had died – what might your cloned child feel about their reasons for existence? Would it be right to bring something into the world just as a replacement for someone else? What would that do to the clone's idea of self-worth? Anyway is such an idea meaningful? The child you lost would have been more than just DNA. Who he was would be related to the life they had lived – you would have to recreate this life (exactly) to have even the slightest chance of having the 'same' child all over again.

Would clones only be available to the rich?

What about the process? How many mistakes would have to be made while the process was perfected? (if it ever could be). What misery and suffering might be experienced by clones during this stage of development? Could the process ever be completely free from error? Errors which might lead to horrible genetic mutations.

Could it ever be right to 'play God' in this way?

Talk Point

What would be good and bad about a world with designer babies?

Check Your Learning

1 Describe the process which led to the creation of Dolly the Sheep.
2 Why might the fate of Dolly make us question the idea of cloning?
3 Explain TWO differences between therapeutic and reproductive cloning.
4 Choose ONE possible advantage and danger of therapeutic cloning and explain your own views on these.
5 Do you think reproductive cloning is 'playing God'?
6 In your opinion, do you ever think that reproductive cloning could be acceptable?

Moral Implications of Cloning

Can, Should and Might...

As you see, part of the problem is that science fiction has often become confused with science fact. Some scientists argue that we shouldn't throw the (cloned?) baby out with the bathwater. In other words, just because cloning *could* lead to all sorts of horrors, doesn't mean that it *will*. To reject the many medical benefits of therapeutic cloning because it *might* lead to the problems associated with reproductive cloning would be very wrong. Every scientific advance could be used for good or bad (the wheel can be on an ambulance or a cannon), we can't stop making progress just because some people will possibly abuse the results. However, some people argue that the possibilities and dangers linked to cloning are just so great that in this case we might have to throw the baby out with the bathwater.

Playing God

Every scientific advance allows us to 'play God'. But every time we make one choice instead of another we also 'play God'. Every time we take a pill we 'play God'. Cloning gives us control over something very powerful, but what's wrong with that? Humans risk the lives of other humans for all sorts of reasons – during war for example – what is any more wrong about taking similar risks but with the hope of real medical benefits at the end? Opponents say that things like cloning go beyond the normal range of moral thinking. It is literally fiddling about with life itself – and life which would have no say about how it is treated either as a clone, or as a potential life in the form of a cloned embryo. Life is something which should not be meddled with in this way – the risks are too great and the responsibility too vast. As

one commentator once said: 'If I can't trust the government to collect my dustbin on the right day why should I trust them to make laws about how we should treat a potential human being'.

The Limits of Human Freedom

Every time we stop at traffic lights we accept that our freedom sometimes has to be limited for the greater good. Perhaps this is also true of cloning. No matter what the benefits might be, maybe they're still outweighed by the dangers. So, we have to stop ourselves using this technology before it gets out of hand. How far does human freedom go? Do we really have the right to 'interfere with nature' in these kinds of ways? Are humans really ready for the decisions which will have to be made once it becomes possible to clone a person and give them life? Do we really understand the moral importance of the cloned embryo well enough at the moment to carry on with therapeutic cloning? Should we limit our own freedom until we've worked out what all these developments mean?

Three Other Forms of Genetic Engineering

Cloning is only one way in which genetic information can be manipulated. The following two methods are more accurately genetic engineering because they result in a change to DNA, some argue an improvement. The third form does not currently involve alteration of the DNA structure but is a way of deciding if the DNA structure is 'suitable' or not.

Somatic Genetic Engineering (Somatic Gene Transfer Therapy)

Here, cells with defective genes are removed from a patient (not always necessary – sometimes the new gene is simply injected into the patient or inhaled as an aerosol). The patient, for example, might not be able to regulate their insulin production resulting in diabetes. A 'viral vector' (a virus like structure) containing a healthy replacement gene is introduced into the defective cell so that the new healthy gene is added to the old ones. With a bit of luck, as the defective cells are replaced they will be replaced with the new healthy form of the cell. Hopefully then this new healthy gene will eventually lead to the patient being able to regulate insulin in the proper way, as the proper DNA 'message' will now get through.

This process has many applications like treating cystic fibrosis and may in future treat many more illnesses caused by defective genes. The trouble is that it's a bit unpredictable – sometimes the healthy DNA can't get into the unhealthy cells and even when it does, the cells don't often do the job they should in enough quantity. Supporters argue that this is no more than giving 'medicine' at the genetic level and so is a valuable addition to medical treatments. One important feature of this is that the changed cells only affect the sufferer – these new cells cannot be passed on to future generations as gene therapy on gametes is currently banned (as is genetic modification of embryos).

Benefits

Where it works this is an effective treatment which is non-invasive and the potential medical benefits are great.

The treatment affects only the sufferer – there are no implications for generations to come.

Dangers

It's not impossible that the altered viral vectors, or the unhealthy cells, could themselves mutate and cause unexpected problems (currently the viral vectors are modified to prevent this but who knows if the odd one might find a way around this).

Not exactly a danger – more a limitation. This therapy still only treats the symptoms not the causes of the illness and only works for the individual sufferer. However, for the sufferer that's probably more than enough!

Germline Therapy

Here, the same scientific principles are used to change unhealthy genes into healthy ones. The difference here however is that the gametes ('sex cells') are the cells affected. This makes a crucial difference because the new healthy gene will now be passed on to all the following generations through the reproductive process. This means that illnesses which are normally passed on genetically won't be any more, healthy cells will be instead. This therapy could either be targeted at an individual adult or could even in future be directed towards a pre-implantation embryo – making it different to how it would have been naturally. Currently such procedures are not permitted.

Benefits

A genetic disorder could be eradicated forever – no one need ever worry about passing on some illness to their children.

If carried out on an adult then the technique is relatively safe for them and there should be no issue about the new healthy cells being passed on to succeeding generations.

Dangers

Does anyone have the right to manipulate genetic information in this way without the consent of those who will be affected? Obviously treating one person is a bit different to treating all succeeding generations.

Who knows how such artificially modified gametes might interact with others during the normal processes of reproduction. Perhaps solving one problem for one generation might actually lead to far greater problems for generations to come.

The healthy DNA has to come from somewhere other than the sufferer. This could mean that your offspring would technically have three parents – the two involved in the reproductive process and the other one who provided the healthy bit of DNA!

(The BIG ONE?) Many argue that germline therapy would be the first step in the production of 'designer babies'. This might start in the form of medical improvements – like ending genetically transmitted illness – but eventually it might lead to 'cosmetic' improvements being applied. For example, once human DNA is fully mapped, we will know what DNA leads to what properties – so you might be able to 'order' some DNA for germline therapy which matched the kind of offspring you want – male or female, blue or brown eyes etc. This might lead to a society where everyone was genetically altered and where there could be a distinction between those who were genetically 'rich' and those who were genetically 'poor' (watch the film Gattaca!). This would favour the rich and work against the poor (financially this time) because probably only the rich could afford it. Some scientists

even argue that such genetically altered people may not even be able to reproduce in combination with people who were not genetically modified (not that they'd probably want to anyway!). This could lead – eventually to the creation of two (or more) very different human species.

You can see why germline therapy is *currently* banned...

Talk Point

What do you think might lead to a change in the current ban on reproductive cloning?

Pre-Implantation Genetic Diagnosis and Selection (PGD)

This involves the use of embryos produced through IVF (*in vitro* fertilisation). A single cell is removed from the embryo (at the eight-cell stage) and tested for genetic disorders. Usually this is in the case of families with known inherited genetic disorders. If the embryo is free of the genetic disorder it is implanted and allowed to go through to full term – if not then it is not implanted. At the moment, no manipulation of the embryo's DNA is permitted, as in the above two examples, where the embryo is to be implanted. So the only 'engineering' going on here would be deciding whether or not the embryo was to be implanted or not based on the genetic evidence. Currently the HFEA regulates this process, allowing it for a wide range of genetically transmitted illnesses. However, it does say that it will treat each case on its own merits and that if one patient is allowed a test for one condition, it does not mean that every patient who may request it would be entitled to the same test.

Benefits

It would ensure that a child born would not suffer from an inherited illness and so bring happiness to a couple knowing that their child would have a normal healthy life free from their own genetic disorder.

Many abortions take place late on in a pregnancy when parents discover that their child has an inherited disease. PGD would allow parents to find out if their child has an inherited disease much earlier in the pregnancy. This could, perhaps, lessen the emotional impact of the abortion.

It could allow the birth of a child who could save an already existing brother or sister with an illness (the so-called 'saviour siblings').

Dangers

It can lead to the destruction of embryos if they are found to carry the genetic disorder – some argue that this is abortion and so wrong. Whatever your view on this, it does mean that someone has to make decisions about which embryo lives and which doesn't. Some think of this as wrong because it is 'playing God' over life and death.

This also involves attaching a 'value' to some condition. At the moment only certain genetic illnesses are included in the HFEA guidelines, but more may be added and perhaps less 'serious' ones. Some say that the process leads to devaluing people who have certain illnesses – suggesting that their illness makes them not worthy of life and ignoring the other contributions they might make to the world.

It could also lead to 'designer babies'. Already, in some countries, it is used to sort out male and female embryos, with only the desired gender being implanted – perhaps in future we could simply select the 'best' embryo from the bunch for implantation – and 'best' could mean whatever we want it to be.

The procedure is complicated and risky. After it has been done any implanted embryo might be at a greater risk of something going wrong as a result of this procedure.

What would a 'saviour sibling' think about the fact that they had only been brought into the world for their brother or sister's benefit? What about their own self-worth?

Perhaps, of course, abortion is wrong and PGD just makes this more likely.

The Use of Human Embryos

Long before cloning, the use of normally fertilised human embryos for research purposes was common. Such embryos were most often the products of abortion or the 'leftovers' from IVF treatments (though they can also be donated eggs fertilised with donated sperm). In IVF, women are often given drugs which lead to super-ovulation, the production of many eggs at a time. These are then fertilised *in vitro* (in a petri dish not a test tube). The fertilised ova then divide and develop in the normal way and the most viable is re-implanted in the woman with the hope that it will grow into a normal healthy child. The ones which are not implanted are allowed to be used up to the 14th day of their development for research purposes, after which they must be destroyed. Fertilised embryos can, however be stored frozen for a number of years

The leftover embryos can be used for all sorts of scientific testing (outlined below) in the hope that what is learned might help develop better fertility treatments or

Check Your Learning

1. What might someone mean by saying that cloning is 'playing God'? Would you agree?
2. Would it be even more wrong to reject the benefits of cloning just because of what they *might* lead to?
3. Explain what is meant by somatic genetic engineering.
4. Describe ONE benefit and one danger of this kind of genetic engineering.
5. How is germline therapy different to somatic genetic engineering?
6. In you opinion, which is the more morally justifiable of the two? Explain your answer.
7. Why might someone want PGD?
8. If you were offered PGD because you were in a risk category, would you want it? Explain your answer.
9. When can an embryo be used for scientific research purposes?

lead to helpful medical discoveries. This research is licensed and guided by the Human Fertilisation and Embryology Authority (HFEA).

HFEA Guidelines

This organisation licences and monitors fertility treatments and embryo research throughout the UK (see www.hfea.gov.uk). Its work is governed by the *Human Fertilisation and Embryology Act 1990* (see www.opsi.gov.uk). It also ensures that licensed centres carrying out IVF treatments and embryo research stick to the laws as laid out in this act. It allows the use of embryos for research up to the 14-day point. After 14 days the cells of the embryo specialise into different body organs and so it is argued that after this point the embryo might 'feel pain'. This point is sometimes called the appearance of the 'primitive streak'.

Research on embryos up to the 14 day limit must be 'necessary' or 'desirable' for at least one of these reasons:

- promoting advances in infertility treatment
- increasing knowledge about congenital (inherited) disease
- increasing knowledge about the causes of miscarriage
- developing better contraception techniques
- developing better ways to recognise genetic abnormalities in embryos before implantation.

Currently, it is supposed to be the case that the research must have a specific purpose related to one of these points. Research which has no specific aim in mind (research purely for the sake of research) is not allowed, although obviously if when you are researching into any of the areas above you might end up finding out things you never meant to.

The HFEA is designed to ensure that all use of embryonic material conforms to these guidelines and the terms of the act, and that research carried out on them follows the standard procedures for ethical scientific research. This includes the methods and equipment used, the storage and disposal of the embryos, the premises in which the research is carried out and so on. It also covers the ways in which the embryos are obtained, for example, they cannot be bought or sold and consent of the providers should be obtained.

UK Law

This is summed up in the *Human Fertilisation and Embryology Act 1990*, which strictly controls what can and cannot be done in relation to embryos and cloning. In short, this Act ensures that all work with embryos is strictly regulated by the HFEA and conforms to the HFEA guidelines. It also prohibits many other related areas such as ensuring that no one benefits financially from the sale or purchase of embryos. As well as this it ensures that there is never any likelihood of human and animal genetic material becoming mixed up through implanting any human genetic material into animals or animal into human.

Therapeutic cloning is allowed by the HFEA, but subject to the granting of a licence on strict terms as well as regular review (the first ever licence for this was given to the Roslin Research Institute). Reproductive cloning is completely banned. Obviously, in relation to embryos, there are very different guidelines linked to embryos which are to be implanted to go through a normal pregnancy and those where the embryo is to be disposed of after the 14-day limit. Any research done using the embryos has to follow strict guidelines about what is and isn't possible and it must be done in order to lead to clear benefits through better understanding of the science of genetics.

Moral Implications of Genetic Engineering and the Use of Embryos

The Rights of the Embryo

Whether we're fiddling about with its genetic material, choosing whether it lives or not or just using it for research purposes, the issue of the rights of the embryo is central. Currently, the embryo has no rights at all up to the 14-day limit, after this point it has limited rights, it can still be aborted up to the 24th week of pregnancy. After that the foetus has full human rights because it is considered a viable life. And there's the issue. Many believe that life begins at the very moment of conception. Everything that the person can be is there in the form of genetic information –s/he is a fully potential person. Therefore, any interference with such a person would be wrong, and definitely so where the person might be destroyed because s/he didn't match up with what we think is desirable. It would be equally wrong to use this embryo to carry out research to help others – we don't use adults to do that without their consent – why should we use an embryo? Surely using an embryo is even worse because the embryo can't speak up for itself. Religious people often argue that the embryo is a being in the image of God, and once it has life it should be given the full protection of the law. Non-religious people too might argue that if we accept treating one 'kind' of human (embryos) in one way and other kinds (anything other than an embryo) in another way then we take grave risks with what is morally

justifiable. Of course, opponents say that the embryo is not a person and so is not due rights. It is also something which can be used to benefit society as a whole and so it is morally justifiable to 'sacrifice' its welfare for that reason.

Meddling with Nature

Altering genetic information might be clever but not very wise. It might get out of hand – treating disease today might be choosing intelligence tomorrow, and so lead to a genetically modified world where some are more valuable than others. Who knows what kind of a society this might lead to? Also, can we really completely control all the possibilities? Sexual reproduction is good because it produces variety, and variety makes us more likely to survive as a species. Genetic engineering might lead to a world full of genetically far too similar beings who might end up being far more susceptible to the least wee change in the environment than the variety we have today. Genetic modification might also lead to unexpected change. Nature has a way of levelling things out: what responses might nature 'choose' to make to a genetically modified world? We might not like them! Even the technology we use for these examples – we assume that it'll improve in the future – but what mistakes will we have to accept until we get to that point? Is it really worth it? Maybe there should be limits on our ability to choose the future we'd like. Although some say we have always meddled with nature, the speed of change available with genetic engineering is far greater than the other forms of 'selective breeding' and it is this which causes the problem.

Check Your Learning

1. What does the HFEA do and how does it do it?
2. What is important about the 14th day of the embryo's development?
3. Why is this the legal boundary for research on embryos?
4. What areas does the *HFE Act 1990* cover?
5. In your opinion, when does human life begin?
6. Explain when you think an embryo should have rights and what those rights should be.
7. Is genetic engineering and the use of embryos 'meddling with nature'?
8. 'The problem with the area of genetic engineering is not what we can do, but what it might lead to us being able to do'. Do you agree? Explain your answer fully.

Christian Views

Christians have very mixed views about this very complex and varied area. In general the argument boils down to two issues:

- When does life begin? And what is morally acceptable to do to something once is has life?
- Should humans take over the life-creative role which perhaps only belongs to God.

Most Christians agree that life does begin at conception. From this moment on everything that is needed to make a potential person is there. However, some Christians accept this but also accept that an embryo can be used up until the 14th day of development. The argument is that although this is a person, as a society we sometimes agree that sacrifice for the greater good is necessary and desirable. The Church of Scotland, for example, sets out its position in the document: *Pre-conceived ideas – a Christian Perspective on IVF and Embryology (1996)*. Here, it argues that the 'divine ideal' would obviously be a world where there was no need for embryo research or any of the technologies in this section. However, it contrasts this with the 'human reality' where, living in a fallen world, we sometimes have to make difficult choices about how to use our abilities for wider human benefit. It suggests that 'dogmatic pronouncements' should not be made and that individuals should make up their own minds based on prayer, reflection and study of the issues. The Church claims that it doesn't want to 'burden further the already taxed consciences of those working in the field'. So, it argues that while the embryo is a person, it can be used according to HFEA guidelines. The Church has set up the world-famous Science, Religion and Technology Project (SRTP) in Edinburgh which grapples with the moral and religious issues raised by the topics in this section. This recognises that one of the central religious issues is the one about 'playing God', which could apply to all the topics in this section.

Source 3

The popular notion that genetic engineering is playing God can be seen in two ways. Humans could be said to be called to imitate God's creative example, in which case why draw a line forbidding transgenesis rather than any other intervention in nature? On the other hand would it be assuming a role which was not ours to have? ... To exclude genetic engineering as unnatural begs the question of what is meant by natural after centuries of human activity in the biosphere...

Engineering Genesis: Earthscan, Bruce D & Bruce A (Eds), 1998 p276

Talk Point 4

Is anything you've studied in this section 'playing God' really that wrong?

The Church updated its views in May 2006 where it looked at the SRTP Report on stem cell research and embryology and agreed with the report's main conclusions:

- Embryo research is permitted up to 14 days using surplus embryos (from PGD/IVF) but only for a very good reason.
- To oppose the creation of IVF or cloned embryos for research, except under exceptional circumstances.
- To oppose animal-human hybrid and parthenogenic embryos.

It also urges the government not to relax the present regulations governing embryo research in the forthcoming legislation (www.srtp.org.uk/cloning.shtml).

The Church made a very full response to the government's consultation on the review of the *HFE Act 1990* (at www.srtp.org.uk/hfea-review.doc). Here it states that the Church of Scotland has no formal view on germline therapy (yet). It agrees that this technology could lead to modifying 'the human germline for non-medical purposes of 'human enhancement' and to eugenic concerns'. All of these, in its opinion would be wrong.

However, the Roman Catholic Church takes a very different view, at least as far as the use of embryos is concerned. It has an absolute prohibition on abortion – called 'a grave violation of the law of God' by a former Pope, John Paul II. Obviously, destroying spare embryos after research could be considered to be abortion, it would also be wrong to create 'spare' embryos for research purposes. The right to life begins at conception and the defencelessness of the embryo calls for special protection. As far as cloning is concerned the Roman Catholic Church is pretty clear about its condemnation of all aspects of it:

Source 4

The Pontifica Academia Pro Vita has looked into the issues of cloning and argues:

The threat of the use of cloning for eugenic purposes should make us wary of it
It alters the natural process of sexual reproduction
It possibly involves the exploitation of women throughout the process
It could lead to the 'radical rupture of these bonds' – i.e. of normal human relationships
It 'mimics' nature but ignores the fact that 'man surpasses his biological components'
It leads to people being judged worthy only because of their biological make-up
How valuable would a clone feel – knowing that they are just a copy of someone else?
Using embryos to develop this technology is an abuse of a person
It concludes: 'The difference should again be pointed out between the conception of life as a gift of love and the view of the human being as an industrial product'

(see also the Vatican documents, *Evangelium Vitae and Donum Vitae* 1987, on the Vatican website)

www.vatican.va

Buddhist Views

There is no clearly stated Buddhist position on cloning. Some argue that if it brings benefits then it should not be discounted out of hand, but the suffering caused along the way before it is perfected might not be worth it in the end and it certainly would not be showing compassion to all living beings.

Obviously the argument of 'playing God' does not apply here, though that's not to say that Buddhists would accept the possibility that humans can behave in any way they want. Buddhists would welcome genetic technologies which could help people, but as far as cloning is concerned, they might always argue that cloning is by definition self-serving and egotistical. Buddhists argue that life can begin in many ways. It is claimed that the Dalai Lama once agreed that the creation of a perfectly good person would be a good idea because it would help in the process of rebirth and liberation. However, this does not mean that he was giving his support to all aspects of cloning by expressing this wish! As far as genetic engineering is concerned, again the Buddhist principle of compassion could lead to supporting specific therapies. However, a Buddhist might be concerned at the use of embryonic DNA, as an embryo can't give its permission to allow this. It might also be concerned at the possible negative kamma associated with the use of embryos for research or the possible uses to which genetic engineering might be put. The Dalai Lama has said that abortion should be 'approved or disapproved according to each circumstance'. Perhaps therefore he would support the use of embryos in research because of the possible benefits this might bring – but always the principle will be one of making sure that good kamma results from the action and its intention – not bad.

Viewpoints Independent of Religious Belief

The British Humanist Association (BHA) argues that the argument about playing God is a silly one – humans have always 'played God' through medical advancements. Humanists consider two issues:

- What are the rights of an embryo?
- Does embryo research produce more good than harm?

The BHA sees no problem with the use of embryos which would otherwise be destroyed, at last some good could come out of their existence. It has no problem either with therapeutic cloning provided that some limits are set about when the use of the embryo should end – currently the BHA supports the HFEA 14-day limit. However, it rejects reproductive cloning suggesting that such clones could suffer physically and psychologically due to their cloned status. In fact, it argues that reproductive cloning, 'in many ways seems like a vanity project'. The BHA goes on to argue that humans have many kinds of, 'knowledge and capabilities which we have decided that it would be better not to use'. It states, 'knowing how to do something does not mean that we necessarily have to do it'.

The BHA website cites an article by the well-known humanist, Richard Dawkins. This article is entitled 'Who's afraid of the Frankenstein wolf?' In this, Dawkins

argues that 'genetic engineering is not, of itself, bad or good. It depends on what you engineer'. He argues that in our selective breeding processes throughout history we have changed nature in many ways: 'Are spaniels and whippets Frankenstein wolves?'

The BHA follows a summary of his argument by stating that the Humanist response to the genetic engineering and embryo research is most likely to be based on consequentialist/Utilitarian arguments. In short, will the benefits of cloning, genetic engineering or the use of embryos outweigh the dangers. If so, then they are morally acceptable. It argues: 'Almost all the potential benefits of genetic engineering have the potential to cause problems. Getting hold of and understanding the facts, assessing the risks realistically, and balancing the possible benefits against the possible harms, must be the basis of ethical decision making' (based on information and quotes from www.humanism.org.uk).

Check Your Learning

1 Why might someone say that the Church of Scotland is confused about its views on the rights of the embryo?

2 In your opinion, does the quote from the SRTP support or reject genetic engineering?

3 Does the Church of Scotland oppose germline therapy or not?

4 Explain the ways in which the Roman Catholic Church's view is different to the Church of Scotland's.

5 How does the Catholic view of abortion link to the topics you've looked at in this section?

6 Explain why a Buddhist might accept or reject genetic engineering/cloning.

7 What TWO things does the BHA take into account when deciding about the morality of genetic engineering?

8 What is Richard Dawkins' view of genetic engineering?

Extension Activities

Knowledge, Understanding and Evaluation through Practical Activities

1 Write an imaginative essay following your purchase of a MIRRORME®™. You can make this humorous or as dark and serious as you like.

2 Make your own advertising poster for the MIRRORME®™.

3 If possible, watch the films *Gattaca* and *The Island*. Write reviews for these films based on how well you think they handle the issues you have studied in this section.

4 Design illustrated information leaflets showing the science behind cloning, genetic engineering and embryo research. Make sure that you make clear the importance of DNA in these.

5 Find out how humans have selectively bred throughout history. Prepare a display board on this – you could focus on agriculture or on pet dogs!

6 Write an interview between a doctor and a patient where the doctor explains the possibility of a cure for the patient's illness using therapeutic cloning. What questions might the patient ask? What answers would s/he be given?

7 Have a class debate: 'Reproductive cloning should never be legalised'.

8 You are a scientist working on therapeutic cloning. A couple come to speak to you. They have lost their only child as the result of an accident. They are unable to have any more children. They are very wealthy and want you to be the first person ever to clone a human being. Script a dialogue between the couple and the scientist (who does not intend to do it).

9 Write an imaginative story based on the following idea and fully use your imagination: It is 3000AD. Following the legalisation of germline therapy in 2010, society is now split into two types of human – GenePositives and GeneNegatives. PThomas (a GenePositive) meets NStacey (a GeneNegative) and falls in love – but of course love between GenePositives and GeneNegatives has been banned too. . .

10 Go to the HFEA website and find out more about HFEA Guidelines and the HFE Act 1990. Make up a brief fact file about the guidelines and the law about the topics you've studied in this section.

11 Split into three groups. Each group will make up a short TV magazine item – which you can even film – explaining the views of one of the following groups on the topics you have studied here: Christians, Buddhists, Humanists. You may need to do some further research and some planning first.

Unit Assessment Question

Intermediate 1: Describe TWO types of genetic engineering **4KU**

Intermediate 2: Explain the difference between therapeutic and reproductive cloning **6KU**

Higher: How does the HFEA regulate the treatment of embryos? **6KU**

Sample Exam Question

Intermediate 1: 'The use of human embryos for research is morally wrong' Do you agree? Give TWO reasons for your answer. **4KU**

Intermediate 2: 'Cloning is never morally justifiable.' Explain how TWO religious viewpoints might respond to this statement. **4KU 4AE**

Higher: 'Genetic engineering is a morally justifiable means to an end.' Explain how ONE religious viewpoint and ONE viewpoint independent of religious belief might respond to this statement. **4KU 4AE**

Homework

Devise a questionnaire on one of the issues you have looked at in this section. Write up your findings.

Personal Reflection

How would you feel and what would you do if you discovered that someone had cloned you and your clone was walking around somewhere?

CHAPTER 9 Medical Ethics: Euthanasia

Can Any Forms of Euthanasia be Morally Justified?

When I'm lying on my bed and life for me is done
I hope you'll help me at that time by bringing me a gun
You see I don't want to end my life all twisted and in pain
With all my life, my hopes and fears, all muddled in my brain

Or maybe some nice pills would more cleanly end it all
A kindly doctor with a needle and plenty of gall
To take his duties seriously and spare me my death throes
And save my family from guilt to add to all their woes

To kill or cure's the subject of the Hippocratic Oath
Is it either/or or more very likely both
He'll send me swiftly to a peaceful gentle kindly death
My eyes will close, my pain will go, then finally my breath

So even if in those last days without even my voice
Remember that – as it was in life – in death it is my choice
And once my life is over my untimely death pronounced
I'll make my way to heaven – albeit unannounced

I know you say 'it's dying not death' that really is my worry
That love and care will see me to the end, no need for hurry
There's always hope – a cure, a miracle which might delay my going
But I just can't rely on that as there's no way of knowing

➔

So let me die with dignity at my own time and place
Let me choose when I last look with love upon your face
If I'm aware or if I'm not I hope you'll clearly see
If I could speak I'd surely say 'this life belongs to me'

Talk Point

Does your life 'belong' to anyone or anything?

Euthanasia

Before looking at the specific forms of euthanasia let's be quite clear about the different ways in which it might be carried out. Euthanasia is the idea that life can be ended by choice. It is sometimes referred to as a 'gentle, easy death' and also 'physician-assisted suicide'. What it means is that your life is ended as a matter of choice by you or by people acting on your behalf. Euthanasia can be:

Active

This means that positive steps are taken to end your life. You are given something on purpose which will bring your life to an end. This can be done by a doctor, a relative or even by yourself by pressing buttons on a machine rigged up by a doctor which delivers a deadly dose of poison into your bloodstream. This can also be done by giving you more of a drug which is prescribed for you with the intention that it ends your life.

Passive

Here something is not done which will ultimately lead to your death. For example, medicines may be withheld which you need for your survival, or life support systems which keep your vital organs working or your nutrition levels right may be 'switched off' so that death takes its more natural course.

These are very important distinctions because, for many people, there is a very great difference between 'killing' and 'allowing to die'. For many this is the crucial issue in the whole topic of euthanasia.

Talk Point

Do you think there is any real difference between a doctor actively killing a patient or allowing their patient to die through withdrawing treatment or being inactive in some other way?

Voluntary Euthanasia

Voluntary euthanasia is where you have made a conscious choice to end your life. It might be during an illness when you realise there's no hope of recovery. It might be long before that where you make a conscious decision while perfectly well that in the event of you becoming ill, and with no likelihood of either recovery or of a peaceful natural death, that your death is 'brought forward' by your own actions – or by others acting on your instructions. It differs from straight suicide in that it usually involves you seeking professional medical help to end your life rather than just doing your own DIY job.

When might voluntary euthanasia be a potential option?

In a situation where you are terminally ill (illness with no hope for recovery and which will end in your death), some people believe that it is a better option to choose the time and place of your dying rather than wait for the inevitable, possibly prolonged and possibly painful process of death.

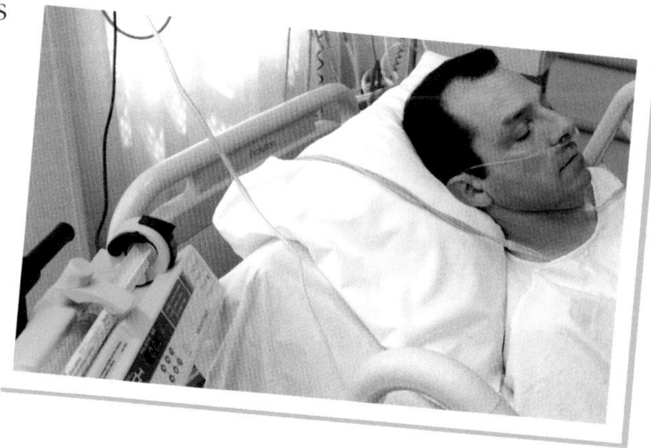

In a situation where your terminal illness is likely to lead to some deterioration in what you see as the quality of your life. This could of course be physical pain which you want to avoid – but it could also be mental suffering or the fear of losing touch with what you see as yourself through memory loss or brain deterioration leading to you becoming unable to live as you. You might also choose euthanasia in a situation where medical opinion tells you that you are likely to lapse into a Persistent Vegetative State (PVS) from which you would never recover.

Some might wish the option of voluntary euthanasia where they feel that for some reason the quality of their life is no longer worth living – even though they are not terminally ill. This would vary widely between people, but let's say that you were a professional sportsperson and through accident you became quadriplegic (unable to move through your own efforts) – you might consider your life no longer worth living because the things which matter most to you in life are no longer possible. So, you might want the option of voluntary euthanasia.

Some people might want this option because they don't want to burden their family with looking after them through a long and difficult illness. They also don't want to give their family the awful responsibility of ending their life and so they turn to doctors to do this. Doctors (arguably) have the medical skill to help end your life painlessly and they are probably not emotionally tied to you – at least not in the same way as your family.

These are the 'practical reasons' why someone might want voluntary euthanasia, but there are other reasons which are more 'theoretical'.

The belief that life and death is something which we should all have individual control over. If you have a headache you take a pill to get rid of it. Some argue that ending your life with a doctor's help is just the same – you're getting rid of the 'headache' which is your life or the current circumstances of your life. Your life is yours and you should be able to rationally choose when you no longer want it.

Some argue that euthanasia is about the issue of the quality of life. As a human being perhaps it is your decision when you think your life is no longer worth living. Why should anyone have the right to deny you this choice? In life, your freedom is usually only restricted by the law when exercising your freedom might harm others. If you choose to end your life, is that harming someone? Should you not be allowed to do so to protect that person or those people? Supporters argue that ending your life is a personal choice which affects no one but you and therefore should not be subject to any kind of restriction.

Besides, the reasons for your choices are no one else's business. Who can decide but you if the choice is a good one or not? Maybe it's perfectly acceptable for you to end your life because you want your remaining relatives to be spared supporting the dying you – or even the you which no longer wants to live.

Do people have the right to die?

So what do people think are the possible benefits and dangers of voluntary euthanasia?

Benefits

It gives us all control over all aspects of our lives. Why should we have almost complete freedom throughout life but absolutely no freedom over our deaths?

It means that vital healthcare resources don't need to be pointlessly used up on people who actually don't want to live.

It stops people from having to take their own lives without medical help – because this can result in painful deaths and often mistakes leading to prolonged suffering. Physician-assisted suicide is a far more humane form of ending a life. We put animals down who are in misery – why can't we do the same for humans?

If it's all done legally and in a controlled way then we don't have to put relatives in the awful position of having to do this for us – and live with the memory for the rest of their lives (which could be especially horrible if they make mistakes and your end is agonising and traumatic).

If it's legal then no one risks prosecution (as they do now) by assisting you to die.

Even if it is 'unnaturally ending a life' what's wrong with that? Many things we do are pretty unnatural. In fact, every time we accept medical care in life we act unnaturally. Is there any difference between that and using our medical knowledge to humanely carry out people's voluntary wish to die?

Dignitas Suicide flat, Zurich, Switzerland

Supporters say it allows us to 'die with dignity'. They argue that the process of dying can often be long and painful. It can be accompanied by personal mental distress as you lose control over yourself. A conscious choice to end your life before this happens is far more desirable.

If it were widely available it means that we can all live our lives safe in the knowledge that we'll never have to suffer unnecessarily because our lives can be ended before that point. This will make society a much happier place. Currently, people in the UK who want voluntary euthanasia have to travel to other countries to obtain it. Wouldn't it be much more kind and supportive if we could get such a service in our own home surrounded by our families instead of in some foreign land surrounded by medical stuff?

It allows everyone to make their own choices about this important aspect of life. This respects the rights of all people and allows them to be in control of every aspect of their life.

However, many argue that this rosy picture isn't quite right. It's not just a case of letting everyone decide for themselves because there are dangers linked to what seems to be your choice alone.

Dangers

Is it ever right to put doctors in such a situation? They do have the medical expertise but do we have the moral right to ask them to use this by ending lives? Helping someone to take their life is quite a responsibility and may have harmful effects for the doctors involved – does anyone have the right to expect a doctor to use his knowledge and skills in this way? Shouldn't doctors be curing not killing?

Is everyone who decides that they want to end their life in the same mental state when they choose to do so? If you choose long before you're ill then you assume you'll think the same way when you are older (or when you become ill) as you do now. What if you decide on voluntary euthanasia when you're twenty and then a year later become terminally ill, but unfortunately lose the power of communication. You change your mind and there's no way of letting anyone know.

Doesn't society have a duty to protect people – maybe even from themselves? You'd obviously have to be 'of sound mind' to decide you wanted voluntary euthanasia. Who decides when someone is of sound mind and when they're not? Maybe someone would opt for voluntary euthanasia because they want to spare their family the burden of looking after them. Maybe they don't really want to die but are just doing what they think is the right thing. Also, this might mean that poorer people would be likely to make this decision more often than the wealthy, because the rich will probably find it easier to look after their ill relatives than the poor. Apart from this, how might we know when someone's decision was a real choice and not a cry for help, or something which their family were forcing them to do so that they could inherit all their money?

Also, during illness people go through all sorts of emotions. Maybe they would ask for voluntary euthanasia during a 'low period' – should it be automatically granted? And, during severe illness people aren't always in complete control of their thinking. Someone would have to judge whether the person was 'thinking straight' or not – what a responsibility.

Isn't voluntary euthanasia the first step on a slippery moral slope? If society allows people to end their own lives with medical help for whatever reason, does this make it more likely that we will come to respect and value human life less? Might this lead to some people having euthanasia suggested to them as a sensible option –maybe by stressed doctors working in a health service with limited resources?

Wouldn't it just mean that we deal with many of society's problems – poverty, care for the elderly, support for the sick and dying by getting rid of them through voluntary (or 'voluntary') euthanasia? What might this do to the relationship between doctor and patient. You might worry that your doctor is looking at you wondering if voluntary euthanasia might be the best thing – even if you'd never considered it yourself.

If voluntary euthanasia becomes commonplace, what does this say about quality of life? Is society upholding this idea or making it worthless? Isn't life valuable no matter what or is it only valuable if we think it is in certain circumstances? This could send out very confusing messages to people because if voluntary euthanasia was something everyone could go for, then maybe some people might feel pressurised into voluntary euthanasia 'because everyone else seems to be doing it when…'

People are scared of dying not death – there are viable alternatives to euthanasia. Hospice care, improved medical treatments and so on. If we rush into accepting euthanasia then some medical treatments might never be developed because there's not the same urgency if euthanasia is an option.

Talk Point

3

Do you think legalising euthanasia is a slippery moral slope?

Check Your Learning

1 What other words/phrases are used to describe euthanasia?

2 Describe ONE situation where voluntary euthanasia might be considered as an option.

3 Why might someone think voluntary euthanasia is 'unnatural' and why might someone think the opposite?

4 Do you think a person has the right to choose when to end their own life?

5 Explain ONE possible benefit of voluntary euthanasia.

6 Explain ONE possible danger of voluntary euthanasia.

7 What alternatives are there to euthanasia?

8 Should voluntary euthanasia be made legal in the UK?

Involuntary Euthanasia

Involuntary euthanasia is where the choice to end your life is not made by you but by others. This is generally in cases of terminal illness with no hope of recovery, and where you are unable to take part in the decision yourself for whatever reason – usually linked to a PVS. However, such decisions are sometimes made where medical opinion suggests that a person's quality of life is now, or is predicted to be, so poor that their life is not worth living. Generally speaking, the medical people involved will try to get the relatives' permission to carry out an act of euthanasia. This is usually the case in terminal illness.

However, relatives do sometimes refuse and hospitals may well go to the courts asking for permission to override the relatives' decision. The courts have to decide here what the person would have wanted if they had been able to choose for themselves. They take into account as much information as possible about the medical circumstances but also the person's beliefs and values in relation to the importance of life. This is often difficult because most of us don't give much thought to what we'd like to happen if someone was deciding whether or not our life should continue in a PVS or with no prospect of quality of life. It's also difficult as sometimes the patient is a new-born child with no history of beliefs or values – should the parent's beliefs and values override the medical circumstances here. Recent cases in Scotland suggest not.

When might involuntary euthanasia be a potential option?

- Where a person is in a persistent vegetative state (PVS) with no predicted hope of recovery. This could be as a result of illness or accident.
- Where a person is terminally ill and suffering greatly but unable to communicate their wishes for some other reason.
- Where a person's life is judged to be of such poor quality as not to be worth living any more. This, for example might well be the case where a child has been born with some serious mental or physical deformity which is so grave as to threaten their continued existence or suggest a life which will be full or pain or suffering in some way.

It's unfortunate but a fact of life that doctors do have to make choices about life and death every day. There are only so many resources available and doctors do have to decide how best to use them. So, sometimes, doctors may want to opt for involuntary euthanasia because otherwise precious medical resources are being used on a patient with no hope, instead of on a patient where the resources might help them to survive and live a normal life.

There are 'theoretical' elements to this just as there are for voluntary euthanasia.

- Society has a duty to protect the weak and prevent unnecessary suffering. If we have the medical technology to prevent suffering then we should use that, even if in some cases this means humanely ending someone's life rather than trying to unnecessarily prolong it.
- Maybe society has to make choices about the quality of life, not to do so would be morally indefensible. If a child was born with such severe mental and physical deformities that the child's life could never be anything anywhere near 'normal' then maybe we have a duty to use the resources available to us to end that child's life in as humane a way as possible. Maybe the parents are thinking about themselves and not the child and so there is a duty to override their wishes in some cases.
- Involuntary euthanasia might just be what the person would want but can't say – so we have a duty to act on their behalf to end their suffering as they would if they could.

Benefits

Perhaps carrying out involuntary euthanasia is the last act of kindness that anyone can perform for someone, whether it's a relative or a doctor using his skill to end pain and suffering when curing is impossible.

So, if it were made legal it would take away the fear that this act of kindness might result in your prosecution. Many doctors say that the practice of involuntary euthanasia is already common with doctors risking a great deal to do what they think is right. Making it legal (with suitable guidelines) would protect them and others who carry it out for the right reasons.

Such medically controlled euthanasia avoids relatives having to try this for themselves, possibly resulting in a botched job.

It might help us all to know that we would never die in great agony, especially if we couldn't express our wish to take up the option of voluntary euthanasia. This would make a more caring society if we knew that our doctors could decide when it was the right thing to do.

It would be much better for our relatives to see us slip away in a peaceful controlled way than in obvious distress.

It does mean, like it or not, that we could 'free up' much needed resources for people who have a chance of recovery from illness.

Dangers

Would doctors always make the right decision? They might feel pressurised because of the money it costs to maintain someone in a PVS – or they might be persuaded that it's right by greedy relatives, eager for the death to get their hands on an inheritance. There are always choices to be made about quality of life or hope of recovery. Has anyone the right to end someone's life based on one choice rather than another?

Doctors might also make mistakes in their diagnosis. It wouldn't be the first time that 'someone in a PVS with no hope of recovery' amazingly comes out of it and goes on to have a long and happy life.

Maybe it's not an act of kindness but one of hopelessness. Modern medicine should prevent pain and suffering until death comes naturally – so why the need to hurry it along?

The process of the dying of a relative is an important time for those they leave behind. Maybe being too hasty with the involuntary euthanasia doesn't give them time to properly adjust – and might leave them wondering if they had agreed to the right thing for the rest of their life. Also, when decisions have to be made about involuntary euthanasia, people's emotions are high and maybe they're not thinking straight. Perhaps this is not the best time to be making such monumental decisions.

Of course, if it's not carried out by a doctor, then the person might live under a cloud of guilt for the rest of their lives.

No matter who does it – at the current time they risk prosecution in this country.

Maybe there's always hope for a cure – or a miracle – which isn't going to be much use after euthanasia has been carried out.

Sometimes the courts have to decide what the person in question would have wanted. Is this ever possible? And does society have the right to give some judge the responsibility of passing a 'death sentence'?

Maybe it makes society a less caring place. We would know that if we were ever in a situation where involuntary euthanasia was an option that it might be rushed into without much thought. That might not give us great confidence in our doctors – or our relatives.

Talk Point 4

Do we ever have the right to make decisions about whether someone should die or not?

Check Your Learning

1 Explain the differences between voluntary and involuntary euthanasia.
2 Who might have to make the decision about involuntary euthanasia?
3 What is a PVS?
4 What is meant by the phrase: 'doctors are always having to make life and death decisions' and how does this relate to euthanasia?
5 Explain ONE possible benefit of involuntary euthanasia.
6 In your opinion, do the dangers of involuntary euthanasia outweigh the benefits? Explain your answer fully.
7 Does a person have the right to choose when to die?

The Moral Implications of Euthanasia

In general, euthanasia, no matter what its form centres on just a few moral arguments.

The Meaning of Life

When is a life worth living? Some argue that *quality of life* is what matters. There comes a point where what you are experiencing can no longer be thought of as living in the proper sense. This might be because your personality has changed so much through a degenerative disease or because you are incapacitated, or in such pain that nothing else about life really matters. You may no longer be a conscious, thinking being – even though your heart is beating and your blood is moving around your body. What lies in a PVS might not be in any sense 'you' any more.

Supporters of euthanasia often argue that it should be an option where a person's quality of life is so poor that there's no point in them going on 'living'. In such a situation, your own previously expressed wish to die or that of your relatives should be respected. Doctors already make judgements about quality of life in some cases – why not at the end of life? Others argue that what is important about life is the *sanctity of life*. Such people argue that life is valuable as long as you are alive, no matter what its quality (and of course we can't always make judgements about its quality because we don't have all the facts). Life is sacred and should always be preserved as long as possible by whatever means possible. No one has the right to make judgements about quality of life and so end your life. Life is inviolable. This idea is closely linked to the second major moral argument.

Time Out 

Do you think life is sacred? What for you would be a good/poor quality of life?

Whose Life is it Anyway?

Personal freedom is the issue here. Should everyone have the right to choose when and how they die? Supporters of euthanasia usually argue that we should, though there should be safeguards to protect people who don't agree. If you choose to end your life or have it ended then that should be up to you – it doesn't mean that the same thing should apply to everyone in the same situation – just to you. So, there are no dangers to anyone else from your choice. People who argue this way point out that human beings have freedom over every other aspect of their life, something we value highly throughout life, so why take this freedom away in relation to your death? Supporters of the sanctity of life argument often argue that our life is not our own – it belongs to God, and isn't ours to do with as we please. God will decide when our life is at an end, not us. There are limits to our freedom over ourselves. This means that no one has the right to end a life in an unnatural way, such decisions should be left to God.

The Moral and Practical Consequences of Euthanasia

Some argue that the morality of euthanasia comes down to its likely consequences. If it led to a society which is more caring then it is right – but if it leads to a society more thoughtless about the value of life then it's wrong. It's really to do with the balance of the benefits and dangers above. Its rightness or wrongness comes down to whether the benefits outweigh the dangers. For example, is it more morally correct to make a doctor use his skill to end a life or to force him to watch helplessly while his patient suffers an unnecessarily painful death? Or is it right to refuse one person's freely chosen voluntary euthanasia because it might pressurise someone else into doing the same thing? Is there any real moral difference between killing (when it's an expressed wish) and allowing to die?

UK Law on Euthanasia

For these complex reasons, UK law covers the issue of euthanasia. There have been many high profile cases where people have tried to use their own situation to force the government to change its view on euthanasia, for example, the case of Diane Pretty (http://news.bbc.co.uk/1/hi/english/static/in_depth/health/2001/euthanasia/default.stm). In the case of Tony Bland, it looked as if the courts might have been moving towards legalising 'allowing to die', but each case is still treated on its own merits, there's no general legal ruling to follow. If someone wants euthanasia they must go abroad to obtain it – or risk prosecution of those involved here. The House of Lords has been quite clear in stating that although euthanasia might be right for some it does not follow that it's right for all.

Source 1

Intentional killing, including at the individual's request, is a serious criminal offence currently carrying a mandatory life sentence. Various attempts have been made to introduce into Parliament draft legislation to permit voluntary euthanasia. The BMA has opposed these and, in its evidence to the House of Lords Select Committee on Medical Ethics, also declined to support any weakening of the mandatory life penalty upon conviction.

Suicide is not an offence. In England, Wales and Northern Ireland, assisting suicide is a crime carrying a potential sentence of 14 years' imprisonment. It appears, however, that juries are reluctant to convict since many cases involve close relatives claiming to have acted in good faith to curtail suffering. No UK doctor has been convicted of assisting suicide although some admit to doing so.

Physician assisted suicide is no different in law to any other person helping another to commit suicide. A misconception has grown that physician assisted suicide is legal in Scotland. This arose from the fact that in Scotland there has not been any legislation on suicide and therefore the act of suicide was never illegal. In 1961, England and Wales passed the Suicide Act decriminalising suicide but at the same time enacting:

s2(1) A person who aids, abets, counsels or procures the suicide of another, or an attempt of another to commit suicide, shall be liable on conviction to imprisonment for a term not exceeding fourteen years.

Like its counterpart in England and Wales, The Criminal Justice (N.I.) Act 1966, decriminalised suicide in Northern Ireland but specifically retained the offence of complicity in the suicide of another. The absence of any corresponding legal provision in Scotland has led some people to believe that assisting suicide is legal there. This is not the case. Whereas in England and Wales, those who assist another to commit or attempt suicide are usually prosecuted on a charge of manslaughter (although they could be prosecuted under the Suicide Act), in Scotland they are usually charged with culpable homicide for the same action.

www.bma.org.uk/ap.nsf/Content/Euthanasiaphysicianassistedsuicide~Legal

Talk Point

5

Do some background research – should Diane Pretty have been granted the right to die?

Euthanasia in the Netherlands

The Netherlands was the first country in the world to legalise euthanasia. For a full explanation of the Dutch legal position see www.minbuza.nl/en/welcome/Netherlands/social,index.html. It was being carried on by doctors long before it was legalised, and sometimes quite openly, but the liberal-minded Dutch rarely prosecuted anyone for it despite its illegality. However, even although it is now legal there are still very careful safeguards around it to make sure that it is not abused:

- the patient must be terminally ill with no hope for recovery
- the patient must personally request euthanasia and this must be in the context of a professional relationship with a doctor who is aware of the case history and therefore the person's mental state
- euthanasia must be a 'last resort' – every form of treatment having been exhausted
- it must be agreed by two doctors that this is the best option for this specific patient.

This is expressed in Dutch law in the following way:

1 In order to comply with the due care criteria referred to in article 293, paragraph 2, of the Criminal Code, the attending physician must:

   a) be satisfied that the patient has made a voluntary and carefully considered request;

   b) be satisfied that the patient's suffering was unbearable, and that there was no prospect of improvement;

   c) have informed the patient about his situation and his prospects;

   d) have come to the conclusion, together with the patient, that there is no reasonable alternative in the light of the patient's situation;

   e) have consulted at least one other, independent physician, who must have seen the patient and given a written opinion on the due care criteria referred to in a. to d. above; and

   f) have terminated the patient's life or provided assistance with suicide with due medical care and attention.

Termination of Life on Request and Assisted Suicide (Review Procedures) Act
For the full text of this law and a full explanation of the Dutch legal position see www.minbuz.nl/en/welcome/Netherlands/social,index.html).

One other interesting feature of debate here is that in the Netherlands terminally ill children aged between 12 and 15 can also obtain euthanasia – with parental permission. (Beyond 16 it is entirely your choice.) Some argue that this is far too young to fully understand the issues.

All of these regulations mean that it's not just available 'on demand'. The aim is to respect the wishes of individuals in individual cases but to avoid opening the doors to everyone for any reason. Many argue that this sensible approach respects human freedom to choose and avoids the dangers of unregulated euthanasia – but opponents say that it still makes euthanasia too readily available and some of the abuses people fear actually occur in the Netherlands. Also, it is claimed, the 'slippery slope' argument is in evidence here with many cases not sticking completely to the guidelines, and in fact many cases not being reported at all. After assisting with a suicide, doctors are required to make a full report to the Royal Dutch Medical Association as well as the legal authorities. Many claim that this does not always happen.

Talk Point 6

If euthanasia were made legal in the UK, at what age should you be able to opt for it?

Source 2

Approximately 4,000 patients a year die through active euthanasia in the form of a lethal injection that kills in minutes. Over half of Dutch doctors have performed mercy killings with the required consent and consultation and at least 90 per cent of the population support euthanasia. The BMJ study found that in 1995 almost two thirds of cases of euthanasia and physician-assisted suicide went unreported. One in five cases of euthanasia occurred without the patient's explicit request, and in 17 per cent of such cases, alternative treatment was available in contravention of the guidelines. Dutch law requires patients to experience 'unbearable suffering' to justify euthanasia. But more than half the doctors surveyed said the main reason given by patients for the request was 'loss of dignity'. Almost half said they took action 'to prevent further suffering'. The researchers concluded: 'The reality is that a clear majority of cases of euthanasia, both with and without request, go unreported and unchecked. Dutch claims of effective regulation ring hollow'.

http://news.bbc.co.uk

Check Your Learning

1. Explain the differences between the quality and sanctity of life arguments
2. How is the issue of euthanasia (possibly) linked to the idea of personal freedom?
3. Should decisions about euthanasia be restricted to each individual case alone?
4. Outline the UK's legal position on euthanasia.
5. Explain how the legal position in the Netherlands is different to the UK.
6. What safeguards does Dutch law have to ensure that euthanasia is not abused?
7. According to the source, is the law on euthanasia in the Netherlands working?
8. Should the UK change its laws on euthanasia?

The BMA Guidelines on Euthanasia

Because euthanasia is so morally complicated and doctors are meant to be healers not philosophers, the British Medical Association (BMA) has drawn up guidelines about euthanasia. It makes a clear distinction between active euthanasia and allowing patients to die:

'The BMA does not believe that it is appropriate to prolong life at all costs, with no regard to its quality or the burdens of the intervention... The guiding principles underlying any such decision must be to protect the dignity, comfort and rights of the patient; to take into account any known wishes of the patient and the views of people close to patients who lack capacity.'

So clearly the BMA sees some value in allowing people to die where there is no hope of recovery.

However, as far as assisted suicide is concerned, it's a very different story:

'Traditionally, the BMA opposed any form of assisted dying but in 2005 its annual representative meeting (its policy-making body) recognised that there were diverse opinions within society and the profession. So, for a time the BMA took a neutral stance, agreeing that it would support whatever changes in law in relation to assisted suicide which the government might make...'

In 2006, however, BMA members voting at the annual meeting made clear that the majority opposed such [legalising assisted suicide]. Therefore the BMA dropped its neutral stance and again opposes all forms of assisted dying.

The current policy is that the BMA:

believes that the ongoing improvement in palliative care allows patients to die with dignity;
insists that physician-assisted suicide should not be made legal in the UK;
insists that voluntary euthanasia should not be made legal in the UK;
insists that non-voluntary euthanasia should not be made legal in the UK; and,
insists that if euthanasia were legalised, there should be a clear demarcation between those doctors who would be involved in it and those who would not.

(www.bma.org.uk)

Obviously the BMA's job is to look after the interests of doctors who, after all, would be most directly affected in any change of UK law. It wants to safeguard a doctor's right not to be involved in euthanasia if s/he does not want to.

Christians on Euthanasia

Christians are divided on the issue of euthanasia. Some argue that all forms of euthanasia, active or passive go against the will of God. God gives life and God is the only one who will decide when it should end. Euthanasia has therefore been described as 'rushing into God's presence unannounced'. The Church of Scotland is quite clear in its opposition to the legalisation of euthanasia:

Source 3

Legalisation of euthanasia will not produce a solution to the needs of the individual sufferer; or address the healthcare challenges of contemporary society. It is the expression of an attitude to life which belittles the sovereignty of God, diminishes the importance of sustaining relationships, and inhibits the pursuit of life-affirming answers for people in need and distress. Christians must be active in promoting positive alternatives derived from Biblical truth, so that the momentum towards intentional killing may be curbed. The Church has an obligation before God to assert God's interest in life, rather than in death...to exercise Christian compassion towards suffering the disabled and the dying and to encourage the relief of symptoms and the improvement in the quality of life for such people. The Church cannot support euthanasia as a means to any of these ends, and rejects the introduction of death as a treatment option in any clinical situation.

Euthanasia: A Christian Perspective: The Church of Scotland 1997

Some Christians distinguish between ordinary and extraordinary medical treatment, drawing a difference between killing and allowing to die. For some Christians there does come a point where extraordinary measures should not be taken to preserve life. Instead, life should be allowed to follow its natural course, and so, in fact allow God's will to be done. It is said that the death of Pope John Paul II was an example of this – when it became clear that his recovery was unlikely, extraordinary measures to keep him alive were not taken. This was cited by the Roman Catholic Church as a faithful example of how to meet death, and as an example of trusting in God instead of 'doubting his goodness' by taking control over your own death through euthanasia.

Source 4

In the end the Catholic position ultimately rests on the kind of community we become. Our convictions about sovereignty, stewardship, sanctity of life, suffering and mercy call us to witness to the powerlessness that comes with the limits of human control over life and death. It also comes by responding to the conditions of hopelessness which make euthanasia so attractive. Responding to the fears of losing control, meaning and company by becoming a caring community will be a witness to the hope that, although life may be hard, it can still be lived. Supporting euthanasia would be a rejection of the abiding presence of God manifest in the covenantal commitments of being a community committed to caring mercifully for those who cannot be cured.

Euthanasia, Moral & Pastoral Perspectives, Gula. RM, Paulist Press 1994 p68

Buddhists on Euthanasia

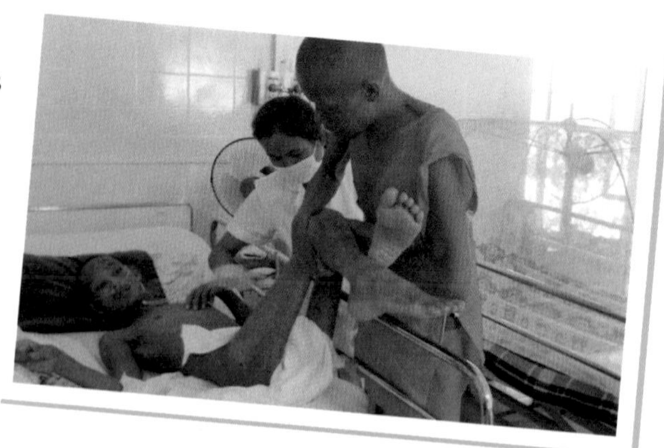

131. He who seeking his own happiness punishes or kills beings who also long for happiness, will not find happiness after death.

Dhammapada

Some Buddhists would reject all forms of euthanasia as the negative kamma associated with such premeditated killing would be so great. If the killing was motivated by the wrong thoughts then this would be even more serious, for example, if the decision was made on the basis of freeing up medical resources for some more 'hopeful' case, or avoiding the burden of supporting a dying person to his natural end. In the case of voluntary euthanasia there would be the issue of causing another being to take or help take your life which would bring them bad kamma – so this should be rejected as far as possible. Buddhists believe that the best approach is to care for the dying in the best possible way so as to minimise their pain and suffering and let nature take its course. Both the outcome as well as the intention of your actions are important.

However, Buddhists also stress the importance of the concept of compassion in all aspects of life. If the Buddhist was convinced that euthanasia was the most compassionate thing to do then he might accept it. Again, this comes down to skilful means – what is the right thing to do in this situation. This is specific to each case, and so Buddhists would be unlikely to support any view of euthanasia which tried to apply the same principles to all cases. One (maybe the most important) Buddhist precept is avoiding harming living things – obviously sometimes in life this has to happen (in self-defence, or even in order to eat) – so perhaps there are cases where this precept has to be suspended. If, for example, euthanasia would mean preventing even greater suffering then perhaps it is an appropriate option.

A Viewpoint Independent of Religious Belief

The modern Utilitarian, Peter Singer is well-known for his views about euthanasia. He stresses the importance of quality of life, arguing that there are times when a person's life is no longer worth living and so euthanasia should be an option open to them – or to society on their behalf. He makes no specific distinction between killing and allowing to die, because for him, once euthanasia seems appropriate, the patient can no longer be considered a person in the proper sense. He says:

> *We often use 'person' as if it meant the same as 'human being'. In recent discussions in bioethics, however, 'person' is now often used to mean a being with certain characteristics such as rationality and self-awareness.*
>
> *Rethinking Life & Death*, Singer P, OUP 1994 p180

Singer's view is that without the qualities of rationality and self-awareness we can't describe someone as a person and therefore they aren't necessarily entitled to the same moral rights as persons. Singer argues that the sanctity of life argument is weak because there are many cases, war for example, where those who uphold the sanctity of life seem quite able to ignore the idea for what they see as the greater good. He does not see therefore that suspending the notion of the sanctity of life is any different in the case of euthanasia. He argues too that the 'slippery slope' argument is weak because it doesn't seem to have resulted in widescale abuse in the Netherlands, nor in other countries where euthanasia is carried out by doctors illegally. Singer also cites the decisions in the case of Tony Bland which seem to support his own view of the quality of life argument. He rejects the idea that all human life is of equal worth, instead suggesting that:

> *We should recognise that the worth of human life varies...When we reject [the idea that all human life is of equal worth] we will instead focus on ethically relevant characteristics like the capacity for enjoyable experiences, for interacting with others, or for having preferences about continued life. Without consciousness none of these are possible: therefore, once we are certain that consciousness has been irrevocably lost, it is not ethically relevant that there is still some hormonal brain function, for hormonal brain function without consciousness cannot benefit a patient... So our decision about how to treat such a patient should not depend upon lofty rhetoric about the equal worth of all human life, but on the views of families and partners... If a patient in a PVS has previously expressed wishes about what should happen to her or him in such circumstances... At the same time... we cannot ignore the limits set by the finite nature of our medical resources...*
>
> *Rethinking Life & Death*, Singer P; OUP 1994 p192

This is classic preference Utilitarianism – making the moral decision based on the interests of those directly involved, but it is also a more classic form of utilitarianism at the same time. The greatest good for the greatest number cannot, in Singer's view, be served by keeping 'alive' someone who is no longer a human person, even if they remain a human being. Also, if when you are a person, you make a rational choice to opt for euthanasia should you ever cease to be a person (even if you're still 'alive') then that wish should be respected.

Check Your Learning

1. Explain the BMA's position on euthanasia.
2. Describe TWO contrasting viewpoints on euthanasia within the Christian faith.
3. Is there any difference in Christian belief between 'killing' and 'allowing to die'?
4. What does a religious person mean by the 'sanctity of life argument'?
5. Why might a Buddhist oppose euthanasia?
6. Why might a Buddhist support euthanasia?
7. Explain why Peter Singer thinks euthanasia is acceptable.
8. What are the similarities and differences between Singer's views and those of Buddhists and Christians?

Extension Activities

Knowledge, Understanding and Evaluation through Practical Activities

1. Write a 'living will' where you explain clearly what your views on euthanasia are should you ever be in a situation where you are in a PVS or where your quality of life is judged to be unacceptable.
2. Imagine you are the sole relative of someone who is in a PVS. You are asked for your views on allowing them to die. Write an imaginative essay explaining the thoughts which are going through your head and the reasons for your final decision.
3. Have a class debate 'Life is sacred and should be preserved at all costs'. Try to represent the viewpoints you have studied in this section.
4. An MP comes to your class to explain his reasons for trying to get a bill through parliament which will legalise euthanasia in the UK just as in the Netherlands. Write a script for a drama which you will do in class. Make sure that you have a variety of viewpoints represented both for and against his proposals. Your viewpoints should include religious and non-religious points of view on the topic.
5. Devise an advertising strategy either supporting or opposing this MP's actions. You could make a short TV commercial or a poster campaign.
6. Create a piece of artwork based on the statement 'Euthanasia: The Right to Die?' Your artwork can be for or against any or all kinds of euthanasia.
7. You are a doctor who has been asked by a patient to help end her life. Script the conversation you might have with this patient.
8. Do some research into class/school views on the various types of euthanasia you have studied. Design a questionnaire on the topic and prepare a report on your findings either as a display or as a written report. Perhaps you could issue your questionnaire at a parents' evening.
9. Find out more about the cases of Diane Pretty, Tony Bland and Dr Kervorkian (an American doctor who was imprisoned for openly carrying out acts of euthanasia). Prepare short fact files about these cases and explain how they support or reject the arguments for euthanasia.

Unit Assessment Question

Intermediate 1: How might a religious person support his belief that involuntary euthanasia is sometimes right? **4KU**

Intermediate 2: Explain TWO differences between voluntary and involuntary euthanasia **8KU**

Higher: 'Involuntary euthanasia is all about quality of life.' Do you agree? **6KU 6AE**

Sample Exam Question

Intermediate 1: State TWO ways in which the law on euthanasia in the Netherlands tries to make sure that euthanasia is not abused. **4KU**

Intermediate 2: 'Everyone should have the freedom to choose when and how to die'. Do you agree? Give reasons for your answer. **6AE**

Higher: How might the BMA's guidelines on euthanasia help a doctor? **4KU 4AE**

Homework

Find out about the alternatives to euthanasia offered by hospices. What do they do? Why? Write a report of your findings.

Personal Reflection

Would you support the legalisation of euthanasia in the UK?

CHAPTER 10 War and Peace: Is War Ever Morally Justifiable?

A line of the usual suspects is lined up in the Head teacher's office. Each has been sent along to the Head because of some act of apparently pointless aggression towards a fellow pupil. Sheepishly staring at their feet the Head begins an interrogation worthy of a very dodgy secret police agency in some banana republic where bureaucracy has gone loopy...

Head: Well John McDougall... what did you do this time?

McD: I walloped Gary Smith sir.

Head: And what, pray tell, motivated you to such an act of vacuous barbarity?

McD: Eh?

Head: *[slowly]* Why did you do it?

McD: I thought Gary was going to hit me sir.

Head: So, let me get this clear... You thought you'd knock him senseless because you had a psychic premonition that he was going to damage you in some as yet unspecified way.

McD: No sir, I thought he was going to hit me sir.

Head: So you hit him first?

McD: Yes sir, seemed like the right thing to do at the time.

→

Head: Mmmmmmm indeed, an interesting analysis of the concept of self-defence... *[to another pupil in the lineup]* And you, Karen Girdlings – what made you engage in an all-out slapping offensive against Amy Dodds?

Karen: She was in my seat in Geography.

Head: This seat, you brought it in from home did you, your own self-assembly work from IKEA?

Karen: No, sir, my seat in Geography room 1.

Head: Have you a plaque on this seat which commends the school with gratitude for the many happy days you have spent here?

Karen: No sir, it's plastic.

Head: So in what way, exactly, can it be considered to be your seat?

Karen: I always sit there sir.

Head: So, in response to Amy's invasion of your treasured pvc family heirloom you thought it quite morally in order to give her a 'doing'?

Karen: *[just looks down at her feet]*

Head: And you Taylor?

Taylor: Sir, Ian Connolly was going to beat up my wee brother.

Head: If I recall correctly from my last visit to your 'wee' brother's primary school, your wee brother is considerably bigger than you...

Taylor: But sir...

Head: ...and also the county boxing champion in the light heavyweight division?

Taylor: Yes Sir, but...

Head: And isn't Ian Connolly small, skinny and a trainspotter at the weekend?

Taylor: Yes Sir, but...

Head: Family honour then, I suppose Taylor. *[Looks down at referral on his desk]* Now this one is really interesting... *[looks up at Morgan McPhail]* So McPhail, I'll read this one to you shall I? *[Reads]* 'I had just been speaking to Mr Simpson in his English class when I heard a commotion outside. I found Robert Russell (4BA) in a headlock being exercised by Morgan McPhail (4FA). Morgan was screaming at Robert, enjoining him to say that St. Mirren were, 'top of the league and you're no'. Robert was refusing to comply ranting that Dunfermline would 'stuff that bunch of losers' on Saturday'. How much more of this do I need to read...?

Morgan: Sir, Russell's always going on about our last defeat at the hands of his jammy crew – the ref was against us.

➜

Head: So, in order to preserve your West of Scotland cultural background and general way of life, you decided to attempt to part Robert's mysterious Eastern head from his body in case his influence ultimately leads to your grandchildren shaking Paisley's dust out of their shoes, moving to the Kingdom of Fife and calling everything 'a beezer'?

Morgan: But sir...he...

Head: Right, detention for all. You each have some of the most twisted, warped and generally morally contorted views of what it is and isn't right to fight for. What's going on in that RE department I wonder? Perhaps I'll need to go and 'observe' it – there's a time and a place to engage in unprovoked combat – but not in my school...

Why Do Wars Happen?

You'll need your history department for detailed explanations of specific wars, because how they begin is always after a long and usually mind-bogglingly complicated series of reasons concerning things like which politician said what to whom and where and who wanted to pull a fast one on someone else – that and loads of dull stuff like treaties and conventions and agreements... However, we can put the reasons for fighting wars into broad categories which should help us to understand why wars start more generally. even if all wars do not fit into a nice neat pattern.

Wars are fought for many reasons:

Defending Yourself from Aggression or Securing Your Freedom

Obviously, fighting back against another aggressive country is one reason for war. If someone plans to invade your homeland you can either let them or fight back. Sometimes aggressive acts like this by one country against another just come 'out of the blue', but usually they happen because of a long period of unrest, mistrust and disagreement between countries which eventually boils over into a strike by one against the other. Once the attacked country has decided to fight back – hey presto, you have a war. You should bear in mind that there are international law 'guidelines' about when a conflict officially becomes a war. War is usually declared, but not always. For our purposes, it's the moral stuff we're interested in so go back to your history teacher for the definition of when a war is a war.

In World War II, Poland went to war with Germany to protect itself from the aggressive act of Germany's invasion of Poland. Wars can also break out because one country has been under the rule of another for some time and wants to get free from that country. This could explain something like the American wars of independence. This is also sometimes the case in civil wars where one group within a country feels that another group in the same country is keeping them from being completely 'free' so they go to war with each other to secure their freedom. This freedom can be practical or ideological. The Spanish Civil war was about two competing ideologies, Fascism and Communism and the freedom people had to follow these political ideologies, but it was also about preserving one way of life and not allowing it to be swamped by another.

Defending the Weak From Attack or Preserving Your Way of Life

Sometimes a country may go to war because it thinks that by doing so it is helping to protect another smaller and weaker country which is unable to protect itself. Britain's involvement in World War II was for this reason. It declared war on Germany to come to the aid of countries like Poland and Belgium. This could seem very selfless and noble, and often it is. However, it could also be a long-term form of self-protection. Perhaps if Britain hadn't entered the war when it did then Germany would have got stronger over the years and eventually posed a direct threat to Britain. Many modern conflicts have been about the superpowers: the USA and previously the USSR going to war to protect countries they saw as in need of support. But of course it's not just as simple as being nice and helping others. These conflicts were also partly motivated by ideology and belief. Both superpowers (Capitalist USA and Communist USSR) thought that a good way to preserve their own way of life was to stop the spread of the 'opposite' way of life throughout the world – so the USA helped countries which favoured Capitalism and the USSR countries which favoured communism. The modern version of this, of course, is the 'War against Terror' where some western governments are involved in conflicts in places like Iraq and Afghanistan because they believe these countries pose a threat to the 'Western' way of life. One very silly but possibly very helpful example of this is in the film *Chitty Chitty Bang Bang* where a war has been fought between neighbouring kingdoms over which end of the boiled egg to chop off first, the pointy end or the other end! Maybe that's just as meaningful as political ideology, who knows?

Preserving your way of life can also involve preserving your language, culture and religion. Of course, it is claimed that many wars are caused by religion, but usually such 'religious wars' had much more complicated reasons for starting than just differences of belief – though that might have been an important part of it.

Talk Point 1

Using the ideas above – do you think the current 'war on terrorism' is right?

Taking Back What You Think Is Yours

Some wars begin because country A thinks country B has what belongs to it. This might be land or resources of some kind. Remember that all the world's borders are just manmade ideas and whether you live in one country or another is just the way history has developed. In the UK, for example, the town of Berwick-upon-Tweed has been back and forward between being in Scotland and England throughout its history. Many Middle Eastern conflicts today are based on the fact that the Middle East map was re-drawn after the First and Second World Wars and people still think that what's theirs has been taken from them. The existence of the country of Israel, for example, is either a land which was stolen from the Palestinian people or a rightful return of a land to its true inhabitants. Britain's conflict with Argentina was over the fact that Argentina had invaded the Falklands. Or, if you're Argentinean, it was over the fact that Britain didn't recognise that the Malvinas belongs to Argentina.

Extending Your Country's Power or Resources

The reasons for war given above potentially sound quite noble, but, sometimes, war is just about one country being greedy for more. Perhaps the country next to you has valuable natural resources which you want – or maybe you're just running out of land and want to give your people more space – which the country next to you has (or maybe it doesn't but your government doesn't care about that). One feature of World War II was the idea of *lebensraum* – that Germany 'needed' to expand its borders to allow its people to have a better life. Many say that modern conflicts – such as the conflicts in Iraq – are more about the issue of world oil supply than anything else. It has been said that if Iraq's major resource was bananas then it's not likely that the allies would have invaded it. Oil is an important commodity for the western world – maybe the west was keen to make sure that it could still have access to it and so didn't want it to be controlled by Saddam Hussein. It's said that if global warming becomes a reality, then the next wars will be 'water wars' as countries fight each other to control and get access to vital water supplies. Already, in some Middle Eastern countries there have been tensions because one country builds a dam which harms the water supply of the country downriver. There have often been such economic reasons for wars.

Talk Point

Are wars for gain always wrong?

An Expression of Human Nature

Some argue that war is just human nature. Humans are naturally aggressive and need an outlet for that. War provides this outlet. This would mean that war is inevitable and will always be around. This is often linked to the 'Malthusian' argument which says that war is just one of 'nature's' ways of keeping the population in check. Every now and again, the human population gets to a point where it puts a strain on the earth's available resources. Without something to reduce this strain the system can't cope, and so wars come along to bring the population down to a more manageable level. So, it's maybe not even just human nature, but a part of nature.

The End Result of Lack of Communication

Some argue that wars are caused because countries get the wrong end of the stick. Maybe there's an initially straightforward disagreement which escalates and gets out of hand. Add in national pride and being seen to be politically strong and you have a dangerous recipe for conflict. It is often said that those who fight in a war sometimes don't have much of an idea of what the war is 'for'. Instead they trust that their national leaders are making the right decisions. But does this make sense? Sometimes national leaders have clashes of personality or want to appear strong leaders (or maybe just go down in history as one) – and so wars end up happening because of all this personal stuff. Perhaps if George Bush and Saddam Hussein had got together and baked cakes then the whole conflict in Iraq would never have happened. If it's only misunderstanding which leads to war – or lack of communication, then is that enough to justify a war?

Talk Point 3

Do you think that some reasons for going to war are better than others?

What are the Effects of War?

In any war there are direct and indirect victims. There can be different effects for those who go off to fight wars in foreign lands and those who stay at home, but not always. In countries that are invaded, ordinary citizens can end up being just as much at risk as the military, maybe more so as they don't have the equipment or skill to fight back so well.

Death and Destruction

Obviously people die in wars. Soldiers go off to fight knowing this is possible, but innocent civilians also die in bombing raids and other enemy actions. As well as this, the families of those who are killed, whether military or civilian, may have to live with their loss for the rest of their lives. This can have:

- health effects – as the people suffer depression and mental anguish due to their loss
- economic effects – as the family income is reduced by the loss of a loved one and
- emotional effects – as people struggle to come to terms with their loss.

This obviously relates to those directly affected – but it can go much deeper. Whole towns and societies can be affected by the increase in the number of people harmed by the death of a loved one, as well as bearing the effect of the loss of the people themselves. Also, some people aren't killed in war, but seriously injured either physically or psychologically. This may affect the rest of their life in all sorts of ways – changing how they live and so affecting everything they are linked to for the rest of their life.

As well as these, war usually involves some kind of destruction. This might be to the built environment – buildings old and new as well as infrastructure like schools and hospitals. It could affect ancient historic buildings and their contents (important art, books etc.) and so demoralise people through the destruction of things which are linked to their national identity. It can also involve the destruction of the natural environment. Military activities often release nasty chemicals and the by-products of modern weapons usually aren't environmentally friendly. Local climates can be changed and natural ecosystems altered dramatically. There are also very often leftovers of wars which can harm for many years to come. The occasional World War II unexploded bomb is still sometimes discovered in Scotland, and the placement of hidden landmines in some countries in South East Asia is still a major cause of death in these places.

Social and Economic Effects

Wars can result in widespread poverty. The normal economic functioning of a country is disrupted: it may be unable to trade and manufacture goods, services may not be possible in the normal way. It is also possible that industrial and agricultural practices have to change. This might be because factories and farmland are destroyed by military action (or its by-products). It can also be due to the fact that in war, a country has to put far more of its 'energy' into maintaining the war effort. Factories which made tractors may now have to make tanks and farms produce food for the war effort (or the invaders) rather than the country's own population. All of this can lead to economic change, which may result in widespread poverty. It is argued that a lot of poverty in the developing world is a direct result of time, energy and resources being used to support conflicts rather than improve people's lives. But on the other hand perhaps losing a war in the long-term might be even more disastrous for the country than the short-term troubles the war might bring. A war can often mean that the economic consequences stay with a country for a long time, making it hard for the country to recover properly.

War uses resources up with no regard for the future – and sadly, both the human and physical ones. These resources are not easy to replace and may damage a country long after the war is over. Along with poverty there could well be outbreaks of disease as the country's infrastructure is not able to cope with the demands of the war. Polluted water combined with reduced healthcare make for a very vicious circle of war and misery. When you put all these gloomy consequences together you can end up with very serious social change. A society's normal way of functioning can be completely disrupted by war, and the 'old certainties' of life change forever. People change in how they relate to each other, as well as in how they understand who they are and what their nation stands for. It can also change the nature of other societies. One of the features of war is often the displacement of people as refugees. This is a strain on them obviously and can be difficult for the country that receives them, which may itself be struggling in wartime.

Psychological Effects

War can scar the people involved in many ways. Some soldiers returning from wars are never quite 'themselves' again, having witnessed unimaginable horror (or been expected to commit atrocities themselves). The people left at home can suffer in this way too. A battle zone is one thing, but having your own normally quiet streets bombed and littered with the dead is another. People may suffer specific psychological problems like post traumatic stress disorder (known as 'shell shock' in

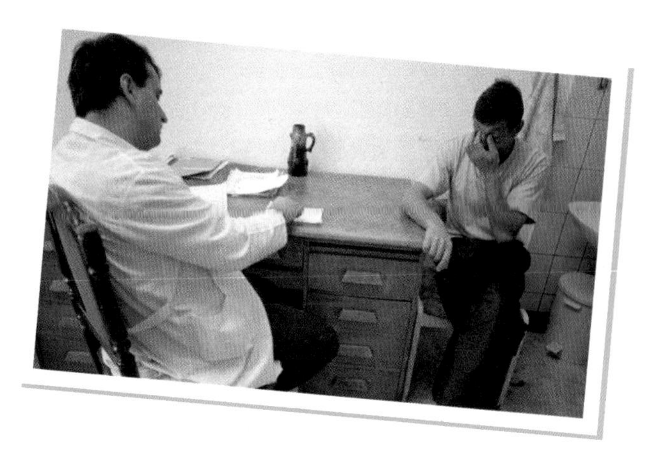

World War I), or just a more general angst about the world. Living through war changes people's whole view about the way the world is and what is good and evil. These effects can change people's personalities and lead to difficulties for them in many ways.

Time Out 1

What do you think are the worst effects of war?

Check Your Learning

1. Explain TWO possible reasons for war beginning.
2. Choose a war that you know about – why did it begin?
3. Do you think war is 'inevitable'?
4. Why can civilians suffer just as much as soldiers during a war?
5. How can war harm the environment and what can this harm lead to?
6. Explain ONE economic effect of war.
7. In what ways can war be psychologically harmful?

The Moral Implications of War

Is It Ever Right To Go To War?

Maybe war is just immoral: what can be right about it? Maybe everyone should just agree never to go to war again and that would be that. By its very nature, war calls into question what is and isn't moral. It involves killing, harming, taking, in fact, just about every kind of human nastiness you can imagine, and on a scale which is usually huge. So perhaps the biggest moral implication of war is war itself. Obviously wars happen and people of all walks of life justify them for different reasons. Some people will argue that war is morally justified because although war is always bad it is sometimes necessary. A Utilitarian position would be that although war causes a lot of pain, the pain is justified because the long-term benefits are greater. Utilitarians value freedom, and wars are sometimes necessary to bring freedom about. So although war causes pain for some people now, unless it is fought, greater pain and suffering might follow for far more people in the future. In this case the ends justify the means. Fighting a war may be necessary to safeguard freedom or a way of life or to protect something of value. A Utilitarian would ask whether, ultimately, the benefits of the war outweighed the drawbacks. If so, then the war can be morally justifiable.

Source 1

> The sole end for which mankind are warranted, individually or collectively, in interfering with the liberty of action of any of their number, is self protection
>
> ***On Liberty*, JS Mill (1859)**

Are Some Wars More Morally Justifiable Than Others?

Perhaps there are some reasons for going to war which make one war more right than another. Maybe going to war for defensive reasons is much more acceptable than for aggressive reasons. Maybe going to war to protect the minority from aggressors is more important than going to war just because you're pals with the country next door – or you want to show off that your country's tough. There's also the issue of fighting for your beliefs as opposed to some more practical ideal like freeing the oppressed. Is it right to fight for your beliefs (religious, political or otherwise)? Is it right for you to be sent off to war to fight for an ideology which you don't actually agree with? Because this is all so morally slippery, many people refer to the Just War Theory to guide them about when it is right to go to war or not. According to Just War Theory, going to war is morally acceptable when:

- there is a good reason for the war – to right wrongs or fight aggression
- it is the last resort – every other method has been tried
- the aim is to restore good over evil.

The problem here is that each of these statements can be thought of differently by different people. Who decides what is a good reason and a bad one? Obviously fighting back at an aggressor may be necessary, but perhaps there might be times when you need to strike first to have a meaningful advantage. If war is the last resort, that's fair enough, provided your enemy hasn't been building up strength while you've been negotiating. And what about good and evil? Does any good outcome really justify the evils of war?

Can There Be Rules About War?

You can be prosecuted after a war for 'war crimes' – odd you might think when killing's going on all over the place. However, it is agreed that there are certain rules which should be followed even during war. Part of the reason for this is so that wars are more likely to end. If people ignore the rules then the revenge and reprisals could go on forever. Again, the Just War Theory covers some of the principles of what's right and wrong during war:

- it should be proportional: you should do only what you need to do to achieve your objectives, no more
- military and civilian targets should be clearly separated, and prisoners and people who are invaded during war are entitled to some basic human rights – war isn't a licence to treat people any way you like

- certain methods are permitted in war and others aren't
- weapons should not be used indiscriminately, but directed at military targets.

Again, the problem is that during war people tend to act impulsively and don't think about the consequences of their actions. Usually too, each side thinks it will win and so won't have to worry about being prosecuted for war crimes afterwards. Also, the distinction between civilians and the military isn't always clear. What if it is suspected that civilians are protecting soldiers – do the civilians then become justifiable targets?

How Can We Respond To Aggression?

Responding to aggression in the form of war isn't too different from responding to aggression in any other situation. You see that the aggression forms a threat to you somehow and so you respond to that. This is all very similar to those in the Head's office at the start of this Chapter.

Attack

Obviously you can 'respond' to aggression by striking first.

The benefits of this are:

- you have the upper hand at the beginning and maybe disable your enemy's ability to strike back
- your enemy hasn't had any time to prepare for your attack so you can inflict more damage than you would have if they'd been ready for you
- you make your enemy re-think: they might decide that you mean business and aren't prepared to take you on, so a full-blown war might never begin
- your readiness for war is up and running while theirs is limping along – this might see you through to victory in the end.

The drawbacks are:

- maybe your enemy will see this as an unfair start and it'll really get them riled – their response to you therefore might be much worse than it would have been in the first place
- your enemy's friends might jump to their aid more quickly because of this sneaky way you've started the conflict off – this might ultimately be bad news for you
- maybe you've got it wrong and your enemy was bluffing (they had no intention of engaging in military action) and the world's sympathy is now with your enemy
- maybe you're not as tough as you think you are – your enemy responds to you more forcefully than you expected and you are left battered and bruised – this gives courage to the enemy and weakens your resolve.

Attack as a strategy is always a risky business. You have to be sure that it's the right thing to do and that you're going to do it right, otherwise you might have made a huge mistake.

Defence

This, of course, might not be something you choose, you just might have to do it.

The benefits of this are:
- you make sure that your enemy realises that if they're going to attack you then they'd better be ready for what you'll do to them in return
- it mobilises your people and makes them join the cause: maybe they'll have a new-found sense of national pride if their nation rises up against an aggressor
- you get your ability to fight back into gear: if you waited too long and planned it all out too carefully you might lose any advantage which you otherwise might have had
- you can choose what to protect first instead of waiting until the enemy had a stranglehold on you and the choice was made for you.

The drawbacks are:
- you may respond too soon and too weakly giving the enemy the advantage, you might actually lose out through not planning and preparing properly to respond to the aggressor
- your response might be a hopeless one – you might never be a match for the enemy and so it would be much more sensible for you just to give in and hope for the best
- you might just make the aggressor more aggressive, which might lead to them being even more nasty to you than they had planned to be
- you might draw the aggressor's allies into the fight, whereas if you didn't fight back they would stay out of it – so your defence might lead to escalation of the conflict.

Defence seems like the most obvious thing to do, but it might not be the right thing to do. Maybe it'll just make the situation worse.

Negotiation

Many wars have a period of negotiation before them (but not all). The really tricky thing here is to know how far to take the negotiation and to know if and when the negotiation has got to the stage where it's pointless.

The benefits of this are:
- the longer you negotiate, the longer you put off the war: if you're all sitting round the table

discussing things then you're not lobbing grenades at each other, which has the tendency to interfere with reasonable conversation
- while negotiating, you show to the world that you are reasonable and fair – this might gather up world sympathy for you, which you might need if the negotiations break down
- negotiation might stop the war from breaking out: maybe it is all a misunderstanding – maybe you can come to an agreement
- maybe negotiation can give you time to ready your armies and get the vulnerable to safety – maybe it just gives you time to be better prepared for an inevitable war.

The drawbacks are:
- the longer you talk, the more preparation time you lose and if you think the negotiation will work then maybe you don't get your military response properly ready – and if the negotiations fail then you'll be caught out
- maybe you're not being reasonable in the negotiations, giving your enemy vital political 'ammunition' to claim that you are being unfair – this could lead to you losing out on world sympathy and so not being supported when the time comes for war
- perhaps the negotiations will lead to you having to give up things you don't want to – things that you might not have lost during a war – so the negotiations were less effective for you than a war would have been
- perhaps your enemy is messing you about and has no intention of negotiating at all but instead is using it as a way to find as much about your weaknesses as possible.

Check Your Learning

1 Why might a Utilitarian support war?

2 Explain what the Just War Theory says about going to war.

3 Should there be rules observed during war?

4 Is 'attacking first' morally justifiable?

5 Should a country always defend itself from attack?

6 Do the drawbacks of negotiation outweigh the benefits?

The Pacifist Response to War

Throughout history there have been many who have felt that the causes of war were never enough to justify going to war and the effects of war were just too great to be justified for any reason. Such people have often worked against war in all sorts of ways, many have taken the view that pacifism is the correct response to war. Pacifism is where someone simply refuses to fight. Some pacifists think that there might be cases where you can defend yourself against a specific and individual threat, though others would disagree even with this. All pacifists are united in the belief that fighting in war is wrong – how can you fight against someone you don't even know just because your government says it is the right thing to do? Pacifists believe that violence is not the answer, reasonable negotiation is. If everyone just refused to fight then of course all wars would stop.

A Short History of Pacifism – the Conscientious Objectors

There have probably always been pacifists. The motivation for being a pacifist has taken many forms throughout history. There have always been people who refused to fight others, either for religious reasons or because they believed that fighting wasn't the right way to solve a problem or because they just believed that fighting against fellow human beings was wrong. Pacifism as a widely held ideal probably came to most people's attention during World War I with the conscientious objectors. Conscientious objectors were people who refused to take part in war. This was often for religious reasons, for example, the Society of Friends (also known as the Quakers) believe strongly in the idea of pacifism and so if you were a Quaker then you were most likely a pacifist – many conscientious objectors were Quakers.

However, many conscientious objectors were not religious people, but refused to fight because they believed that fighting is wrong as well as ineffective. Many were Humanists and they believe in the common humanity of all people – fairness, equality and so on. This led these conscientious objectors to refuse to fight because it went against their beliefs about human relationships and what makes society 'work'. World War I involved conscription, meaning that ordinary people could be 'called up' to fight even if they'd had nothing to do with the military before. Some conscientious objectors refused to have anything to do with the military – and that meant working in *any* job which had military links no matter how indirect – like making metal which would end up being made into guns. Some didn't go that far but simply refused to join the military in any shape or form. Some did join the military, but refused to do anything which involved combat. Many served as medical assistants – helping the wounded and dying. In fact, some carried out great acts of bravery to come to the aid of injured soldiers, but these acts of bravery were rarely reported or publicly rewarded. Many took the chance whenever possible to aid enemy troops too. Even on the battleground, some refused to wear any

kind of uniform, which in itself was a danger. A captured prisoner of war in uniform was generally treated fairly in those days, but a non-uniform captive would often be shot right away as a spy.

Source 2

Desmond T. Doss Sr., 87, an Army medic on Okinawa during World War II saved more than 75 wounded soldiers at great personal peril and became the first conscientious objector to receive the Medal of Honour. At the time, he was in the medical detachment of the 77th Infantry Division. A battalion of his comrades was fired on by the Japanese as its members scaled a 400-foot escarpment.

Refusing cover, Mr. Doss carried each of the 75 casualties one-by-one to the edge of the cliff and helped lower them by rope to safety. He continued similar rescue missions over the following days, also tending to the wounded by administering plasma as mortar fire struck around him.

During a nighttime attack May 21 near Shuri, he received injuries from a grenade blast. Instead of risking the larger mission, he spent hours nursing his wounds. Seeing a soldier in worse condition nearby, he directed help to tend to that man first. Still in range of enemy fire, he was hit and suffered a compound fracture in an arm.

'With magnificent fortitude he bound a rifle stock to his shattered arm as a splint and then crawled 300 yards over rough terrain to the aid station,' his Medal of Honor citation read.

'Through his outstanding bravery and unflinching determination in the face of desperately dangerous conditions Pfc. Doss saved the lives of many soldiers,' the citation continued. 'His name became a symbol throughout the 77th Infantry Division for outstanding gallantry far above and beyond the call of duty.'

www.washingtonpost.com/wp-dyn/content/article/2006/03/25/AR2006032501181.html

Many conscientious objectors saw the war through in these ways. However, most conscientious objectors had a very difficult time of it at home. Many were imprisoned (some remained in prison after the war had ended) and in prison were treated very badly – some lost their minds as their spirits were broken. Even if they survived military prison, many found it just as hard on the 'outside' after the war. They had difficulty getting jobs and were generally victimised by society. The reason was quite simple: people believed that they were cowards hiding behind their beliefs by refusing to fight and so put themselves in danger. Also, in times of war national pride becomes important to people. Conscientious objectors were seen as unpatriotic and people who brought shame to the UK by their 'cowardice'.

Of course it's not impossible that some people claimed to be conscientious objectors to escape fighting because of fear, but the overwhelming majority were not like this. The treatment they received in prison and at home was very difficult and it took great courage to stand up for your beliefs in this way. World War I was a new kind of warfare, even for professional soldiers, and there were many cases of 'shell-shocked' (often professional) soldiers refusing to return to the battlefields and then being shot for cowardice. It's only in the last few years that the government has issued apologies to the families of men treated in this way, and there's never really been any official government acknowledgment that the treatment of the conscientious objectors was wrong.

Contemporary Pacifism

Pacifism probably got its second lease of life in the peace-loving 1960s. Here, conflicts like Vietnam and the Cold War between the USA and the USSR made people very concerned about the future.

Conscription in the UK is over today so the need for conscientious objection is not currently present. However, pacifism remains alive and well around the world. Nowadays, it usually takes the form of protest groups campaigning against current conflicts. It can also take the form of going into war zones and helping those affected – like the organisation *Medicin Sans Frontiers*. The 'War on Terror' is currently on everyone's lips and has resulted in the invasion of Iraq. Afghanistan still bubbles away with the threat of escalation and there are tensions between the west and Iran. The Middle East remains a hotbed of possible strife and around the world there is always the threat of new skirmishes and tensions leading to war. Pacifists campaign for peaceful resolutions to conflict. They might do this through acting as pressure groups or through taking part in the political process – or just through educating others, often by doing no more than living a pacifist lifestyle.

Check Your Learning

1. What is pacifism?
2. What are the similarities and differences between religious and non-religious pacifists?
3. What do you think the UK government should do for the families of pacifists who were badly treated during World Wars I and II?
4. Do you think pacifism is a reasonable position to hold?

The UN Charter and Conventions on War

The United Nations sees itself as a peacekeeping organisation. Members of the UN get together to agree on international laws, and other ways of ensuring that fairness and justice is available for all. This means that the UN puts a great deal of energy into trying to make the world a fairer place so that the tensions and conflicts of modern life are less likely to lead to war, for example, helping countries with their economies and education systems. The **UN Charter** has, as its principal aims:

- to practice tolerance and live together in peace with one another as good neighbours
- to unite our strength to maintain international peace and security
- to ensure, by the acceptance of principles and the institution of methods, that armed force shall not be used, save in the common interest
- to employ international machinery for the promotion of the economic and social advancement of all peoples (www.un.org/aboutun.charter/).

But the UN also realises that sometimes wars happen and, when war does break out, it often steps in to try to restore peace and order. This is done through the UN Security Council which may impose economic or diplomatic sanctions on any country which is acting aggressively or breaching UN guidelines in some way. If these do not work, then the UN can take action to restore international peace.

Article 39

The Security Council shall determine the existence of any threat to the peace, breach of the peace, or act of aggression and shall make recommendations, or decide what measures shall be taken in accordance with Articles 41 and 42, to maintain or restore international peace and security.

The UN aims to avoid military action as much as possible, though sometimes it can't be avoided and so...

Article 42

Should the Security Council consider that measures provided for in Article 41 would be inadequate or have proved to be inadequate, it may take such action by air, sea, or land forces as may be necessary to maintain or restore international peace and security. Such action may include demonstrations, blockade, and other operations by air, sea, or land forces of members of the United Nations.

For the full text of the UN Charter see: www.un.org/aboutun/charter/

So, the UN may go into a country to restore order and engage in armed conflict, even if it sees itself as a peacekeeper. Some argue that the UN is too tightly controlled by the major world powers, like the USA, and so is more likely to act in the interests of those powers than other countries, though the UN has many checks on its activities which are designed to avoid this.

In the case of a World War, or where war breaks out and continues despite UN involvement, there are international conventions about what is acceptable during war. The aim of all of these is to ensure that, even in war, some level of humanity is retained and that wars don't just become a case of do whatever you want. For example, the **Geneva Convention** is concerned with the conduct of war: who is and isn't a proper target, how prisoners of war should be treated and so on. It takes the view that during war there are still rules about how the war should be conducted so that the war ends as quickly as possible and doesn't drag on in a spiral of revenge because of atrocities committed during the war. It states:

1 Persons taking no active part in the hostilities, including members of armed forces who have laid down their arms and those placed hors de combat by sickness, wounds, detention, or any other cause, shall in all circumstances be treated humanely, without any adverse distinction founded on race, colour, religion or faith, sex, birth or wealth, or any other similar criteria (www.unhchr.org/english/law/prisonerwar.htm).

As well as these there are many other conventions concerning both going to war and what is acceptable during war. The **Hague Convention**, for example seeks to set out rules about the protection of cultural property in the event of armed conflict. This relates to the treatment of historic buildings as well as works of art and the like.

Talk Point 4

Should we be concerned about what happens to historic buildings during a war?

There are many international law guidelines about war – far too many to go into here – all covering different aspects of war. But they all aim to do the same thing – ensure that war involves as little suffering as possible and that life returns to normal as soon as possible. For a full list of some relevant international law see: www.hrweb.org/legal/undocs.html.

Christian Views of War

Source 3

The Methodist Church teaches that war is contrary to the spirit, teaching and purpose of Jesus Christ. On the other hand Jesus did not condemn the Centurion (Luke 7:1–10) or even Pilate himself for being part of the military arm. Instead he reminded Pilate that he had received his authority from a greater power and remained accountable to that power (John 19:10–11). The Christian pacifist does not necessarily condemn the use of every kind of force, but refuses to employ force unaccountably or to destroy others, for example in either personal or State violence.

The Christian non-pacifist does not justify every war, but reluctantly recognises that violence (force) may be used when authorised to defend against aggression, to rectify a breach of a boundary, or to restrain or replace a 'notorious and tyrannical' despot. The Church upholds the right of individual members conscientiously to choose between these positions, and offers pastoral support to those on both sides of the debate.

www.methodist.org.uk/static/factsheets/fs_peaceandwar.htm

This balanced quote makes it quite clear that Christians have a variety of views about war. Generally Christians would prefer there never to be war, because their faith is based on love for others, kindness humane treatment of all and war tends to be the opposite of these. The Christian teaching 'turn the other cheek' seems to suggest that Jesus himself was a pacifist, as even after a personal attack he seems to say that the Christian should not retaliate with further violence.

However, he does not tell soldiers to give up their warrior ways – just that they should be careful about how they behave as soldiers. Throughout history, Christians have been involved in wars – the religious orders of the middle ages like the Knights Templar were odd mixtures of holy men and warriors – in their opinion, fighting for their faith. Modern Christianity includes absolute pacifists like the Quakers, as well as military chaplains from many forms of Christianity and ordinary soldiers who believe that fighting a war for the right reasons is perfectly compatible with their Christian faith.

Buddhist Views of War

Buddhism is often thought to be a religion which is completely peace-loving. This is partly true. Most Buddhists are likely to be pacifists because one of the central beliefs of Buddhism is not harming any other living being. Aggression is completely contrary to Buddhist teaching. Buddhists however might argue that it is acceptable to defend yourself. Many Buddhist temples are famous for their martial arts. Karate, for example, means 'open hand': a way of defending yourself without weapons and based on the idea of inflicting no more harm on an aggressor than is necessary. The

Dalai Lama has never asked the people of Tibet to fight back against what he sees as the Chinese invaders. Instead he has always taught that understanding and compassion are the only ways forward.

The Buddhist monk has many additional precepts which must be followed, most of which would make it impossible to take part as a combatant in a war. Also, famously, some Buddhist monks voluntarily burned themselves to death as a protest at the Vietnam war, which would suggest that your own death is preferable to fighting back. It's not that simple though. Buddhists believe in the idea of skilful actions and it is this which might allow a Buddhist to engage in war. Skilful actions is the idea that what is right in any situation might be different according to the situation, the people involved and so on. So, for example if the Buddhist was convinced that a war was the only way to prevent even more violence and horror for a long time to come then he might, regretfully, take part in it. The skilful thing to do in a situation might be to defend the weak and this might mean taking part in violent action to prevent a greater tragedy.

Source 4

Dalai Lama's acceptance speech for his Nobel Prize for Peace Oslo 1989

As a Buddhist monk, my concern extends to all members of the human family and, indeed, to all sentient beings who suffer. I believe all suffering is caused by ignorance. People inflict pain on others in the selfish pursuit of their happiness or satisfaction. Yet true happiness comes from a sense of brotherhood and sisterhood. We need to cultivate a universal responsibility for one another and the planet we share. Although I have found my own Buddhist religion helpful in generating love and compassion, even for those we consider our enemies, I am convinced that everyone can develop a good heart and a sense of universal responsibility with or without religion.

www.tibet.com/DL/nobelaccept.html

All tremble at violence; all fear death. Putting oneself in the place of another, one should not kill nor cause another to kill

Dhammapada 129

Viewpoints Independent of Religious Belief and War

Many WWI conscientious objectors were humanists, and many organisations campaigning for peace today are based on non-religious ideals. Humanists believe that while war may sometimes be necessary, it is always something society should try to avoid as far as possible. There should be more peaceful ways to settle disagreements and our common humanity should guide us about what's right. Human reason and intelligence can help us to understand how wars come about, and so also help us to avoid them. Many Humanists might take a Utilitarian view of war (although Buddhists and Christians might do this too!), that although the 'cost' of war is often terrible, the cost of not going to war might be even greater. This means that wars may have to be fought for 'the greater good'. The sacrifice of some may have to be the price paid for the safe future of many.

Source 5

Professor Richard Norman of The British Humanist Association states:

All too often wars achieve nothing except terrible suffering, leaving a legacy of bitterness which sows the seeds of future wars. Most humanists are likely to say that, because we should value every human life as something unique and precious, we should look sceptically at the reasons governments give for inflicting death and destruction in war. But most humanists would also say that we have to look hard at each individual case, for just occasionally war might be the lesser evil.

www.humanism.org.uk

Check Your Learning

1. What are the basic elements of the UN Charter?
2. What does the Geneva Convention aim to do?
3. What is the Hague Convention?
4. Do you think that people pay much attention to these charters and conventions during wartime?
5. Should a Christian support war?
6. How would a Buddhist argue that it might be necessary to fight in a war?
7. Why might a Humanist oppose war?
8. What are the differences and similarities between the viewpoints about war you have looked at in this section?

Extension Activities

Knowledge, Understanding and Evaluation through Practical Activities

1 For each of the characters in the stimulus material, how might a Christian, Buddhist and viewpoint independent of religious belief respond to what each character did (and their 'excuse')?

2 Do some research about the start of a war. How did it begin? What were the major causes of war in this case? In what ways was it attempted to avoid war? Write a report of your findings.

3 Carry out some further research into a recent conflict/war. Using the headings about the effects of war in this section, explain what the effects of war were in this conflict. You should write this up as an illustrated report using images and eyewitness accounts where possible.

4 Write a short information leaflet for Christians OR Buddhists OR Humanists answering the question 'Is it ever right to go to war?' Try to explore a range of viewpoints within your chosen faith/belief system.

5 Design a display board about conscientious objectors. Explain what the beliefs behind it are, as well as giving some real-life examples of how conscientious objectors were treated at home. You should also include information about objectors who were awarded bravery medals (see www.bbc.co.uk/ww2peopleswar/stories/43/a3697743.shtml for an example of a British conscientious objector/war hero).

6 Prepare a short talk about the UN and war. You should try to refer to current conflicts as well as UN documentation.

7 A Christian, a Buddhist and a Humanist get together to talk about the most recent war/conflict. Research their viewpoints further and write the conversation they might have.

8 Find some examples of pro- and anti-war music and create a presentation on this. You could perhaps do a Powerpoint display here, incorporating the songs as well as the words.

Unit Assessment Question

Intermediate 1: Explain what is meant by a conscientious objector. **4KU**

Intermediate 2: Explain TWO things the UN Charter prohibits during war. **4KU**

Higher: Describe how ONE religious viewpoint might support the idea of war. **4KU**

Sample Exam Question

Intermediate 1: Should a religious person fight in a war? Give TWO reasons for your answer. **4AE**

Intermediate 2: Describe TWO ways in which war can affect soldiers. **4KU**

Higher: Referring to UN Charters and Conventions in your answer, how might these Charters and Conventions protect people during war? **4KU 4AE**

Homework

Your country is at war. You have been called up for active service as you were once a member of the armed forces. However, you are now a conscientious objector. Write a letter to the government explaining your position and what you intend to do about your call-up.

Personal Reflection

Would you fight in a war for your country? Are there some things you would fight for and some you wouldn't? What would you do if you were called up for war tomorrow?

CHAPTER 11 War and Peace: Modern Armaments

Is It Morally Justifiable To Use Modern Armaments In Warfare?

Memo

To: Rear Admiral General Sir George Lord Fortescue-Pole, Chief of Defence.
From: Janey de Valiumci, Public Relations Senior Creative Director, Real PR Solutions Co. ('Creatively speaking to the People')
Re: Naming of new smart missile®™

Dear Rear,

With reference to the commissioned brief from her Majesty's government to name the Ministry of Defence's latest smart missile® ™, following extensive consultation we are pleased to present you with our suggestion.

Getting it right is our business and we're aware that selling a product like this to the public (and certainly to its consumers!) is always going to be tricky. Therefore we think it right to share with you a little of our creative process, and we don't do this for all our clients I can assure you! We began thinking along the lines of mythological beings of great power and authority – Zeus, Titan, Medusa, Thor – but we feel this approach is so lame these days having been done so often before. Then we considered something a little quirkier – stressing the power of this weapon through the reverse psychology of a name which might bring a chuckle. As it's a

➜

'smart' weapon and links with the idea of intelligence, we came up with countdown, blockbuster, High IQ, scrabble (as it certainly would make people scrabble and you'll no doubt flatten a few blocks with it!).

However, we thought this might be a little too subtle for the military. We moved then from the properties of the weapon to its location. From your brief we gather that as the weapon contains highly dangerous radioactive uranium, it will be based in Scotland so as to cause minimal damage in the event of any malfunction. We also realised that no weapon has been given a specifically Scottish name and felt that this might endear it to the Scottish people and cause them to welcome its deployment right in the centre of Edinburgh (somewhere called Gilmoretown we believe). An inspired idea incidentally, locating it in an underground vault beneath a secondary school and building the school a swimming pool as a cover for the construction work – there are obviously some people in your organisation who would fit right into ours!

So, to the Scottish-flavoured names: Obviously the Big Man was a possibility as was the Hard Man. In the interests of gender equality, we briefly considered Big Senga. However, we're all agreed on the final choice which we know will meet with your approval. We think it combines the Big idea with a distinctively Scottish feel. So – our name for this new piece of weaponry is... the Pure Big Hairy Bampot. Of course, if desired, this can be referred to publicly as the PBHB Missile, but its full title is sure to bring a smile to our home troops every time it is deployed!

We look forward to your response.

Janey

Janey de Valiumci, DPHBCNM (Hons)

Time Out

What would you name a powerful new missile?

Sticks and Stones

Obviously, if you think war is wrong then it doesn't matter if you fight armed with a smart missile or a big stick. Modern warfare, however, has become highly technologically advanced. Killing can be quicker, easier, more efficient and altogether less personal than it used to be. Its one thing to hack someone to death with a two-handed sword and quite another to drop a bomb on a city, kill thousands and be home again in time for tea. With the application of modern technology, a whole new range of moral issues become important even if the original moral issue remains the same – is it right to take life during a war?

Some argue that modern armaments make war more efficient by ending the war more quickly than conventional weapons. They argue that such weapons can more effectively target military sites and avoid civilian casualties ('collateral damage' they call this). They also argue that such weapons pose less of a threat to those who use them, as opposed to the dangers of finding that your gun has run out of ammunition as the enemy comes charging towards you. How true is all of this? Are modern armaments really a step forward or a return to darker, more callous days? Is an impersonal war less morally justifiable than one that has the personal touch?

Talk Point 1

Is war any different according to how it is fought?

Conventional Weapons

World War I probably saw the first deployment of modern technology on a grand scale. This was more notable because there was a clear contrast between countries which had it and those who didn't. Tales are told of one nation's horse-riding cavalry being mown down by another's tanks and artillery. Multi-round machine guns are more than a match for guns which need reloading after each shot (and remember to keep your gunpowder dry). Here also, little light aircraft could swoop over a battlefield and the pilot could chuck bombs down on the soldiers below. Cannons became more mobile, more accurate and more deadly. Instead of a lump of lead being fired, shells were lobbed which exploded on impact spreading their deadly contents much further than the average cannonball. Of course, guns and cannons had been a feature of warfare for hundreds of years by this time, but their efficiency by the early 20th Century was much improved.

By World War II, things had moved on even further. Buzz bombs capable of being fired over long distances were developed and air raids became a common feature of the war in Europe with mass destruction in towns and cities caused by bombers who could easily complete a mission and return home within a few hours. Jet engines replaced propellers, submarines replaced ships. Even so, troops on the ground were still deployed with rifles and grenades, though these too were much better than before. Also, World War II ended, in the Pacific at any rate, with the deployment of nuclear weapons against Japan – the world's first use of weapons of mass destruction. After this war, many other conflicts involved new weaponry being used: chemical weapons in Vietnam, 'agent orange' and smart missiles in Kosovo and the war in Iraq. It's probable that the future will see more of this, with remote controlled bombs, guided from the comfort of an office, falling on far off targets. Perhaps even the failed 'star wars' plans of the USA might return – where satellites armed with laser technology could destroy whole cities at the press of a button. But that's for the future, or rather hopefully not. Let's have a closer look at conventional weapons first.

Benefits

The line between conventional weapons and modern armaments is quite subtle, but let's make the distinction the amount of personal involvement the weapon requires. For our purposes therefore, a conventional weapon is one which needs to be used directly by a military operative – so it could be a night-sighted, laser-guided, hand-held rocket launcher or it could be a sharp bayonet. It could also be a tank or a piece of rolling field artillery.

The major benefit of such a weapon is that its use is directly under the control of the person who wields it. This means that he (or she, but let's not get into that moral issue here) can choose when to fire it and when not to fire it. He has control over when it's used and who it is used against. This means that he's more likely to direct it against an enemy threat in the form of the enemy military than against a group of schoolchildren who just happen to come from the enemy's country.

So, such weapons can be targeted specifically at strategic enemy targets, make military gains quickly and bring a battle to a swift end. Weapons like this are unlikely to hit civilian targets or be discharged by accident. They will 'take out' specific targets as directed. This all means that the fighting is restricted to fighting between soldiers and that innocent civilians are protected as far as possible. It also means that the weapon does what it is required to do and no more – it can kill one soldier or twenty, but not more than this if that's not militarily necessary.

Dangers

On the other hand, such weapons require direct human control. This puts warriors in the front line and exposes them to a great deal of personal danger when you compare standing in a machine gun placement with sitting in a computer control room directing long-range missiles. Conventional weapons involve risking your own military in more direct action.

As well as this, such weapons still depend on individual decisions by military operatives. Although they are designed to be used against specific military targets, in a battle zone you're probably not likely to be thinking very reasonably and not taking too much time to work out if someone or something is a military threat or not.

The modern efficiency of such weapons is also a drawback – one little pull on a trigger can release an awful lot of destruction, and you might just make a mistake. Modern battles are as likely to take place in towns and cities as on open rolling fields, and here it isn't always easy to make a quick and accurate decision about whether someone is a justifiable military target or an innocent civilian. There are often cases where an enemy military might use a 'human shield' – hiding behind civilians or in civilian buildings. Therefore the use of a conventional weapon always includes the possibility that it might result in a mistake and the intended target confused with an unintended one.

Also, even if the target is clearly military, it is still possible that innocent civilians will be harmed as a side-effect. Aerial bombing is conventional weaponry but throughout its use has always resulted in errors and unintended side effects which kills and harms innocent civilians.

Conventional weapons therefore suffer from the problem that their use can be indiscriminate. One of the rules of war is that military action should discriminate between justifiable (military) targets and unjustifiable (civilian) targets. Though of course, it's never that simple. During the Vietnam conflict, the USA argued that the indiscriminate bombing of towns and villages was justified because 'innocent civilians' were protecting the enemy military. Modern bombing has often been justified by the claim that enemy warriors are using non-military buildings from which to launch attacks.

There are more general dangers associated with the use of any weapons – like the possibility that the use of any weapon is more likely to lead to an escalation of violence, or that even conventional weapons are a drain on a country's economy and resources.

There are also psychological dangers. With the use of conventional weapons the military operative is more closely involved – he can often see immediately the gruesome outcome of his use of a weapon. This probably results in long-lasting mental scars which the use of modern armaments might avoid.

So, in response to the limitations of conventional weapons, governments have turned to modern technology and applied it to warfare. The broad aim of modern armaments therefore is:

- to pose a greater threat to an enemy and so perhaps prevent conflict arising in the first place by their deterrence value
- to bring any existing conflict to a quicker end
- to inflict more damage more efficiently and more specifically against military targets
- to be able to be used with less direct danger to those using them.

To this end, many world governments have invested heavily in the development of modern armaments in the hope that their existence might be more likely to keep the peace rather than lead to war and, if war does break out, be more likely to lead to success in the war for your country as opposed to the enemy's.

Talk Point **2**

Do the dangers of conventional weapons outweigh their advantages?

Check Your Learning

1 What might the 'original moral issue' about war be?
2 How did the technology of war change from World War I onwards?
3 What was the 'Star Wars' programme?
4 Why do you think it was eventually cancelled by the US government?
5 Explain ONE benefit of a conventional weapon.
6 Explain ONE danger of a conventional weapon.
7 Why do you think some governments think that modern armaments are an improvement upon conventional weapons? Do you agree?

Modern Armaments

Smart Missiles

This is basically a missile which has highly developed computer guidance systems within the missile.

Benefits

It can be programmed to strike a specific target by entering coordinates, perhaps using global satellite positioning systems or map references. This makes it much more likely that it will strike only its specified target.

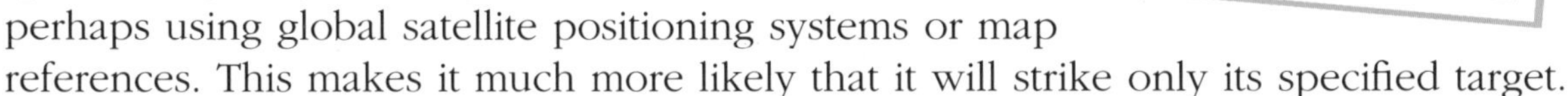

It can be programmed to seek out certain properties – like heat seeking missiles which can 'chase' a moving enemy target like a jet. This means that it is more likely to strike its target as it can change course to match the target's movements.

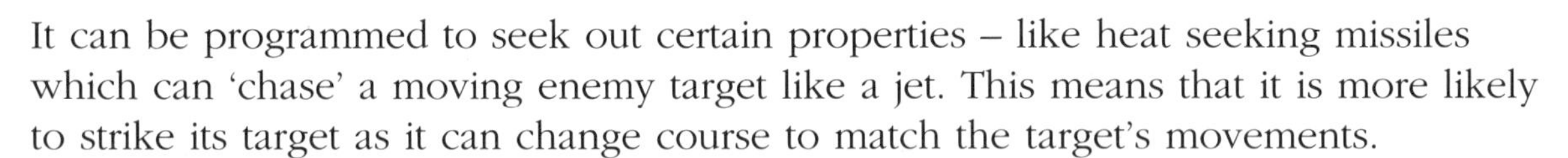

It can be guided remotely towards its target.

There is minimal danger to the people controlling the missile as the missiles can be launched from a very long range, well out of the way of potential enemy fire. The missile may be destroyed, but the person controlling it will be far away and safe from harm. This also means that the controller avoids the more traumatic and bloodier side to war, making it more like a computer game than the messy business of conventional battle.

If properly programmed the missile should hit its target and nothing else – it should therefore not harm civilians.

It can be used immediately whereas getting conventional weapons to a war zone takes time, is costly and dangerous. Smart missiles are quick and require minimum fuss to deploy.

Simply possessing such weapons may make an enemy less likely to strike. If they know that your country can respond in this highly effective and very destructive way they might not enter into action in the first place, especially if their country is still dependent on conventional weapons which may take a long time to get organised (by which time you'll have smart-bombed them into submission). So, they're a good deterrent.

Dangers

No matter how efficient you think they are, they're rarely 100 per cent accurate. In places where they have been used there are still examples of them going wrong and hitting the wrong targets because the technology fails, resulting in widespread civilian casualties, or friendly fire incidents where your own military or your allies are the unintentional targets.

Even if they were 100 per cent accurate, you would still need to be completely sure that the target you were going for was actually a military target, so your military intelligence must be right. Again, there have been many cases where smart missiles have hit the right target but it turns out that this shouldn't have been the target in the first place.

The storage of such weapons is always a potential danger. They have to be stored away from the reaches of a potential enemy – malfunctions might lead to accidental deployment against someone who is not your enemy – resulting in the start of an unintended war, or the weapon may go off in storage causing destruction.

Weapons like this are costly, they put a strain on your country's resources. Even if they are never used, just having them has major cost implications. They have to be housed, maintained, tested and so on – all of which doesn't come cheap. Is it right to be spending big money on such things when that money could be spent elsewhere in your country, perhaps on more worthwhile things? It's hard to find out just how expensive a smart missile is, but it has been suggested that that average cost for an AGM130A smart missile is $300,000.

Finally, one of the benefits might also be a danger. When you turn warfare into nothing more than a glorified computer game by using missiles such as this you make warfare impersonal and seemingly unreal. Perhaps you might make it easier therefore for wars to begin and continue, because the warriors will never see the direct results of their actions and so not be aware of the horror which is the result of the deployment of a smart missile. This might make wars both more likely and more likely to last longer.

Talk Point

3

Is a smart missile worth the money?

Weapons of Mass Destruction (WMDs): Chemical Weapons

Source 1

The Evangelical Christian John Stott calls chemical, biological and nuclear weapons:

'ABC weapons; they surely constitute the most gruesome alphabet ever conceived'

Citing an Ecumenical group in the USA who examined the morality of Weapons of Mass Destruction he says:

'What these Christian groups affirm about nuclear weapons is equally applicable to chemical and biological weapons. For all three, being indiscriminate in their effects, are indefensible in their use'

New Issues Facing Christians Today, Stott J, Marshall Pickering 1995 pp 109 & 110

According to the Parliamentary Office of Science and Technology of the UK government, there are thousands of poisonous substances which could be use as chemical weapons, but only a few are actually usable in practice. These act quickly and cause very serious reactions including almost instant death. They can be grouped as follows:

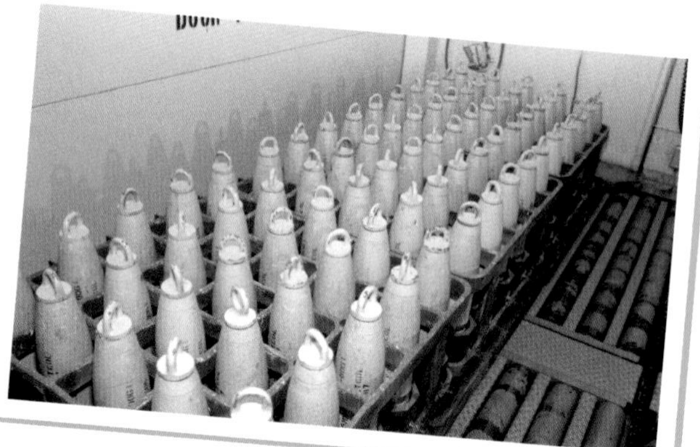

- choking agents, for example, chlorine gas which causes your lungs to fill with fluid meaning you can't absorb oxygen
- blood agents, for example, hydrogen cyanide which stops your cells using oxygen
- nerve agents, for example, sarin which interferes with normal nerve functioning
- blister agents, for example, mustard gas which can cause harm to the lining of the lungs.

For a fuller list of chemical weapons see www.parliament.uk.

Chemical weapons have been around for a long time – it is believed that the Spartans used sulphur fumes against the enemy in 400BC. Mustard gas was used in World War I and the defoliant Agent Orange used during the Vietnam War. Interestingly, chemical weapons were not used during World War II. Some claim that this was because Adolf Hitler experienced their use as a German soldier in World War I and refused to use them in battle as a result (though, of course, the Nazis used cyanide gas in the concentration camp gas chambers).

Benefits

Chemical weapons can be highly effective. It doesn't take much to inflict a great number of casualties. They can be deadly even in very small amounts and large quantities of them can often be made quite quickly and cheaply compared to other weapons.

They don't cause any destruction: you could in theory destroy every living thing in a city, but leave the city standing unaffected. This would mean that, once the chemical had cleared, you could take everything which was in the city as the spoils of war.

They can be delivered over a great distance in fairly cheap conventional missiles.

They can disable instead of kill, enabling you to move in and complete the job with very little danger to your troops.

They can be introduced to a location in simple and covert ways, like being introduced through an air-conditioning system or in a water supply. You can even kill using anthrax by sending it through the post in an ordinary envelope. In this way, they can be very specific: you kill only the intended target and there are no innocent casualties.

They might well act as a deterrent, putting your enemies off going to war with you out of fear that you might use chemical weapons.

Dangers

At all times during the production and deployment of such chemical agents there is the danger of an accidental release. This might kill people who are on your side – military or innocent civilians – and this can be widespread. This is just as likely when you just possess such weapons as when you're actually using them.

Chemical reactions are often unpredictable in certain environmental conditions. Your chemical weapons may, therefore, not target those they should and end up killing the wrong people entirely. Once released, unlike a gun or a bomb, chemical weapons can end up doing unpredictable things – things which are out of your control.

If such weapons fall into enemy hands they could be used against you. This is true of course of all weapons, but chemical weapons can kill in very small quantities and kill vast numbers. If you have a corrupt scientist working on the building of a bomb it is far less easy for him to hand one of those over to the enemy, this is not so with a few small bottles of sarin nerve gas.

Chemical weapons are probably too easy to create and so might end up in the hands of all sorts of dodgy people.

As soon as you use chemical weapons you send the signal to your enemy that it is acceptable to use them and this might lead to the rapid escalation of a conflict into an even more widespread and deadly war with far more casualties.

Chemical weapons are probably inhumane ways to kill – sarin gas can take up to 30 agonising minutes to kill the victim – remember that most world governments agree that even in war there have to be some rules. Killing enemies in this way goes against many of those rules.

Weapons of Mass Destruction (WMDs): Biological Weapons

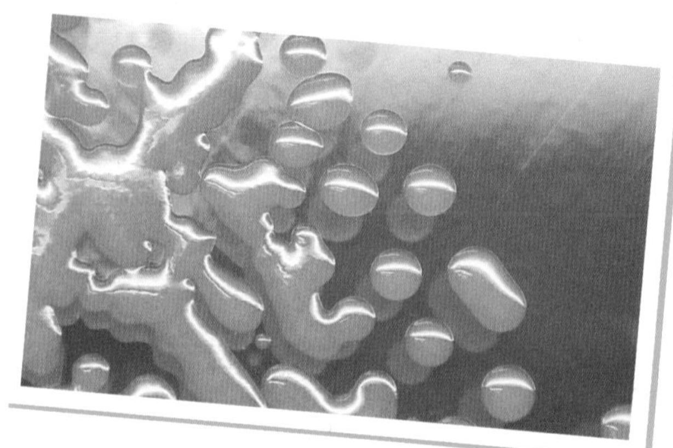

This can be anything from a naturally occurring infectious disease to a toxin specifically created as a weapon. It is said that in the Middle Ages, corpses of those who had died of bubonic plague were catapulted into castles so they would infect the population inside the castle. Harmful biological agents occur quite widely in nature and don't take much to have them able to be used in a war situation. Anthrax, hantavirus and smallpox are all examples of biological nasties which can be turned into weapons and let loose on an unsuspecting enemy.

Benefits

Biological weapons are quite easy to introduce into a system: they can be introduced to a water supply and slowly infect those who drink the water. They can be deployed without any need for acts of aggression, so your enemy doesn't know they've been attacked until it is far too late.

They are very easy to make and comparatively quite cheap.

They can be very effective: once released they can either kill only the intended target (like anthrax) or spread and infect whole populations with only the need for one carrier, for example, hantavirus.

They too can kill living things while leaving buildings and property intact. Once the danger has passed, what was your enemy's is now yours.

They can be introduced to animals, people or crops – this means that you could destroy your enemy's economy or ability to survive – leaving them unable to retaliate in the event of a military attack by you

They possibly have very good deterrent value. If your enemy knows you have them and would use them it might put them off attacking you, especially if they don't have such weapons.

Dangers

Like chemical weapons, there's always the danger of infecting your own people by accident during production or deployment.

Even more than chemical weapons, biological weapons can easily mutate out of your control. You may start off with something which just kills your enemy, but this biological entity might mutate and end up killing all life on earth, biological weapons are very unpredictable.

Using biological weapons might lead to the rapid escalation of a conflict once the

enemy knows what you have done. They may respond even more violently based on the belief that now they are infected they don't have much to lose by responding with all they've got – you might end up getting more than you bargained for – this might mean that they use their biological weapons too.

Using biological weapons means you can't always choose who you kill, this goes against the rules of war where you should target only military targets and even then only in proportion to what needs to get the job done. Biological weapons go way beyond both of those principles.

Whereas chemical weapons can 'clear up' with time, biological weapons may lead to consequences which last for a very long time indeed, especially because of their unpredictability. Perhaps your action will lead to an enemy population which could infect your population for hundreds of years to come. Perhaps your enemy might wait until those who survive the attacks can regroup (and it is always possible that some targets could develop a random immunity to the weapon – that's evolution after all), then they might strike back and your population will get it all back.

Time Out 2

Some believe that the biggest problem of chemical and biological weapons is that they might fall into the hands of terrorists. What do you think?

Check Your Learning

1. Explain what a 'smart missile' is.
2. Describe TWO possible benefits and dangers of a smart missile.
3. Do you think a government should spend money on smart missiles instead of conventional weapons?
4. Give ONE example of how chemical weapons have already been used in war.
5. What do you think is the greatest possible danger of chemical weapons?
6. What do you think is the greatest possible advantage of biological weapons?
7. If you were an MP, would you support the use of chemical or biological weapons? Explain your views.

Weapons of Mass Destruction (WMDs): Nuclear Weapons

During the Cold War between the superpowers, the USA and USSR's collections of WMDs either kept us all on our toes and held back conflict, or were just an accident waiting to happen – depending upon your point of view. At the end of the cold war, WMDs of the nuclear variety were decommissioned (put out of action) or so it is said... Most recently, Iran has been the target of complaints that it is doing nuclear research, maybe with a view to having a stock of nuclear WMDs and North Korea has been testing its own, all raising international tensions.

A nuclear weapon is basically a big bomb. The explosive power of this is phenomenal, because it is the result of a nuclear chain reaction which releases an incredible amount of destructive energy instantly. Nuclear weapons kill targets in a staged way depending upon how close you are to the point where the bomb lands. Those at the point of detonation will be vaporised immediately. Those further away may be killed by the force of the blast, others by various forms of radiation, some of which will damage cells and take a very long time to kill you very painfully. In fact, exposure to nuclear radiation might not kill you but damage body cells in such a way that your children and children's children might be genetically damaged for many generations to come. In short, a nuclear blast can kill millions, immediately or over a long period of time – and that's without mentioning the side-effects of destruction and damage to the economy and long-term stability of a country. For a full explanation of the effects of a nuclear blast see http://en.wikipedia.org/wiki/Nuclear_explosion#Direct_effects.

Benefits

Nuclear weapons are just about as deadly as you get. They kill over a wide range with ruthless effectiveness, crippling a city or even a country in an instant. After the detonation of the nuclear weapons in Japan in World War II, Japan immediately surrendered.

Nuclear weapon deployment might bring a conflict to a speedy end – so sparing the possible casualties of a war which could go on for a long time.

As long as the site of the detonation is far from your country and your armies there's not much risk to your own people from the detonation of the bomb.

One bomb can cause utter devastation of life and property. After the bombing of Hiroshima in World War II there wasn't much left standing in the city, this can not only cripple a country but demoralise a whole nation.

Nuclear technology is costly but not completely out of the average country's grasp. The actual science is quite straightforward, in fact you can find out how to put a nuclear bomb together on some Internet sites. As long as you get hold of some plutonium you're away. Given too that one weapon can be so effective, it won't take long before you're up and running.

Some argue that the very existence of nuclear weapons keeps the peace, because they act as a deterrent. If you and your enemy has them, neither will use them because they'll fear you striking back. This idea went by the glorious name of Mutually Assured Destruction (yes, that's MAD) and was the idea that if one country used nuclear weapons its target would use them in return – and as nuclear weapons launches were often computer controlled, in immediate response to the detection of a first strike, an nuclear war could begin without any human ever making a choice to fire or not.

Dangers

Again, the production, storage and deployment of such weapons always involves potential risk to your own people, either the scientists developing the bombs or the military deploying them. The materials which make up nuclear weapons (like radioactive uranium) are very damaging to human health, causing cellular destruction and alteration. This can lead to cancers as well as genetic defects which can be passed on to generations to come.

Also, nuclear weapon by-products like nuclear waste are very difficult to control and store – nuclear waste lasts for thousands and thousands of years. So for one bomb today you put people's lives at home at risk for a long time to come.

Nuclear weapons still cost money – maybe you could be doing better things with that money.

There's always the danger of accidental launch. It is claimed that this happened more than once during the Cold War and that World War III almost began by accident, either that or some crazy world leader gives the order for an attack which leads to world war.

Nuclear fallout might still affect your troops or your country – even if your bomb goes off halfway around the world. The radiation can be absorbed by particulate matter and weather systems can take it all around the world. This happened after the nuclear accident at the Chernobyl Nuclear power plant. Such radiation has long-lasting and potentially deadly effects. Also, the force of a nuclear blast could be enough to set off seismic activity across the world or alter weather patterns around the world and so on.

The problem is that you can never quite tell what the effects of a nuclear blast might be.

There's always the danger of nuclear capabilities falling into the hands of the 'wrong people' like terrorist groups. After the break-up of the USSR, nuclear weapons technology was often sold off to inappropriate people by unscrupulous people...

After a nuclear blast the site of the blast might be contaminated with nuclear radiation for some time to come and so the site will be useless to you. That and the fact that all the buildings will be flattened and the land useless for cultivation etc.

Talk Point 4

Is there any point in having nuclear weapons if you're never going to use them?

Moral Implications

What is above is more related to the military and practical implications of WMDs, but what about the moral issues that they raise?

Harming the Innocent

WMDs are non-specific – they kill indiscriminately. While some chemical weapons can be quite specific you still don't have total control over who they kill or harm. This means that it's fairly likely that using them will involve the deaths of innocent civilians, which goes against the most basic rule of war. Of course, some argue that in war there's no such thing as an innocent civilian – everyone in the enemy's country is a justifiable target because in some way they could all support the enemy's war effort (either now or in the future).

But, WMDs are by definition super-powerful and difficult to be very specific with. Perhaps anything does go in war and maybe using such weapons will bring a war to a quick end – in the long run this might save more lives than it costs – including innocent civilians. So, you might sacrifice some to save many more in future. The nuclear bombs dropped in World War II brought the war in Japan to an end. It's true that many innocent civilians were killed, but how many more might have been killed in conventional warfare had the war not been stopped in this way? Remember, too, that many of these WMDs have harmful effects which can go on long after deployment – is it really right for generations to come to suffer the effects of a war which had nothing to do with them? This too would also apply to the continued existence of landmines in a place which had once been a war zone.

Proportionality

One of the rules of war is that you do just what you need to achieve your objective. Aren't WMDs just a little over the top? You can't really control the casualties affected by a WMD and, even if you could, the destructive power of WMDs make you wonder if the ends justify the means. Is it morally justifiable to kill so many so brutally to achieve your goal? Is the deployment of WMDs not always going to be far more than is necessary?

Deterrence Value

WMDs may act as a deterrent, they may not, but is that the point? A world based on the fear of their use is a pretty horrible world to imagine. Is it right to keep the peace through the threat of war? Do we have the right to hold people to ransom by threatening to rain down WMDs on them if they don't do what we want them to? This would be a very morally dubious world – the message would be even to the youngest child that it's okay to threaten someone to make them behave the way you want to. Is living in peace as the result of threatening war a true peace?

Threat of Escalation

Maybe the more WMDs there are in the world the greater is the chance of war breaking out. Instead of keeping the peace they might be more likely to lead to war! If your enemy has WMDs then you're probably going to try to develop them yourself. Maybe you wouldn't have if your enemy didn't have them. So, maybe by having them you risk making the situation worse instead of better. Also, wars can start for all sorts of reasons and perhaps the existence of WMDs in the world might lead to the war getting much too serious much too soon as everyone is afraid that the enemy will be the first to use them.

Drain on Resources

WMDs, even the cheapest ones, involve costs (as do conventional weapons). Is this what governments should be spending their money on? Perhaps all the money spent on weapons would be better spent on schoolbooks (much better idea) or healthcare or making people's lives better in many different ways. Whatever weapons we have involve cost, maybe we should be investing it in making the world a better place instead (through social improvements) rather than in making the world a more dangerous place (through putting our money into weapons).

Possessing and Using

Some people argue that it is not morally wrong to possess weapons (of any kind), but it is morally wrong to use them. Of course, the response to this is what is the use of having something if everyone knows you never have any intention of using it? This doesn't seem logical and seems like an awful lot of time and money spent and risk taken for an idea which will never happen.

You Can't Un-Invent Them

WMDs exist – you can't turn back the clock and make them go away. It would be fine if everyone agreed to get rid of them completely, but human mistrust makes this unlikely. It might actually make things worse if some countries gave up their WMDs while some did not. This might result in an imbalance of power which might mean that a war becomes more likely. Perhaps even if we disagree with the existence of WMDs we have to appreciate that they might be here to stay, and so surround them with suitable safeguards to protect us all from all the dangers they represent.

Weapons generally, and WMDs in particular, raise issues about when it is and isn't acceptable to go to war and what is and isn't acceptable during war. All WMDs do is give us a far greater capacity for death and destruction, but maybe the moral point is the same because some might argue that it's just as wrong to kill one person as it is to kill millions... Many argue that WMDs are no different to any other kind of weapon because they take lives and this is perfectly acceptable during war. A country has the right to defend itself in the most effective way it can after all. Also, some would say that just having WMDs has kept the world more peaceful in recent history because no one wants to risk anyone unleashing these horrible weapons and so everyone has kept the peace and not gone to war – an uneasy peace is better than no peace at all.

Check Your Learning

1. Why do some people argue that nuclear weapons are the biggest threat to peace there has ever been?
2. Why do some people argue that nuclear weapons have kept the peace since WWII?
3. Is there (morally) any difference between possessing and using nuclear weapons?
4. In your opinion, is it morally justifiable for a country to have WMDs?
5. What do you think is the most important moral implication linked to WMDs?

Talk Point 5

Does it make any difference whether killing is done with conventional weapons or WMDs?

International Conventions on WMDs

Because of the dangers of these weapons, the international community has got together and come up with laws and regulations which try to control the possession and possible use of these weapons. Again, the aim is to observe some level of decency during war and avoid going too far – as well as hopefully stop wars beginning in the first place.

Way back in 1856, the Hague Conventions prohibited the use of certain weapons in warfare, trying to ensure that wars were fought with at least some attention to human rights as far as that was possible. It was after World War I that the international community really got going with trying to tidy up international law on weapons use during war.

1925 Geneva Protocol

This too goes by the glorious title:
PROTOCOL FOR THE PROHIBITION OF THE USE IN WAR OF ASPHYXIATING, POISONOUS OR OTHER GASES, AND OF BACTERIOLOGICAL METHODS OF WARFARE
And states:

The undersigned Plenipotentiaries, in the name of their respective governments:
Whereas the use in war of asphyxiating, poisonous or other gases, and of all analogous liquids, materials or devices, has been justly condemned by the general opinion of the civilised world; and
Whereas the prohibition of such use has been declared in Treaties to which the majority of Powers of the world are Parties; and
To the end that this prohibition shall be universally accepted as a part of International Law, binding alike the conscience and the practice of nations;
Quoted at http://fas-www.harvard.edu/~hsp/1925.html

This was a response, at least partly, to the use of poisonous gas in World War I and bans the use of such weapons in wartime. However, because it didn't say anything about possessing such weapons (back to the question of why you would have them if you weren't going to use them...) other conventions were developed to cover these aspects.

Chemical Weapons Convention 1997

Now this Convention covers pretty much every possibility linked to chemical weapons...

> The Convention prohibits all development, production, acquisition, stockpiling, transfer, and use of chemical weapons. It requires each State Party to destroy chemical weapons and chemical weapons production facilities it possesses, as well as any chemical weapons it may have abandoned on the territory of another State Party. The verification provisions of the CWC not only affect the military sector but also the civilian chemical industry, world-wide, through certain restrictions and obligations regarding the production, processing and consumption of chemicals that are considered relevant to the objectives of the Convention.
>
> www.un.org/Depts/dda/WMD/cwc/

So this means that not only should you not use chemical weapons, you shouldn't make them or store them or dump them where you think no one's looking. It also prohibits the use of certain chemical processes which even hint that you might be sneakily putting chemical weapons together. This last part is important, because many disputes over chemical weapons in the recent past have been where countries are suspected of making them. These accused countries often respond that they're not making weapons but developing technologies for peaceful purposes.

The Ottawa Treaty 1997

This bans the use of anti-personnel landmines as well as their production and storage. It also encourages countries to help those affected by landmines and clear their country of any remaining landmines in former war zones. It also suggests that countries can help other countries to deal with their landmines.

UN Convention on Certain Conventional Weapons 1980

To give it its rather mouthy title this is properly known as:

> The *Convention on Prohibitions or Restrictions on the Use of Certain Conventional Weapons Which May Be Deemed to Be Excessively Injurious or to Have Indiscriminate Effects as amended on 21 December 2001* (CCW) is also known as the Convention on Certain Conventional Weapons.
>
> The purpose of the Convention is to ban or restrict the use of specific types of weapons that are considered to cause unnecessary or unjustifiable suffering to combatants or to affect civilians indiscriminately.
>
> www.unog.ch

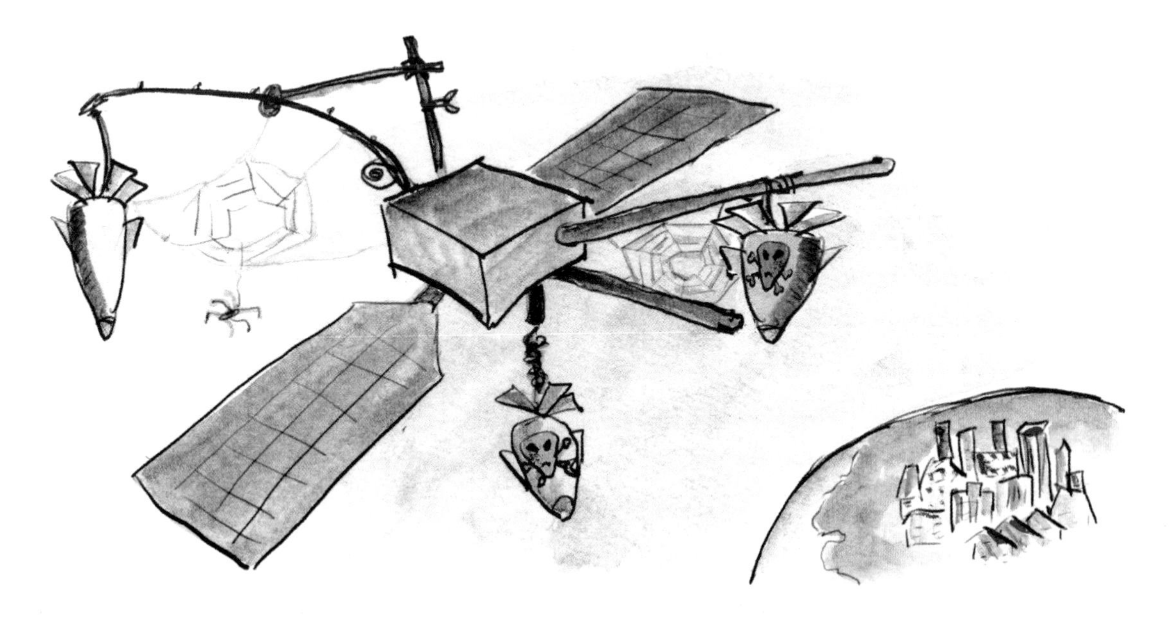

This means that countries who have signed up to this agree not to use weapons which cause more harm and damage than is necessary to achieve a successful military outcome and not to use weapons which target non-military personnel. In practice this means all kinds of weapons from booby-traps to landmines. A fairly recent addition to this is the *Protocol IV on Blinding Laser Weapons*

> It is prohibited to employ laser weapons specifically designed, as their sole combat function or as one of their combat functions, to cause permanent blindness to unenhanced vision, that is to the naked eye or to the eye with corrective eyesight devices. The High Contracting Parties shall not transfer such weapons to any State or non-State entity.
>
> www.unog.ch

The most recent amendment has been the 2003 addition of *Protocol V on the Explosive Remnants of War.* This aims to reduce the effects of unexploded weapons interfering with humanitarian aid efforts. Of course, this is not only about indiscriminate killing, it's also about containing the effects of war to wartime as opposed to allowing people to be harmed after the war has ended. Like all UN conventions, this is only really binding on those countries who sign up to it, but it does express the views of the international community and so countries who do not sign up are unlikely to be helped by the UN in other ways.

Finally, because of the sheer horror of the possibility of nuclear war, the UN also has guidelines about nuclear weapons. This obviously covers their use but again covers everything from possessing them to doing more or less anything which might make it look as if you're trying to develop nuclear capability.

The Treaty on the Non-Proliferation of Nuclear Weapons

Considering the devastation that would be visited upon all mankind by a nuclear war and the consequent need to make every effort to avert the danger of such a war and to take measures to safeguard the security of peoples,

Believing that the proliferation of nuclear weapons would seriously enhance the danger of nuclear war,
In conformity with resolutions of the United Nations General Assembly calling for the conclusion of an agreement on the prevention of wider dissemination of nuclear weapons,
Undertaking to co-operate in facilitating the application of International Atomic Energy Agency safeguards on peaceful nuclear activities...
Declaring their intention to achieve at the earliest possible date the cessation of the nuclear arms race and to undertake effective measures in the direction of nuclear disarmament. For the full text of this treaty see: www.un.org/events/npt2005/npttreaty.html

In short, if your country already has nuclear weapons (referred to in the Treaty as a *nuclear weapons state*) then you should do nothing to help any other which doesn't have them (*non-nuclear weapons state*) country develop them – including helping them get access to nuclear materials. Every country is allowed to develop nuclear energy for peaceful means but not for the construction of weapons. One of the most recent problems about this however has been that some countries have been developing nuclear energy programmes which other countries claim are just covers for the development of nuclear weapons. UN inspectors are able to go into a country and check things out – but this isn't always made very easy for them. The aim of this treaty is to ensure that nuclear weapons don't become more widespread throughout the world as the UN is quite clear that the more nuclear weapons there are around the more likely it is that this will result in war.

These treaties and conventions are all very well and express the will of the international community. If you want to be part of that club, and so get a slice of the benefits linked to it, then you will agree to these treaties. However, when wars break out it is usually because things have reached the point where argument and international law have broken down, and at this point governments might not give these treaties their due respect. However, others will argue that these international laws help to keep the peace just like any law keeps the peace – you'll get your occasional law-breakers but most folks will stick to the law – especially if they think it's in their interests to do so.

Talk Point 6

How helpful do you think all these treaties and conventions are in avoiding war?

Christian View of Modern Armaments

There are many different Christian views on war. Some reject it totally while others see it as a terrible, but sometimes necessary, evil. As far as WMDs are concerned, most Christians agree that the use of weapons during war should inflict no more suffering than is necessary and should certainly avoid killing innocent victims as far as possible. It is a difficult area because of the argument that some would use which says that it is worth the human cost of deploying WMDs because it saves the lives of far more people in the long run. Christians in Scotland have often been at the forefront of protest against nuclear weapons because of the existence of the nuclear base at Faslane on the Clyde. Here, Trident nuclear weapons are stored.

Source 2

Among the Churches advocating the non replacement of Trident is the Church of Scotland, whose position is one of 'sustained opposition' to nuclear weapons. On 23 May 2001, the Church called on the UK Government 'to abandon the Trident programme'. In May 2006, churches in Scotland united in their opposition to a replacement of the Trident nuclear weapons system. The Church of Scotland, the Catholic Church and Episcopal Church signed the petition at Holyrood, Edinburgh, stating 'We urge the government of the United Kingdom not to invest in a replacement for the Trident system and to begin now the process of decommissioning these weapons with the intention of diverting the sums spent on nuclear weaponry to programmes of aid and development.'

www.churchofscotland.org.uk

This kind of response is echoed by the Christian Campaign for Nuclear Disarmament:

Source 3

Christian CND's Mission Statement

Believing that nuclear weapons are intrinsically evil, Christian CND works ecumenically to convince people of this and to strive towards their abolition; we believe that this aim is attainable.

Our Vision as people of faith:

we believe that the wholesale destruction threatened by these weapons makes their possession and use an offence against God and humanity

we deplore the nuclear arms race and the blasphemous assumptions on which it relies

we are challenged in our worship of God and our commitment to Jesus Christ by the existence and spread of nuclear weapons

we trust in God, not nuclear weapons

we turn our lives towards a culture of peace and non-violence

we cooperate with all who want to work for the goal of abolition of nuclear weapons

http://ccnd.gn.apc.org/mission%20statement.html

It's hard to get hold of any official group within Christianity which publicly supports the possession and possible use of WMDs, except for some extreme right wing groups in the USA. But there are no doubt some Christians who would argue that in some cases the benefits of WMDs might well outweigh their dangers and disadvantages. Their argument would be that just as Christians can, regretfully, accept that war is sometimes necessary, it's therefore not impossible that it is sometimes necessary to use particular kinds of weapons. In wars, disproportionate things happen and innocent civilians do get killed. It might be wrong to specifically target the innocent in such ways, but when it comes down to it, for a Christian, it's just as bad to kill enemy soldiers as it is to kill enemy civilians – so this distinction doesn't make much sense. Perhaps Christians would simply argue that the horrible destructive power of nuclear weapons just shows how wrong war, in all its shapes and forms actually is.

Buddhist View of Modern Armaments

The Dalai Lama has spoken out against what he claims are China's plans to build and store nuclear weapons in Tibet. He asks for the:

Source 4

Restoration and protection of Tibet's natural environment and the abandonment of China's use of Tibet for the production of nuclear weapons and dumping of nuclear waste;

He asks for this based on his belief that:

Tibetans have a great respect for all forms of life. This inherent feeling is enhanced by the Buddhist faith, which prohibits the harming of all sentient beings, whether human or animal.

In a New York Times interview with the Dalai Lama in 1993 he made the following statement was made which gives some idea of the Dalai Lama's views on nuclear weapons:

Q: Did you say that killing sometimes is acceptable?

A: Comparatively. In human society, some people do get killed, for a variety of reasons. However, when you have an established army, and countries with those armies go to war, the casualties are immense. It's not one or two casualties, it's thousands. And with nuclear weapons, it's millions, really millions. For that reason, the arms trade is really irresponsible. Irresponsible! Global demilitarisation is essential.

www.tew.org/dalailama/hhdl.five.pt.html
www.sacred-texts.com/bud/tib/nytimes.htm

Again, in Buddhism, it would be considered wrong to use such weapons – a whole bucketload of bad kamma would follow the deployment of a nuclear bomb – but the principle of skilful means might apply here too. Although Buddhists would prefer the world to be based on loving kindness of all beings towards each other – that's sometimes a difficult ideal. Maybe sometimes peace can be kept through the threat and deterrent value of WMDs of all kinds. If they do keep the peace then their existence could be morally justifiable for the Buddhist.

Viewpoints Independent of Religious Belief

A Utilitarian view of WMDs (in fact, conventional weapons too) could either be in favour of or against them. If they keep the peace then they might be undesirable, but effective, even if that peace is an uneasy one. This benefits the majority in the long run. However, a Utilitarian could also agree with their use – if that use was likely to end a war quickly and so prevent far more suffering for years to come. This would mean that the minority now could be sacrificed for the sake of the majority in the future. On the other hand, a Utilitarian might argue that the potential destructive nature of WMDs is so great that it could never be justifiable, it would just cause far too much misery. Also, biological weapons could get out of hand and end up destroying everyone – not at all the greatest good for the greatest number. The Humanist Carl Sagan made his disgust at the waste that is preparing for war clear:

> The world today spends $1 trillion a year on military preparations, most of it on conventional arms... Much of that money is spent only because the nations of the world are unable to take the unbearable step of reconciliation with their adversaries (and some of it because governments need forces to suppress and intimidate their own people) That trillion dollars a year takes food from the mouths of poor people. It cripples potentially effective economies. It is a scandalous waste and we should not countenance it.
>
> *Billions and Billions*, Sagan, C, Hodder Headline, 1998 p203

Check Your Learning

1. Describe ONE international treaty/convention on modern armaments.
2. Do you think such treaties/conventions are successful? Explain your view.
3. What conflicting views of modern armaments might Christians have?
4. How might a Buddhist explain supporting the possession of nuclear weapons?
5. Explain whether you agree with Carl Sagan or not.
6. What are the similarities and differences between the three viewpoints?

Extension Activities

Knowledge, Understanding and Evaluation through Practical Activities

1 Imagine you are Rear Admiral General Sir George. Write a response to Janey's suggestion.

2 Make up a display board separating conventional weapons from modern armaments.

3 Write up a short report explaining the difference between modern and ancient warfare. Explain the similarities and differences between these two types of war.

4 Imagine you are Rear Admiral General Sir George, again. You are trying to persuade politicians to invest big money in a new smart missile system. Write a speech you might make to them to persuade them to spend the money.

5 Debate in class: 'There's no point in having chemical and biological weapons because we should never use them'.

6 Create a piece of artwork which either supports or rejects the possession and/or use of WMDs.

7 Carry out some research into the bombings of Hiroshima and Nagasaki in World War II. What happened? Why was it done? What were the effects? Why did some argue that it was the right course of action? Write your own illustrated report.

8 Find out about CND and similar organisations – if you can find a pro-nuclear weapons organisation use that too. Design a flyer outlining the organisation, its aims and beliefs.

9 Find out what happens when a country who has signed up to an international Treaty or Convention breaks its rules.

10 Write an imaginative story based on the following idea.

The Kingdom of Hyperbole has recently acquired biological weapons expertise. The King of this small nation is quite mad and has absolute power. He gives the order to use this against the UK because the British Prime Minister once called him a great big lazy pudding.

Unit Assessment Question

Intermediate 1: Should a religious person support the possession of nuclear weapons? **4KU 4AE**

Intermediate 2: Describe ONE difference between a conventional weapon and a WMD. **2KU**

Higher: 'A religious person would never support the possession of nuclear weapons' How accurate is this statement? **2KU 6AE**

Sample Exam Question

Intermediate 1: 'Using biological weapons can never be justified'. Do you agree? Give TWO reasons for your answer. **4AE**

Intermediate 2: Explain how one international treaty or convention has tried to regulate the use of weapons in war. **4KU**

Higher: 'The existence of WMDs makes war less likely'. Would a religious person agree? **6KU 6AE**

Homework

Your country has decided that it might get rid of all its nuclear weapons, but only after a referendum. Imagine two people going to vote. One is going to vote for nuclear weapons to go and the other for them to stay. Both however have some doubts about the vote they're about to cast. Write two short pieces which describe what's going through their heads as they approach the ballot paper...

Personal Reflection

Should the UK possess WMDs?

CHAPTER 12 Revision and Study Guide

What Has This Course Been For?

The course has a number of broad aims:

- To help you understand how people make moral decisions in the modern world and what kinds of things they might base these moral decisions on.
- To help you learn the facts about the specific moral issues you have studied.
- To help you 'weigh up' the issues by looking at various 'pros and cons' in relation to the issue and the arguments.
- To help you understand various viewpoints about each issue – some from a religious standpoint and others from viewpoints independent of religious belief.

Throughout all of this, it is hoped that you will explore your own views of each topic and come to your own conclusions about each moral issue. Beyond that, this might change the way you think about things and so what you do. Perhaps this will lead to you changing the world!

How Can I Decide?

The issues in this book are very complex and even the 'experts' don't always agree. People can study these topics in depth for many years and still not know what the 'answer' is. The same people can change their opinions on the topics based on reason, argument, or a different understanding of they way they make their moral decisions. What is important is that people continue to look into these topics and discuss them. Only then might we eventually get closer to the truth, or at least how we should respond to the issue. Moral issues are probably therefore more of a journey than a destination. Bear in mind, too, that these moral issues change with time, and the 'current thinking' might be different next year or in ten years time. Every single topic in this book is a 'live' issue about which people have to make decisions everyday, sometimes difficult decisions. Hopefully what you have studied will help you to contribute to the debate and discussion.

Learning Outcomes

There are slight differences between Intermediate 1, 2 and Higher. Make sure your over-worked teacher has the latest arrangements documents from the SQA or check them yourself at www.sqa.org.uk. To help you, the differences in wording for the Morality in the Modern World Unit have been put in **bold**.

Intermediate 1

Demonstrate knowledge and understanding of contemporary moral issues.
Explain the reasons for differences in viewpoints on contemporary moral issues.
Express a reasoned opinion about viewpoints on contemporary moral issues.

Intermediate 2

Demonstrate knowledge and understanding of contemporary moral issues.
Compare and contrast viewpoints on contemporary moral issues.
Justify conclusions about viewpoints on contemporary moral issues.

Higher

Demonstrate knowledge and understanding of **theories about the relationship between religious and moral values**.
Analyse viewpoints on contemporary moral issues.
Evaluate viewpoints on contemporary moral issues.

Description to Analysis

There is a 'pecking order' of skills you have to demonstrate in this course from the simplest which is stating a fact or opinion to the most complex which is assessing a viewpoint or analysing an issue. In this unit, you are expected to be able to demonstrate knowledge and understanding of the facts, the viewpoints and the pros and cons of each issue. You are also supposed to be able to analyse and evaluate all of these, expressing your own view too on occasion. You must always do this in a reasonable way and support your answers with evidence wherever you can. It's easy in these topics just to give your opinion or to criticise someone else's, but you must make sure that you do so with supporting reasons which justify your opinion or criticism. The balance of this KU to AE varies according to your level of study:

The split of marks in the **Unit Assessments** (NABs to you) reflects this idea as follows:

NABs Marks Split	Knowledge and Understanding	Analysis and Evaluation
Intermediate 1	**70%**	**30%**
Intermediate 2	**60%**	**40%**
Higher	**60%**	**40%**

In the **final exam**, the split is like this:

Final Exam Marks Split	Knowledge and Understanding	Analysis and Evaluation
Intermediate 1	**60%**	**40%**
Intermediate 2	**50%**	**50%**
Higher	**50%**	**50%**

As for the exam, by the time you've read this book there should be a few past papers for you to look at. Your teacher will have a Specimen Exam Paper from the SQA. This will help them to make up the prelim and give you an idea of what the actual exam might be like. You should look at the SQA website too, because the nice people there have very helpfully put the past exam papers on the site with the marking instructions that the markers use. There's also a thing called the SQA Standards website – remind your teacher about this one!

Sample Assessment Questions with Sample Answers

Here are three sample assessment questions with three sample marking schemes. These are in note-form to give you an idea of the kind of thing which should be included in a good answer. In the exam you should write your answers in prose, but doing a note-form plan is always a good idea – it saves you from wandering off the point, or in the case of moral issues, ending up on the moral high-ground having a rant disguised as your view of the issue. Remember that how clearly you express yourself does matter. The NAB questions aren't significantly different from the exam questions in style so we can use these for practice for both. Remember that your NABs are also practice for the final exam – although the actual questions will be different of course...

Intermediate 1

INTERNATIONAL ISSUES
Reminder: You should answer these questions if you have studied ***International Issues*** in the Morality in the Modern World Unit.

a) Describe ONE effect of poverty. **2KU**

b) State ONE possible cause of poverty. **2KU**

c) Explain ONE advantage and ONE disadvantage of giving food aid to a poor country. **4KU**

d) Name a religion you have studied. What does it teach about helping people in poverty? **2KU**

e) 'Some forms of aid are more useful than others.' Do you agree? Give TWO reasons for your answer. **4AE**

f) What is meant by 'tied aid'? **2KU**

g) 'Charity begins at home.' Do you agree? Give TWO reasons for your answer. **4AE**

Total = 20 Marks

Question	Possible Answer
a) Describe ONE effect of poverty. **2KU**	Examples: ◆ Death ◆ Illness ◆ Disease ◆ Starvation
b) State ONE possible cause of poverty. **2KU**	Examples: ◆ Effects of famine/drought/war etc. ◆ International debt ◆ Corruption ◆ Global trade system etc.
c) Explain ONE advantage and ONE disadvantage of giving food aid to a poor country. **4KU**	Advantage: ◆ A good use of food which would otherwise be wasted ◆ Responds directly to people's needs ◆ Can help a poor country to develop its own sources of food Disadvantage: ◆ Makes developing world dependent upon handouts from the rich ◆ Only a short-term solution ◆ Can be affected by corruption in receiving country
d) Name a religion you have studied. What does it teach about helping people in poverty? **2KU**	Example: ◆ Christianity Poor are favoured by God – duty to help them 'Love one another as I have loved you' Argument: ◆ Duty of the strong to protect the weak etc.
e) 'Some forms of aid are more useful than others.' Do you agree? Give TWO reasons for your answer. **4AE**	Agree: ◆ Emergency aid gets right to the problem immediately ◆ Medical aid helps get people back on their feet towards self-sufficiency ◆ Armaments as aid are not morally justifiable – will make situation worse Disagree: ◆ All forms of aid helpful if that is what is needed ◆ Form of aid should be decided by receiving country so will help ◆ No aid is useful – all leads to increased dependency
f) What is meant by 'tied aid'? **2KU**	◆ Aid with 'strings attached' ◆ Means that receiving countries have to meet certain conditions before the aid is granted ◆ Seen by some as more of benefit to the country giving the aid than the country receiving it ➜

Question	Possible Answer
g) 'Charity begins at home.' Do you agree? Give TWO reasons for your answer. **4AE**	Agree: ◆ Government has a duty to look after its own ◆ Can't deal with poverty abroad and not deal with home issues ◆ Relieving poverty at home first will make relieving poverty abroad easier in the long run DIsagree: ◆ Poverty in developing world is absolute – much more serious and should be dealt with first ◆ Developed world had a hand in causing developing world poverty so should take responsibility for easing it ◆ Relieving poverty around the world will make the world a more stable place for all

Intermediate 2

MEDICAL ETHICS

Reminder: You should answer these questions if you have studied *Medical Ethics* in the Morality in the Modern World Unit.

a) What is voluntary euthanasia? **1KU**

b) Why is voluntary euthanasia a moral issue? **2KU**

c) What does the law in the Netherlands say about euthanasia? **4KU**

d) State one religion you have studied. Why might it oppose voluntary euthanasia? **2AE**

e) What is meant by the quality of life argument? **2AE**

f) Voluntary euthanasia should be made legal. Do you agree? Give TWO reasons for your answer. **4AE**

g) Describe BMA guidelines on euthanasia. **3KU**

h) 'Choice over your own death is a basic human right.' Do you agree? Give reasons for your answer. **2AE**

Total = 20 Marks

Question	Possible Answer
a) What is voluntary euthanasia? **1KU**	◆ When a person chooses to end their own life – often called 'assisted suicide'. ◆ May answer with the right to die etc.
b) Why is voluntary euthanasia a moral issue? **2KU**	◆ Question is whether it is right to control the end of your life or put someone in the position of helping you end your life. ◆ How much control do people have over their own bodies?
c) What does the law in the Netherlands say about euthanasia? **4KU**	◆ Patient must be terminally ill ◆ No hope of recovery ◆ Doctor must be aware of the history of the case ◆ Must use euthanasia as a last resort ◆ Must be agreed by two doctors
d) State one religion you have studied. Why might it oppose voluntary euthanasia? **2AE**	Example: ◆ Christianity Life is a gift from God 'on loan' to humans – cannot do what we want with it Is a slippery moral slope which could lead to abuses
e) What is meant by the quality of life argument? **2AE**	◆ Argument that life is only worth living if the person living it has what s/he thinks is abilities and faculties which make life worth living (as opposed to sanctity of life argument) ◆ Life is worth living only where its quality is 'good enough'
f) Voluntary euthanasia should be made legal. Do you agree? Give TWO reasons for your answer. **4AE**	Agree: ◆ Should be everyone's right to choose when to die ◆ Would take pressure and burden off doctors and relatives ◆ Would make society more compassionate Disagree: ◆ Would lead to abuses like people feeling pressurised into opting for euthanasia ◆ Puts doctors under wrong pressure ◆ Takes away the duty of care for the dying which society should observe ➜

Question	Possible Answer
g) Describe BMA guidelines on euthanasia **3KU**	◆ Does not believe that life should be prolonged at all costs ◆ Should take patient's wishes into account ◆ Opposes legalisation of assisted suicide ◆ Wants support for better care of terminally ills patients
h) 'Choice over your own death is a basic human right.' Do you agree? Give reasons for your answer. **2AE**	Agree: ◆ Choose everything else in life why not death ◆ Your life belongs to you so your choice ◆ Denying you choice is an invasion of your personal freedom Disagree: ◆ Some rights are withheld from the individual for the good of society as a whole – this is one ◆ A dying person is not likely to be in their 'right mind' so should be wary of granting them 'rights' at this point ◆ Our life does not belong to us so it is not a right to do what we want with it

Higher

CRIME AND PUNISHMENT

Reminder: You should answer these questions if you have studied ***Crime and Punishment*** in the Morality in the Modern World Unit.

a) Describe what happened in the case of Timothy Evans. **6KU**

b) Why did the case of Timothy Evans eventually lead to the abolition of capital punishment in the UK? **4KU**

c) What moral issues are raised by capital punishment? **5KU**

d) 'Capital Punishment is morally unjustifiable.' Discuss TWO responses to this statement. One of these responses should be based on a religious viewpoint. **15AE**

Total = 30 Marks

Question	Possible Answer
a) Describe what happened in the case of Timothy Evans. **6KU**	◆ Hanged for murder of wife and daughter ◆ Originally confessed to the murders then changed story to implicate Reginald Christie ◆ Story not believed – he was mentally retarded and changed story raised police suspicion ◆ After Evans hanged more bodies found ◆ Eventually Christie confesses to the murders but too late for Evans
b) Why did the case of Timothy Evans eventually lead to the abolition of capital punishment in the UK? **4KU**	◆ Miscarriage of justice explained ◆ Case not handled well leading to questions in the House of Commons ◆ Showed that when a mistake is made in a conviction, capital punishment takes away the possibility of putting the mistake right as the wrongly accused person has been executed ◆ Capital punishment buries the truth with possible witnesses to the real killer's identity
c) What moral issues are raised by capital punishment? **5KU**	◆ Is it ever right to take a life for any reason? ◆ Illogical way to show that killing is wrong ◆ Wrong to make people kill on society's behalf ◆ Does not allow for the possibility of mistakes ◆ Does not allow society to look back at decisions made in the past and put them right – society's views about right and wrong change – capital punishment is too final for this change to be of any benefit to anyone
d) 'Capital Punishment is morally unjustifiable.' Discuss TWO responses to this statement. One of these responses should be based on a religious viewpoint. **15AE**	Example: ◆ Christianity *Is morally justifiable* ◆ Eye for an eye argument ◆ Justice is seen to be done in the form of retribution ◆ Acts as a good deterrent and so prevents more murders in the future ◆ Saves society the burden of supporting a person in life imprisonment ◆ Makes society safer as killer cannot kill again ◆ Is part of the duty of the strong protecting the weak ➜

Question	Possible Answer
	Is not morally justifiable ◆ Never right to take a life – commandment prohibiting killing should extend to capital punishment too ◆ Does not work – just brutalises society and so opposite of Christian beliefs about love and forgiveness etc ◆ Christians believe that anyone can change and reform – capital punishment doesn't allow for this ◆ Wrong – human life is a sacred gift from God – should not be taken by anyone but God Example: ◆ JS Mill/Utilitarianism *Is morally justifiable* ◆ In the interests of the greater good – sacrifice of a few (one) for the good of the many ◆ Mercifully quick whereas life imprisonment makes a person suffer for much longer ◆ Deters most people from serious crime so protects the majority from harm ◆ Makes society a safer place as the killer cannot kill again *Is not morally justifiable* ◆ Does not deter all serious crime places with capital punishment have no fewer murders than places without it ◆ Could be misused by a corrupt state leading to a more dangerous world for all ◆ Killing always goes against the greater good – even if it is the state who is doing it in response to crime

Final Words

Remember that what you have studied in this course is not just about passing an exam. It is about shaping and informing your view of the world as you grow into adulthood. Perhaps you'll be a great world leader one day and have to deal with some of the issues you have explored in this book. Perhaps you'll be in a position where you have to make a moral decision about something you have studied here. Hopefully, what you have studied should make your decision easier, clearer and better informed. Therefore you should be more confident about your decision, in knowing that you have thought it through very carefully and arrived at your decision after serious reflection. Maybe this will lead to you making better decisions. No matter what you face, making carefully thought-out decisions like that will make the world a better place for us all. Good luck for your exam – and for facing life better prepared …

INDEX